KU-197-845

Historic House Museums

Historic House Museums

A PRACTICAL HANDBOOK FOR THEIR CARE, PRESERVATION, AND MANAGEMENT

Sherry Butcher-Younghans

New York   Oxford
OXFORD UNIVERSITY PRESS
1993

THE BRITISH MUSEUM
THE PAUL HAMLYN LIBRARY

363 690973 BUT

Oxford University Press

Oxford   New York   Toronto
Delhi   Bombay   Calcutta   Madras   Karachi
Kuala Lumpur   Singapore   Hong Kong   Tokyo
Nairobi   Dar es Salaam   Cape Town
Melbourne   Auckland   Madrid

and associated companies in
Berlin   Ibadan

Copyright © 1993 by Oxford University Press, Inc.

Published by Oxford University Press, Inc.,
200 Madison Avenue, New York, New York 10016

Oxford is a registered trademark of Oxford University Press

All rights reserved. No part of this publication may be reproduced,
stored in a retrieval system, or transmitted, in any form or by any means,
electronic, mechanical, photocopying, recording, or otherwise,
without the prior permission of Oxford University Press.

Library of Congress Cataloging-in-Publication Data
Butcher-Younghans, Sherry.
Historic house museums: A practical handbook for their care, preservation,
and management / Sherry
Butcher-Younghans.
p. cm.   ISBN 0-19-506952-8
1. Historical museums—United States—Handbooks, manuals, etc.
2. Museum conservation methods—United States.
3. Dwellings—United States—Conservation and restoration.   I. Title.
E172.B88   1993
363.6′9—dc20   92-14870

1 3 5 7 9 8 6 4 2

Printed in the United States of America
on acid-free paper

FOREWORD

THE MOST NUMEROUS kind of museum in the United States is the historic house museum. Beginning with America's first historic site, the Hasbrouck House at Newburgh, which New York State acquired because it had been one of Washington's Revolutionary War headquarters, Americans have had a penchant for preserving houses of historic importance and turning them into museums. That trend was accelerated in the 1970s and 1980s by a wave of patriotism with the bicentennial of the Revolution and a growing awareness of the tragic destruction of much of our physical heritage in the name of urban renewal. Today, approximately one-half of all museums in the country are history museums; and, among these, historic houses and sites outnumber all the rest.

We who work in the history museum field know these historic house museums to be among the smallest museums in terms of staff and budget. Many of them, in fact, are run entirely by volunteers. It is not surprising, then, that many historic house museums do not meet the professional standards of the museum profession. For some, this is because they lack adequate financial resources. It has been my observation, though, that the inadequacies as often stem from their being run by people who lack the training or knowledge to do the job right. They do not know how, and they do not know who to turn to for the help they need. They feel intimidated by the regional and national professional meetings, which are attended almost entirely by professionals; and they feel that they are looked down upon by the professional museum people who might be able to provide the answers.

It is the good fortune of these historic house museums that a very capable professional, who empathizes with them, has now provided many of the answers to the question: How can we do our job the right way? Sherry Butcher-Younghans, in *Historic House Museums: A Practical Handbook for Their Care, Preservation, and Management* has made a very important contribution to our field. She poses basic questions: What is the mission of the organization? How is it organized? What do trustees do, and how do they relate to the director and staff? Where can you go for help? How do you collect and care for collections? How do you preserve the house for future generations? How do you realize the ultimate purpose of helping the public understand the meaning and importance of the house museum? And finally, how can you use volunteers in accomplishing these things?

Ms. Butcher-Younghans draws on considerable work experience in the museum field, plus a solid academic background in anthropology, museology, and history, to produce a volume that deals effectively with theory and practice, philosophy, and reality. She does not patronize the reader, nor does she gloss over the inadequacies of many house museums. She makes clear the fiduciary responsibilities we all bear for the buildings and objects in our care and makes clear the consequences to future generations of improper conservation and care of the objects and buildings we hold in public trust.

This is a book that belongs on the working book shelf of every historic house museum and, indeed, on the book shelf of every small museum. Its lessons on governance, collecting, conservation, and interpretation apply equally well to museums of all disciplines. We are all indebted to Ms. Butcher-Younghans for an enriching addition to the literature of our field.

December 1991   WILLIAM T. ALDERSON
                                                      Former director,
                                        The American Association for
                                             State and Local History

ACKNOWLEDGMENTS

A BOOK IS RARELY created by the author alone, and this axiom is especially true in this case. Many people freely and generously contributed their time, expertise, and insight in assisting in the making of this manual. To all of them I am grateful.

I am especially indebted to my longtime friend and associate Beverly Schilleman, who read every word (over and over again!!) and offered her skill and intuition at each rewrite.

To my colleagues, who contributed to this volume with their ideas and expertise, my special thanks: John Baule, Steve Laux, Wendy Egan, Marcia Anderson, Lotus Stack, Cyndy Frye-Collins, and Bonnie Wilson. I am grateful to Dr. William T. Alderson for his infinite wisdom and perception, which he so freely shared with me.

On matters of conservation in museums, I was well advised by Ron Harvey and Jim Horns; to both, I am grateful. For his technical advice and straightforward explanations, I thank Charles Nelson, from Minnesota's State Historic Preservation Office.

I appreciate all the assistance I received in the collecting of photographs to illustrate this volume. For their indispensable help, I'd like to especially thank Marita Karlisch, Neil Pose, the folks at the National Trust for Historic Preservation, and the Minnesota Historical Society.

As always my appreciation goes to my mother, Nancy Palmer who filled many of the gaps while I spent extended hours in front of the computer. I, too, am grateful to my father, James Butcher, who suggested to me that I write such a book.

Finally, my deepest gratitude goes to my husband, Tom, and sons, Nick and Neal, who are patient, tolerant, and always forgiving of my absences when I am working on special projects.
My heartfelt thanks to all.

August 1992   S. B.-Y.
Eden Prairie, Minn.

CONTENTS

Historic House Museums

1

Introduction

Take the Art of Building—the strongest—proudest—most orderly—most enduring of the arts of man; that of which the produce is in the surest manner accumulative, and need not perish, or be replaced; but if once well done, will stand more strongly than the unbalanced rocks—more prevalently than the crumbling hills. The art is associated with all civic pride and sacred principle; with which men record their power—satisfy their enthusiasm—make sure their defence—define and make dear their habitation.

John Ruskin, *Selections from the Works of John Ruskin*

RESTORING HOUSES OF the past and establishing them as museums has a long history in this country, a tradition heavily influenced by the English custom of preserving ancient buildings and monuments. The earliest house museums in the United States—Hasbrouck House in Newburgh, New York, and Mount Vernon in Virginia—were both associated with our first president. Each site was saved in the 1850s by insightful and public-minded individuals.

As time went by, more and more houses were rescued from the ravages of time or demolition crews and placed in the hands of trustees who managed the museums for the public. In the 1930s, Laurence Vail Coleman, longtime director of the American Association of Museums, wrote that he could trace the rise of historic houses established as museums "from about twenty open in 1895 to nearly a hundred in 1910 and to more than four hundred now."[1]

By the 1970s, thousands of museum houses across the nation had opened their doors. Since the beginning, about 6,000 historic properties have been preserved.[2] The public's enthusiasm for knowledge of its cultural past had greatly increased as Americans

Winterthur Museum in Winterthur, Delaware, displays two hundred historic-room settings of American decorative arts spanning the time period 1640 to 1840. The staff at Winterthur includes highly trained specialists who care for collections, historic buildings, and gardens. (Photograph courtesy of the Henry Francis du Pont Winterthur Museum)

redefined their attachment to history, especially on personal and local levels. They flocked to historic house museums in great numbers, hoping to capture some of the essence of America's past. It became important to know which house in town was the oldest and which was the former estate of the penniless immigrant who started the successful local industry. These museums are symbolic and bear witness to who we are and where we have come from.

At first, houses were saved because of their association with those who designed or built them, or made them their headquarters. We saved homes that belonged to U.S. presidents, famous authors, infamous frontiersmen, men who amassed great fortunes and built estates to prove it, and men who were in the vanguard of America's wars. These were homes of the elite, usually white and most commonly male, not a representative sample of America's history. Yet a movement has been afoot to balance the view of our past, to bring the lives of everyday people, including minorities, into focus. It is now becoming possible for visitors to see how a coal miner and his family might have lived in a shack in Pennsylvania or where domestic servants lived on the great estate of an industrialist or how enslaved people carried out their lives on antebellum planta-

Log homes are commonly restored and operated as house museums in the midwestern United States. This cabin, built in the dovetail style, was constructed in the 1850s by Swedish immigrants. (Photograph courtesy of V. S. Arrowsmith, Isanti County, Minnesota)

tions. Through the museum experience people's lives can be explored by learning what they thought and believed and how they felt about their world.

The popularity of historic house museums sparks important questions. Who tends these structures and how qualified are they to manage them? How do they obtain the financial support that keeps them in operation? What story are these museums telling the public? Who comes to see them? What is the general quality of historic houses in this country?

Some answers to these questions come from two recent surveys, one on historic properties museums conducted by the National Trust for Historic Preservation, and the other an independent survey of historic house museums in the United States.[3]

Both surveys reveal that today most house museums are being operated with a skeleton crew.[4] Sixty-five percent of historic properties museums have no full-time paid staff, and 19 to 27 percent employ only one full-time staff person.[5] Clearly, volunteers for the most part are running the typical house museum and keeping the doors open to the public. These volunteers—hardworking, and enthusiastic—perform their duties with great devotion and boundless energy, but with no formal training.

Another crucial point revealed in the surveys is that while some house museums have fairly large annual budgets, the majority operate on less than $50,000 annually. With so little money—barely enough to keep the roof repaired and the heat on—many museums are unable to hire the professional help to establish sound exhibits and programs, to care for the furnishings and collections properly, or even adequately to maintain the structure.

Once these museums are established, who visits them and what does the public expect to find? While some museums, such as Mount Vernon and Colonial Williamsburg are visited by over 1 million people yearly, more than half receive fewer than 5,000 a year.[6] Most visitors come to experience the story and learn something about local history, but many come simply for the joy of "being in the historic surroundings."[7]

Finally, what is the overall quality of historic house museums in this country? The answer is that there is a great disparity between the larger and more notable, well-managed and adequately funded museums—such as The Hermitage and Monticello—and their impoverished cousins, the struggling, volunteer-based, poorly funded house museums found in communities everywhere. The former have access to professional staff; evolving historical analyses (reinterpre-

The easily recognizable Governor's Palace, at Colonial Williamsburg in Williamsburg, Virginia. This eighteenth-century village is one of the best-known historic sites in the United States. (Photograph courtesy of the Williamsburg Foundation)

tation); proper care of buildings, furnishings, and collections; professional living history programs; researchers; and support staff. The latter have few, if any, professionally trained staff, survive on shoestring budgets, and often can present only poorly researched and narrowly presented exhibits and programs.

There are many fine examples of historic houses in this country; however, the typical house museum can be described as the poor cousin. This curatorial manual was written with these museums in mind. It is intended for those managers, curators, and directors—both paid and unpaid—who undertake historic house

Museum houses are often operated by hardworking, dedicated volunteers. Without their efforts, many historic sites would not exist. (Photograph courtesy of Laura Ingalls Wilder Memorial Society, Inc., DeSmet, South Dakota)

management with the difficulties and limitations inherent to the small, low-budget museum. I have attempted to examine the universal problems and offer practical, inexpensive, and easy-to-accomplish solutions to increase the professionalism of these museums and close that great gap between the more professional historic house museums and the struggling, less recognized institutions so commonly found across this country.

NOTES

1. Laurence Vail Coleman, *Historic House Museums* (Washington, D.C.: American Association of Museums, 1933), p. 18.
2. Gerald George, "Historic Property Museums: What Are They Preserving?" *Preservation Forum* 3 (Summer 1989): 5.

3. In response to the National Trust survey, George raised some troubling questions about how these properties are being cared for, funded, and who is managing them (ibid., pp. 2–5).

Peggy Coats, while working as the historical resources supervisor and director of Campbell Historical Museum, Campbell, California, polled house museums about governance, programming, operating hours, tours, fees, use policies, staff, budget, and revenues (Peggy Coats, "Survey of Historic House Museums," *History News* 45, no. 1 (1990): 26–28).

4. Coats, "Survey of Historic House Museums," p. 28; George, "Historic Property Museums," p. 3.

5. Coats, "Survey of Historic House Museums," p. 28; George, "Historic Property Museums," p. 3.

6. Coats, "Survey of Historic House Museums," p. 27; George, "Historic Property Museums," p. 3.

7. Coats, "Survey of Historic House Museums," p. 28.

2

Governing
the Historic House Museum

To Govern is to make choices.
Duc de Lévis, *Politique*, XIX

WHETHER YOUR HISTORIC house is just being formed as a museum
or has been established for some time, it is important that those in
positions of authority, such as the site manager, curator, director,
and board of trustees, be aware of laws and regulations that pertain to the museum's management. They are responsible for know-
ing what local, state, and federal laws are pertinent to the successful operation of the organization.

Of particular interest to historic house museums are historic
preservation laws that affect historic structures and museums listed
on the National Register of Historic Places and those of National
Register quality.[1] Any modifications of a historic building must follow regulations set by the Department of the Interior in order to
remain on the National Register.[2] In addition to preservation laws,
museum administrators and trustees must become familiar with and
comply with the local, state, and federal laws dealing with health
and safety in the workplace, building and fire codes, workmen's
compensation, copyright, contract, artists' rights, negligence, attractive nuisance, freedom of expression, and many other issues.

The museum should seek the advice of a qualified lawyer concerning legal liabilities and defining the status of the museum. An
attorney who practices corporate law can assist in filing for nonprofit incorporation, applying for tax-exemption status with the Internal Revenue Service, and explaining the legal responsibilities of

The Lincoln Home in Springfield, Illinois, is one of many house museums dedicated to documenting the lives of past presidents of the United States. The house is pre-served as closely as possible to its original form and includes many furnishings once used by Abraham Lincoln. (Photograph courtesy of the Department of the Interior, National Park Service, Lincoln Home National Historic Site)

the museum's board of trustees. This attorney will interpret all lo-cal, state, and federal laws that affect the organization. It may be possible to find a member of the community who will provide legal services voluntarily; if not, it is worth the money spent to hire a competent lawyer.

Defining the Status of a Museum

Nonprofit Corporations

Historic house museums are usually nonprofit public or private in-stitutions that are classified as "charitable corporations." That is, they control valuable properties and pursue charitable objectives for the benefit of the public.[3] If the museum is not incorporated, it is classified as a charitable trust.

To be classified as a nonprofit corporation, the founders (incorporators) must have articles of incorporation prepared by an attorney and filed with the secretary of the state. If the articles are determined legally sound, a certificate of incorporation is issued and the museum becomes a nonprofit corporation. After the articles have been approved by the board of directors, the museum should apply for tax-exempt status.

Tax-Exempt Status

As a nonprofit, in legal terms, a charitable corporation, a museum qualifies for exemption from federal income taxation. This status is especially attractive to benefactors who are allowed to deduct from their income taxes a portion of their contributions to charitable organizations. Tax-exempt status is also necessary in order to qualify for the Accreditation Program of the American Association of Museums. Accreditation is a mark of excellence recognized throughout the museum community.

In order to obtain tax-exempt status, application must be made to the Internal Revenue Service as a charitable organization, by filing Form 1023. It is important for museum administrators to understand their proper Internal Revenue Code classification and what it means. These stipulations are listed in the Internal Revenue Code under 501(c)(3) organizations.[4] Information on applying for tax-exempt status is provided by the revenue department of each state, and the telephone directory lists a toll-free number for the Internal Revenue Service.

Tax exemption must be sought from the state and local levels as well as the federal. State and local exemptions release a museum from most or all real property taxes and from state taxes on museum income. Museums may also qualify for exemption from state and local sales taxes on items purchased for use in the museum.[5]

The Documents that Govern the Museum

No rational government exists without a document—constitution, charter, or articles of incorporation—that defines its operations and explains the power of those who will regulate it. This document is essential to the governing body in the museum, the board of trustees, because it is responsible, morally as well as legally, for carrying out the purposes of the museum and ensuring its well being. It will determine the allocations of authority and responsibility. Successful management will depend on how carefully the governing document is written and how well it is understood, followed, and respected both by staff and trustees.

The articles of incorporation, constitution, or charter—the term used depends upon how the nonprofit status is filed—define the museum, explain its operations, and describe how authority is organized and limited. It is essential to obtain the services of an attorney when drafting this document. This document should include the following information:

- The name and location of the museum (corporation).
- The purposes for which the museum is organized.
- The system for operating the museum.
- The method of governing the museum.
- A statement of its specific powers to receive gifts, hold property, and enter into contracts.
- The number of trustees, or governors.
- The procedures for selecting the governing officers, the length of their terms in office, and their titles (president, vice president, general council, etc.).
- Provisions for the dissolution of the corporation and disposal of its assets.

Bylaws

Museums also require **bylaws**—the internal rules of the museum that govern its regulation. Bylaws define the roles and responsibilities of the trustees, director, and the staff.[6] The trustees and director—if a director is in place—draw up the bylaws in accordance with state law. An attorney should be consulted when drafting this document. Bylaws must be reviewed, modified, and amended from time to time to reflect changes in the museum's operation. All trustees and staff should be thoroughly familiar with the museum's bylaws, and all new trustees should be given copies to ensure that they clearly understand their roles.

Museum bylaws typically cover:

- Membership. A definition of categories and fees. Procedures for handling delinquent memberships. Formal rules for membership meetings: how they are conducted, where they are held, how members are notified of meetings, and conditions for emergency meetings.
- Board of trustees. The number of members, their qualifications, method of selection (election or other method of appointment), and term of office. When and where the meetings will be held and rules for attendance of trustees and director.
- Officers, staff, and volunteers. The officers' (members of the trustees who are elected or appointed to hold offices such as president, vice president, secretary, and treasurer) responsibilities and procedures for removal. Roles of trustees and both paid and unpaid staff.
- Committees. The basic kinds of committees and their structure, such as their responsibilities, how many members will serve on each, as well as procedures for establishing them.
- Financial provisions. Procedures for keeping account books and records, preparing budgets, and reporting to the trustees on the museum's finances, and a definition of the fiscal year. Provisions for an annual audit of the records and books. Designation of the person(s) who is authorized to sign checks, accept gifts, and enter into contracts with vendors.
- Amendments. Procedures for amending the bylaws themselves.

It may also be useful to include in the bylaws rules for recording proceedings of trustees' meetings, the principal evidence of the board's functioning over the years.[7] Minutes of proceedings are permanent records and must be protected with copies kept in a protective vault or off-site. Someone should be designated as recorder of the minutes, which must be thorough and accurate. Minutes must be distributed with expediency to each of the board members.

Mission Statement

Often included both in the articles of incorporation and in the bylaws, the **mission statement** is a brief summary of the scope and purpose of the museum. It defines the institution—the time period, ethnic group, and geographic area it will represent, and the objects it will collect. The statement is a basic guide and must be well thought out. Funding agencies often will ask to see this document, and it is prudent to have it readily available.

Long-Range Plan

A long-term commitment to its goals helps to secure a museum's future, and advance planning gives it direction and focus. Museum administrators must set priorities and goals that integrate issues of governance, collections management and conservation, educational activities, exhibitions and programs, membership and public relations, and facilities (buildings and grounds). In order to accomplish these aims, the museum must have a detailed strategic plan that states objectives and defines supporting activities and outlines how they are to be financed. The plan should cover at least a five-year period, and each goal should be assigned a specific amount of time for its accomplishment.

The museum director or senior administrator, with the aid of an ad hoc committee or individual trustees, usually drafts the long-range plan.[8] Once it is hammered out, the trustees, who should be thoroughly acquainted with the document, must approve it. The plan should be reevaluated yearly and, if necessary, modified or amended. Some institutions may wish to review their plans biannually. Make the five-year plan an action document; use it and let it work for the museum.

The People Who Govern the Museum

The governing body of a museum is called a board of trustees. The trustees are private citizens who are usually without training in the area of museums. They serve without monetary compensation.

Trustees are so named because of their obligation to the charitable trust, the museum, they administer. They hold a fiduciary relation with the institution whereby each trustee is obligated to the care of the museum and all that it contains for the public's benefit. A trustee must be highly accountable to the museum, serving with complete awareness and understanding of this fiduciary responsibility. His or her role is demanding and time consuming, and the lack of monetary compensation for these services does not free a trustee from liability in the operation of the museum.

Trustees are legally responsible to abide by certain basic duties in administering the trust (charitable corporation).

- Loyalty is a primary legal responsibility of a trustee. Trustees must never take advantage of their position in the museum and must scrupulously avoid any conflict of interest.
- Trustees must exercise care and prudence in making decisions concerning the museum.
- Trustees must not delegate to others tasks that the trustees can perform themselves.[9]

The trustee is accountable and wholly responsible, both ethically and legally, for every aspect of the management of the museum.

Roles and Relationships in the Museum

THE ROLE OF THE TRUSTEES

The role of the trustees and the director must be fully defined in order to avoid the conflict that often occurs in small museums.

One of the board's primary roles is to secure funds for the museum to ensure its status as a nonprofit organization. Trustees must be forward looking and strive to procure a solid financial future for the museum. While the director plays some role in fund-raising— applying for grants and to some degree seeking public support, for example—it is not ordinarily the responsibility of the director to secure capital from the community. All major fund-raising efforts are the responsibility of the board with the assistance of the director.

In practical terms, the board guides the museum by setting policy and seeing that the director and the staff carry it out. In other words, the board acts as the institutional manager or overseer, respectfully allowing the director and staff to conduct the day-to-day operations.[10] For example, if the board approves funding for an educational program, it is the director's responsibility to see that the project is developed and stays on budget, and that the museum's standards are maintained. If the board rejects a program, it would be inappropriate for the director to develop it, just as it would be improper for the trustees to tell the director how to implement the program or the staff how to run it.

Director: Administrative Roles

Carries through museum policy
Assumes accountability for the museum budget
Manages operation of the museum budget
Manages operation of the museum
Creates long-range plans
Implements plans and activities
Hires and coordinates staff

The board of trustees selects and hires the museum director and monitors the director's performance, resolving problems should they arise. The director's performance and the museum's activities should be reviewed and evaluated periodically. The chairman or president of the board usually conducts the review and informs the board members of whether their policies are being properly executed.[11]

THE ROLE OF THE DIRECTOR

A director's role is to hire and to dismiss staff members and to oversee their duties. He or she is ultimately responsible for the performance of the staff. A director creates the long-range plans with the help of the staff. These plans are submitted to and approved by the trustees before they are implemented by the director.

A director should be viewed as a peer of the trustees, not as a servant to carry out their wishes.[12] The astute director will keep the board abreast of the museum's activities and of the functioning of the museum's operation. The president of the board should never feel excluded, and the director should never be kept in the dark about the board's views.[13]

RELATIONSHIP BETWEEN STAFF (PAID AND UNPAID) AND TRUSTEES

The relationship of trustees and museum staff is formal, and both parties should exercise mutual respect in their communications.[14] Just as a director should not dictate to the board, the board should not dictate to the staff. Board members should communicate with the staff through the director, or at the very least with his or her

Board of Trustees: Administrative Roles

Sets museum policy
Ensures funding
Assumes legal responsibility for the museum
Hires director
Monitors the director's performance
Works with the director
Does not work directly with staff

knowledge.[15] This will protect staff from well-meaning, but potentially harmful interference by trustees. Trustees must be careful about what they communicate to staff even in a chance meeting or at a informal gathering. A trustee should never voice a personal opinion to a staff member; such comments might be construed as the view of the board overall. Generally, trustees should not act as individuals; actions should be taken as an entire board.

Staff Management: Policies in the Museum

A Manual of Policies and Procedures

A manual that specifically defines policies and procedures of the institution is essential to the successful operation of the museum. The director should write the manual, involving the staff members in the preparation and incorporating their suggestions. Their participation will help to create a thorough and usable document. The trustees should approve the manual before it is implemented. Updating the manual is important. Periodic evaluation of procedures serves to isolate inadequacies and problems in the system, serves as a self-evaluation, and allows staff to review critically the overall operation.[16]

The manual should contain three detailed sections.

A DESCRIPTION AND HISTORY OF THE MUSEUM

The introduction explains the meaning and origin of the museum's title, provides a brief history of the museum, and defines the symbols or logos used. Also included are the mission statement as well

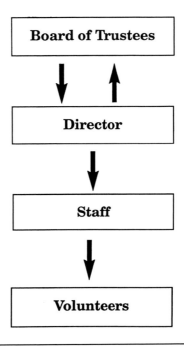

Flow chart showing relationships in small museums.

as a description of what the museum collects, how the collection is used, and the role the museum plays in the community.[17]

PROCEDURES FOR MUSEUM OPERATIONS

The functions of each department and staff responsibilities are a part of the manual, including specific job descriptions for each staff member, paid and unpaid. Outline museum policies regarding opportunities for continuing education and professional development and training and define the relationships between staff members, clarifying lines of authority (an organizational chart may be helpful). In full detail, describe how operations should be carried out, reported, documented, and filed.[18]

Clear instructions are essential regarding security, procedures for emergencies and visitor accidents, handling of special events and complimentary memberships, use of vehicles and telephone, mail services, facsimile machines, and photocopiers. Detailed procedures on securing service contracts, processing of purchase orders, and handling of petty cash must also be established.

THE PERSONNEL POLICY

The museum's personnel policy should contain information about staff rights and responsibilities as well as employee regulations and benefits. These should be carefully written, including provisions for:

- Scheduled work hours.
- Pay periods.
- Definition of full-time and salaried and hourly employees.
- Definition of benefit plans.
- Holidays and vacations.
- Leaves of all types (disability, maternity, emergency, sabbaticals).
- Perquisites for paid and nonpaid staff (complimentary memberships, tickets to special events, parking, museum store discounts).
- Grievance procedures (written set of procedures to deal with personnel complaints and how these should be filed and to whom).
- Business travel.
- Explanation of health and safety rights, such as right-to-know laws concerning chemicals in the workplace.
- Appropriate procedures for reporting accidents and proper steps in dealing with them.
- Legal rights of all employees, from rights regarding harassment to such issues as catastrophic illnesses and smoking in the workplace.

House-Use Policy

The ambience of a historic house often appeals to private individuals, who may request to use them as locations for weddings, birthdays, educational conferences, business meetings, photo shoots, even stage performances.

Some administrators, wishing to add extra income to the museum's coffers, will enthusiastically allow the public to rent the house and grounds for special events. Others will allow restricted usage, depending on the request, and only when certain types of food and beverages are served. (For example, food must not be gooey or sticky, and beverages must be nonstaining.) Other directors, however, hold the view that the historic house museum is an improper location for private engagements because of the potential hazards to interiors and collections, and therefore should not be rented out.

The issue is emotionally charged and one that must be examined carefully. It takes only one hapless incident to mar an important historic structure permanently. A burning candle carelessly placed, an umbrella pointed too close to an oil painting, red wine accidentally spilled on a historic rug will devastate an interior that has been scrupulously preserved and tended for decades.

It is prudent to set firm rules and regulations and to enforce them if private groups and individuals are to use the museum. If the house-use policy restricts the alteration of period rooms for events, then under no circumstance should furniture be relocated, plants rearranged, curtains removed, or other decorations added to the room. No exceptions should be made, or the policy will weaken and eventually be ignored. The rules must apply to everyone. A trustee who asks that a museum room be rearranged to accommodate a photographic session for a son's wedding is overstepping the boundaries.

Having a house-use policy in place will clarify the museum's position to the public. A rental agreement should also be created. Both should be drafted by the director and approved by the trustees. If groups or individuals are interested in renting museum space, they should apply in writing, explaining the purpose for which they intend to use the space. The rental form should list all restrictions for use and state the responsibilities of those entering into the agreement.

A number of issues are important in the creation of a house-use policy.

- Who will be responsible for reviewing and assessing the requests? Who will be responsible for scheduling and monitoring activities? To whom will this person or department report if a problem arises?
- Will the entire museum or only certain areas of the museum be available for private use?
- Will food and beverages be allowed in the museum? If so, what types? Who will be responsible for serving and cleanup and what are the procedures?

- Who will be responsible for security at each event? What procedures will security staff employ?
- What are emergency procedures? Are they accessible to the security staff?
- What activities will take place during the event and what restrictions apply? What specific activities are not allowed in the museum—such as smoking, dancing, amplified music, or photography?
- Which staff member will monitor the specific event and maintain control?
- What are the procedures if damage occurs? For example, an individual from a wedding party renting the house has broken a ceramic planter, inadvertently pushing it over the edge of the veranda. The staff member on duty should inform the renter of the damage. The damage must be documented and fair replacement value established. If the party is unwilling to pay the damage, that amount should be deducted from the damage deposit collected as part of the rental agreement.

After establishing a house-use policy, it should be kept current and adhered to unconditionally.

The legal responsibilities of museums are complicated matters and cannot be explored in detail in this book. The bibliography for Chapter 2 in this book provides a basic listing of publications on the topic. ALI/ABA, the American Law Institute/American Bar Association, Committee on Continuing Professional Education, annually offers a course on legal issues in museums. Resource materials prepared for the course are published in a handbook, and are available—for a fee—by writing to

> ALI/ABA
> 4025 Chestnut Street
> Philadelphia, Pennsylvania 19104

NOTES

1. The National Historic Preservation Act of 1966 and the amendments of 1980 authorize the Secretary of the Interior to maintain the National Register of Historic Landmarks and the National Register of Historic Places. For legal information about historic preservation laws, see

Christopher J. Duerksen, ed., *A Handbook on Historic Preservation Law* (Washington, D.C.: Conservation Foundation and the National Center for Preservation Law, 1983).

2. Refer to *The Secretary of the Interior's Standards for Historic Preservation Projects and Guidelines for Applying the Standards* (Washington, D.C.: Department of the Interior, 1979). It is available through the Government Printing Office.

3. Marie C. Malaro, *A Legal Primer on Managing Museum Collections* (Washington, D.C.: Smithsonian Institution Press, 1985), pp. 4–5.

4. Marilyn Phelan, *Museums and the Law* (Nashville, Tenn.: American Association for State and Local History, 1982), p. 9.

5. Alan Ullberg and Patricia Ullberg, *Museum Trusteeship* (Washington, D.C.: American Association of Museums, 1981), p. 14.

6. Gerald George and Cindy Sherrell-Leo, *Starting Right: A Basic Guide to Museum Planning* (Nashville, Tenn.: American Association for State and Local History, 1986), pp. 81–82.

7. Ullberg and Ullberg, *Museum Trusteeship*, p. 43.

8. Ibid., p. 13.

9. Malaro, *Legal Primer on Managing Museum Collections*, p. 6; Phelan, *Museums and the Law*, p. 156.

10. Ullberg and Ullberg, *Museum Trusteeship*, p. 28.

11. Ibid., p. 60.

12. G. Ellis Burcaw, *Introduction to Museum Work*, 2d ed. (Nashville, Tenn.: American Association for State and Local History, 1983), p. 192.

13. George and Sherrell-Leo, *Starting Right*, p. 85.

14. Ibid.

15. Ullberg and Ullberg, *Museum Trusteeship*, p. 61.

16. Meipu Yang, "Manuals for Museum Policy and Procedures," *Curator* 32, no. 4 (1989): 273–74.

17. Ibid., p. 270.

18. Ibid.

3

//

Where to Find the Help You Need

Help is all about you.

> Gerald George and Cindy Sherrell-Leo, *Starting Right:*
> *A Basic Guide to Museum Planning*

THERE IS AN abundance of information about improving individual museums and enriching the museum field as a whole. These resources provide technical help, assist in locating services, and identify programs for continuing education and possible funding sources. Many are readily available, either at no cost or for a nominal fee.

Yet there are so many places to turn for assistance that it is difficult to choose the right ones. This chapter will help to clarify the information network, which can be somewhat baffling, by identifying and describing institutions that can aid historic house museums. Also listed are annual meetings, workshops, seminars, training courses, and conferences that provide opportunities for information exchange.

National Museum Organizations

The following national associations were formed specifically for the advancement of museums and museum professionals.

American Association of Museums

Founded in 1906, the American Association of Museums (AAM) in Washington, D.C., represents the museum community as a whole

and addresses its needs. As both a professional and a trade association, AAM has more than 2,500 institutional and 8,000 individual
members, nearly 650 corporate affiliates, and 11 standing professional committees. Through AAM, members can also join the International Council of Museums (ICOM), which is dedicated to the
promotion of museums worldwide. Annual meetings, which draw
thousands of participants, are held in various locations around the
nation. Offerings consist of general sessions, panel discussions, and
workshops.

AAM also has six regional conferences that also sponsor annual
meetings in their geographic locations: New England (established
in 1919); Midwest (1928); Western (1942); Northeast (1947);
Southeast (1951); and Mountain Plains (1954). Some publish news-
letters and other periodicals.

AAM publishes a bimonthly periodical, *Museum News,* which
carries articles on current issues and topics in the field, and the
monthly newsletter *Aviso,* which contains information about recent
federal legislation, grant deadlines, job openings, and upcoming
workshops and seminars. *The Museum Directory,* a listing of most of
the museums in the nation, is also issued by AAM.

The Technical Information Service helps members with questions pertaining to career development, staff and board relations,
museum management, professional standards, ethics, and collections preservation. Questions can be posed in writing to this service, which will do limited research and supply appropriate referrals at no fee. (There is a fee for nonmembers.)

AAM also offers two important programs: the Accreditation
Program and the Museum Assessment Programs.

ACCREDITATION PROGRAM

The Accreditation Program was established in 1970 in response to
the need for the profession to develop standards against which the
excellence of individual museums might be measured.

In order to be considered for accreditation, museums must meet
the basic definition of a museum set by the AAM Accreditation
Commission: "an organized and permanent nonprofit institution,
essentially educational or aesthetic in purpose, with professional staff,
which owns or utilizes tangible objects, cares for them and exhibits
them, to the public on some regular schedule."[1] The process involves a rigorous self-examination and peer review of a museum's

administration, curatorship, exhibitions, interpretative programs, and plans. Two questions provide the framework for the review:

- Given the resources available to it, how well does the museum achieve its stated mission and goals?
- How well does the museum's performance meet standards and practices as they are generally understood in the museum field at large?

MUSEUM ASSESSMENT PROGRAMS

To promote high standards in museums, the AAM created the Museum Assessment Programs (MAP) in 1981. MAP is administered by AAM and funded through the Institute of Museum Services (IMS), a federal agency. The programs are designed for museums of all sizes and types, but are particularly helpful for small museums. Grants are noncompetitive and are awarded on a first-come, first-served basis. There are three programs.

- MAP I, Overall Operations and Programs, focuses on an analysis of the museum's entire operations.
- MAP II, Collections Management, aids in establishing policies, procedures, and practices relating to collections management, particularly documentation and preservation.
- MAP III, Public Dimension Assessment, reviews how the museum communicates with the public and assists in improving the variety and quality of public activities.

Museums taking part in a program complete a self-study questionnaire and a grant application. If the museum is eligible, a grant is awarded to cover the cost of a one-day on-site survey and a written report by a qualified professional. The report, which is confidential, defines problems and makes recommendations for immediate and long-range improvements. Using the report as a basis, the museum can make long-range plans, build a network of museum contacts, prepare for accreditation, educate the staff and board, and strengthen fund-raising efforts.

American Association for State and Local History

Established in 1940, the American Association for State and Local History (AASLH) has a strong tradition of serving historical organizations, especially smaller ones. Located in Nashville, Tennessee, AASLH is one of the most valuable resources for historic house museums, offering a variety of services.

- Regional workshops, training sessions, and conferences on current topics of special interest to museum staff.
- Grants-in-aid to researchers working on topics related to state and local history.
- Books, technical reports, leaflets, videotapes, and slide–tape programs through AASLH Press. Topics covered include museum management, interpretation and education, preservation, historical restoration, historical research, living history, exhibits, collections management and care, and funding sources.

Members of AASLH receive the bimonthly *History News,* an award-winning periodical that examines new trends and current issues in the field. Other topics include discussions on challenges in managing common to history museums and news about projects in which other historical agencies and museum are involved. Members also receive the monthly *History News Dispatch,* a newsletter for museum professionals and volunteers that offers news on recent job appointments, placement listings, current developments, and exhibit announcements. AASLH sponsors annual meetings, held at varying locations, where current issues in state and local history, museums, historic preservation and archeology are examined.

National Trust for Historic Preservation

The National Trust, located in Washington, D.C., is the major source of general information on historic preservation that is not a part of the federal government. A nonprofit membership organization chartered by Congress in 1949, its mission is to preserve America's history and culture by encouraging the public to participate in the preservation of America's buildings, historic sites, and monuments and to acquire and preserve historic properties. The organization also acts as a clearinghouse for information on conferences, seminars, and training opportunities. It achieves its mission in a number of ways.

- Providing educational programs on preservation to professionals and volunteers at various locations across the nation.
- Offering technical advice and carrying out preservation activities.
- Serving as an advocate for the country's heritage in state and federal courts.
- Operating special projects to demonstrate how preservation approaches might be used to solve problems and aid revitalization and economic development of the community.
- Acquiring significant American properties and opening them to the public, as house museums. (Currently the National Trust owns and maintains seventeen properties.)
- Sponsoring a national preservation conference held each year in October.
- Granting loans to members.

The National Trust for Historic Preservation offers its members two important publications. *Historic Preservation,* a bimonthly, award-winning magazine, features the National Trust's activities and preservation advice. *Historic Preservation News,* issued monthly, tracks new legislation regarding historic properties and presents current events in the field. A third publication, *Preservation Forum,* is available for upper-level organizational members. It is a bimonthly journal that discusses nonprofit management, funding sources, national and state news, training opportunities, archeology, and historic sites.

The toll-free National Trust Legislation Hotline provides current news on historic preservation legislation and policy. To hear recorded messages call (800)765–NTHP. Callers may also leave messages at this number.

The National Trust provides a number of services.

PRESERVATION SERVICES FUND

The Preservation Services Fund (PSF) provides small grants, usually $1,000 to $1,500, to nonprofit organizations and public agencies to support the initiation of preservation programs. The grants must be matched dollar for dollar by institutions receiving the funds.

PSF funds may be used for professional consultant services, educational programs, and conferences.

NATIONAL PRESERVATION LOAN FUND

Created in 1984, the National Preservation Loan Fund (NPLF) provides nonprofit organizations and public agencies with low-interest loans, loan guarantees, and lines of credit for a wide range of projects, including historic rehabilitation, restoration, and acquisition. For loan and grant information, contact the National Trust office.

CENTER FOR HISTORIC HOUSES

The National Trust also runs the Center for Historic Houses. This agency provides owners of historic houses with guidance on rehabilitating and caring for their properties. The center also provides various educational programs, resource materials, and opportunities for networking with other homeowners.

- Conferences, seminars, lectures, and hands-on workshops presented at locations across the country by well-known preservationists.
- The Great American Home Awards, given annually to nominated individuals who have successfully rehabilitated their historic homes.
- The Old-House Starter Kit, available for a small fee, with literature that answers questions about rehabilitating an old house.
- An insurance program that offers replacement value on historic residences.

National Institute for the Conservation of Cultural Property

The goals of the nonprofit National Institute for the Conservation of Cultural Property (NIC), located in Washington, D.C., are to preserve our nation's cultural heritage. NIC has initiated numerous programs and projects to fulfill their goals.

CONSERVATION ASSESSMENT PROGRAM

The Conservation Assessment Program (CAP), funded by the Institute of Museum Services, provides noncompetitive grants to museums for conservation assessments. CAP grants assist museums in examining their collections, museum environment, and historic structure, and all procedures and policies affecting the collections. The grant supports a two-day on-site visit and written report of a general conservation assessor. This grant is especially useful to historic house museums because it will also provide for an architectural assessor, where appropriate. The report helps to identify overall conservation needs and recommends action both for care and management of collections. CAP is a one-time award granted on a first-come, first-served basis.

COLLECTIONS CARE INFORMATION SERVICE

The Collections Care Information Service (CCIS) provides bibliographic references on preventive conservation and collections care to callers who use its toll-free number. The CCIS database contains more than 1,600 entries and citations. Callers receive an overview of the topic in which they are interested, bibliographic citations, and information on how to obtain publications pertaining to the subject. (Questions pertaining to treatments of individual objects are not handled through this service.) Callers outside Washington, D.C., can dial (800)421–1381. Those calling from the Washington area should use (202)625–1495.

SAVE OUTDOOR SCULPTURE!

Save Outdoor Sculpture! (SOS!) was created by NIC to address the serious problem of neglect of outdoor statues and monuments in this country. The goal of SOS! is to survey all outdoor sculpture throughout the nation using a network of trained volunteers.

BAY COLLECTIONS PILOT TRAINING PROGRAM

The Bay Foundation was established in 1950 by Charles Ulrick and Josephine Bay to support their interests in art restoration and education. A grant from the Bay Foundation supports a series of course curricula on collections-care training, published by NIC. The curricula focus on natural history, fine arts, history, and ethnographic and archeological collections. These teaching materials are available at no charge to museums and organizations that are interested in setting up collections-care training programs within their institutions.

Association for Preservation Technology

The Association for Preservation Technology (APT) was formed in 1968 to provide preservationist professionals from the United States and Canada with a forum for exchanging information on building technologies and exploring new methods for researching and preserving historic structures. APT also publishes the APT *Bulletin,* an academic journal for the preservation specialist, and a bimonthly newsletter, the *Communiqué.*

Federal Agencies that Can Help Historic House Museums

Advisory Council on Historic Preservation

The Advisory Council on Historic Preservation, an independent federal agency in Washington, D.C., is the major policy adviser to the government on historic preservation. The council was established by the National Historic Preservation Act of 1966. Nineteen members make up the council, including the Secretary of the Interior, the Secretary of Agriculture, and other federal agency heads, as well as preservation experts, one mayor, one governor, and private citizens. The council chair and vice chairpersons are appointed by the president of the United States.

The council is responsible for assessing the effectiveness of state, local, and private programs in their implementation of the National Historic Preservation Act. This assessment is reported to the president and Congress. The council also makes recommendations for improving the national historic preservation program, provides testimony and technical advice on legislative proposals relating to historic preservation, reviews federal and federally assisted projects that affect properties on or eligible for the National Register of

Historic Places, and directs inquiries about historic preservation to appropriate preservation organizations.

The council also publishes, at no charge, an important guide, *Where To Look: A Guide to Preservation Information,* which identifies historic preservation resources, and provides general bibliographies, lists preservation organizations, defines legislation and legal control, and discusses economic incentives and many other preservation issues. Numerous other publications about historic preservation are available at no charge through the council.

National Park Service

The National Park Service, a bureau within the Department of the Interior, operates many historic sites throughout the nation. One of its primary functions is to assist government officials and Park Service employees through programs, literature, and continuing-education courses. Some programs offered by the Park Service are available to the public. One of the most valuable training courses for neophyte curators of museums is called Curatorial Methods Training Program. This two-week course, usually offered annually, concentrates on basic information essential to the care of museum collections. Topics covered include scope of collections, museum ethics, museum records, preventive conservation, museum security, fire protection, emergency planning, collections management, planning, programming, and funding. Four curators are selected to participate in each class. Other courses for nonfederal employees are also offered. To receive a catalog of current training courses offered by the National Park Service write to

> Curatorial Methods Course Coordinator
> Stephen T. Mather Employee Development Center
> P.O. Box 77
> Harpers Ferry, West Virginia 25425-0077

PRESERVATION ASSISTANCE DIVISION

The Preservation Assistance Division (PAD), a branch of the National Park Service, develops technical materials on preservation for federal agencies, state and local governments, and individuals. Two PAD series are published: (1) Preservation Briefs, which deal with such topics as energy conservation in historic buildings, roofing, mortar pointing, and the preservation of glazed terra cotta; and (2) Preservation Tech Notes, which treat curatorial issues such as storage environments for objects and the effects of sunlight on historic furnishings. Preservation Briefs are available through the Government Printing Office in Washington, D.C., or through each state's historic preservation office. The cost is about $1 per issue or the basic set for about $9. Preservation Tech Notes can be obtained by writing to

> Preservation Assistance Division
> National Park Service
> P.O. Box 37127
> Washington, D.C. 20013–7127

Single copies are available at no cost.

The PAD staff will also answer questions from individuals pertaining to historic preservation, such as how to conserve energy in historic buildings, how to retrofit a building with fire-safety equipment, and how to care properly for wood shingles. Inquiries can be made by phone or by letter.

State Historic Preservation Office

The State Historic Preservation Office (SHPO) is another important source for historic house museums. Each state has a state historic preservation office; they are often housed in the state historical society or within a government agency such as state parks. SHPO officers, appointed by the federal government, inform citizens about historic preservation standards, report on legal concerns and tax benefits, provide information on grants and loans for historic properties, and nominate properties to the National Register of Historic Places. In some states, the SHPO conducts workshops and consults with individuals about preservation problems. Many keep an up-to-date listing of area contractors and suppliers who specialize in historic restoration.

Regional Organizations that Help

Society for the Preservation of New England Antiquities

William Sumner Appleton, a pioneering preservationist who was concerned with the vanishing material culture of New England, founded the Society for the Preservation of New England Antiquities (SPNEA) in 1910. Today this regional membership society holds true to the traditions that Appleton set forth: to preserve and document New England's past through its art, artifacts, and historic properties.

As part of SPNEA's mission, twenty-three house museums and eleven study properties are preserved and interpreted for public use. Study properties, including ten seventeenth-century houses and one eighteenth-century meetinghouse, are used for architectural research by students and scholars. Visits to these properties are by appointment only. (Nine other properties are owned by SPNEA, but are not open to the public.)

SPNEA offers several important services.

SPNEA RESEARCH AND STUDY COLLECTIONS

SPNEA manages in its properties collections of more than 100,000 household articles that represent 300 years of tradition in New England. Most of the objects in this well-documented collection are household furnishings on view in twenty-three houses, many of the objects original to the houses. The collections also include historic wallpaper, textiles, architectural elements, and other objects. Some of the collections are housed in a storage facility located in Haverhill, Massachusetts. Collections can be studied for research and comparison purposes by appointment.

SPNEA ARCHIVES

SPNEA also maintains an archive of 1.5 million historic photographs, prints, architectural drawings, advertising materials and manuscripts and illustrated publications that reflect New England in former times. The archive staff members can answer inquiries and assist in research. It is located in the Harrison Gray Otis House, 141 Cambridge Street, Boston, Massachusetts.

SPNEA CONSERVATION CENTER

The SPNEA Conservation Center, located at 185 Lyman Street, Waltham, Massachusetts, maintains three divisions: the Architectural Conservation Services, the Furniture Conservation Division, and the Upholstery Conservation Division. The services these divisions offer are available to public agencies, nonprofit organizations, businesses, home owners, and architects.

The **Architectural Conservation Services** can be employed to perform a number of consulting services in historical construction projects.

- Provide architectural history and chronology of changes to buildings.
- Make recommendations for the repair, restoration, and replication of historic structures.
- Write reports on historic structure.
- Supervise conservation and restoration treatments.
- Conduct historical paint research.
- Replicate historical paint colors.
- Re-create original or early decorative finishes.
- Conduct research on historical wallpaper.
- Advise on cleaning, repointing, and replacement of masonry structures.
- Consolidate or replace deteriorated wood.
- Offer courses and lectures on various aspects of technical architectural conservation.

The **Furniture Conservation Division** and the **Upholstery Conservation Division** provide a full range of services, including

- Conserving traditional finishes.
- Performing gilding.
- Identifying fiber content, pigment, and wood.
- Reupholstery: partial or complete traditional reupholstery and noninterventive (stabilizing fabrics without adding or removing anything) upholstery treatments.
- Performing nonabrasive cleaning and repair of hardware.
- Creating suitable finishes where inappropriate finishes are present.

At SPNEA each treatment is adapted to the conservation needs of the object. Conservators are also available for surveying environmental conditions of collections while on exhibit and in storage, as well as long-range conservation planning.

Agencies that Fund Museums

Institute of Museum Services

Institute of Museum Services (IMS) is an independent federal agency in Washington, D.C., that was established in 1976 to improve museum services by issuing grants. IMS currently funds several noncompetitive and competitive programs for which museums are eligible.

- General Operating Support. This grant is given annually in a competitive program created to improve museum operations. Grants, in the amount of 10 percent of the museum's operating budget to a maximum of $75,000, are made by a peer review, focusing on how effectively the museum uses available resources. To apply, write to the American Association of Museums for the GOS application forms.
- Conservation Project Support. This program, also competitive, provides matching grants for projects relating to conserving museum collections. The grants usually do not exceed $25,000. Write to AAM for the application forms.
- Museum Assessment Program. As mentioned earlier in the chapter, the Institute of Museum Services funds MAP, MAP II, and MAP III, and the American Association of Museums administers this program.

National Endowment for the Humanities

A federal program in Washington, D.C., the National Endowment for the Humanities (NEH) is designed to assist museums through grant awards for exemplary work that will advance and disseminate knowledge of the humanities. The grants are made through five divisions (Education, General, Research, and State programs; Fellowships and Seminars) and two offices (Office of Challenge Grants, and Office of Preservation), which support museums and individuals working in museums. Information about the divisions and offices of NEH and instructions on making application are available from the Office of Publications and Public Affairs. You can call (202)786-0438 or write to

> National Endowment for the Humanities
> 1100 Pennsylvania Avenue, NW
> Washington, D.C., 20506

National Endowment for the Arts

Also located in Washington, D.C., the National Endowment for the Arts (NEA) is a federal assistance program that supports projects in the visual and performing arts. Through its Museum Program, application for funding may be made for special exhibitions, utilization of museum resources, care of collections (arts), professional development, museum purchases (to acquire work of living American artists), and an arts and artifacts indemnity program (to obtain insurance for international exhibitions). For additional information and copies of the guidelines, call (202)682–5442, or write to

> National Endowment for the Arts
> 1100 Pennsylvania Avenue, NW
> Washington, D.C. 20506

J. Paul Getty Trust

The Getty Trust is a private foundation in California dedicated to the visual arts and humanities. It administers the J. Paul Getty Museum, as well as six programs: the Getty Center for the History of Art and the Humanities, the Getty Conservation Institute, the Getty Art History Information Program, the Getty Center for Education in the Arts, the Museum Management Institute, and the Program for Art on Film.

GETTY GRANT PROGRAM

The Getty Grant Program provides assistance for projects relating to scholarship in art history, art museums, and conservation. The program's newest category, Architectural Conservation Grants, is of particular interest to house museums. Established in 1988, these grants support the conservation of buildings of outstanding architectural, historical, and cultural significance throughout the world.

In order to qualify for a grant, a building or group of buildings must be owned by a nonprofit entity and open to the public. In the United States, a building also must be designated as a National Landmark and included on the National Register of Historic Places, although in certain instances State Landmark properties included on the National Register will be considered. Approval by the legal owner of the building must be granted in order to qualify for the grant. The proposed conservation project must focus on the repair and conservation of the structure and fabric of the building. Work relating primarily to maintenance, capital improvements, systems upgrading, or adaptive reuse is not eligible for support. Projects usually include on-site training opportunities for specialists in architectural conservation or related crafts. The three funding categories of the architectural conservation grants are Project Identification, Project Preparation, and Project Implementation. Most grants are awarded at the project identification and project preparation stages.

For information on and guidelines for the Architectural Conservation Grants, contact

> Getty Grant Program
> 401 Wilshire Boulevard, Suite 401
> Santa Monica, California 90401

Conservation Organizations

American Institute for Conservation of Historic and Artistic Works

Located in Washington, D.C., The American Institute for Conservation of Historic and Artistic Works (AIC) is a nonprofit professional organization whose goal is to uphold standards of professional conduct and to advance knowledge and improve methods of conservation in preserving cultural property. Through publications and annual meetings, AIC conservation professionals are able to exchange information on conservation practices and share knowledge on new materials and techniques for slowing the decay and deterioration of historic and artistic works.

AIC publishes the *Journal of the American Institute for Conservation*

(JAIC) twice a year, a bimonthly *Newsletter,* and the *AIC Directory,* which lists names and addresses of all members and includes the "AIC Bylaws and Code of Ethics and Standards of Practice" in the field of conservation.

CONSERVATION SERVICES REFERRAL SYSTEM

The Foundation of the American Institute for Conservation of Historic and Artistic Works (FAIC) administers this program, which assists institutions and individuals in making informed choices on a wide range of conservation issues. The staff will undertake a computerized search to identify and locate a professional conservator to assist with specific conservation problems. All conservators in the referral system are members of the American Institute for Conservation of Historic and Artistic Works. Contact the Services Referral System by telephone (202)232–6636, by facsimile: (202)232–6630, or by writing to

> Foundation of the American Institute
>   for Conservation of Historic and Artistic Works
> 1400 16th Street NW
> Suite 340
> Washington, D.C. 20036

Canadian Conservation Institute

The Canadian Conservation Institute (CCI), located in Ottawa, is a division of the Museums and Heritage Branch of the Department of Communications. CCI's mandate is to provide conservation treatment and research service. Although the institute is for use by Canadian institutions, its staff members are willing to share their experience and knowledge with others and will readily answer technical questions and provide advice on materials and commercial products that can be used in museums, on specific treatments and conservation procedures, and on the basic care of collections. Send inquiries about collections care by mail or call.

CCI offers to anyone interested their publications: *CCI Newsletter,* CCI Notes, and a series of technical bulletins. Most are available at no cost and are of great value to the curator because of their practical information and how-to instructions on a wide range of topics such as caring for basketry, methods for displaying books, creating storage systems for paintings, and mounting small, light, flat textiles. For a listing of publications write to

CCI, Extension Services
1030 Innes
Ottawa, Ontario K1A OC8
Canada

Textile Conservation Workshop

The nonprofit Textile Conservation Workshop, in South Salem, New York, provides conservation services in a fully equipped laboratory at minimal cost for museums, historical agencies, and private individuals. The workshop also conducts surveys for smaller museums on the physical condition of textiles collections and makes recommendations for storage, treatment procedures, and exhibition. It offers lectures and informal discussions to interested organizations on the care, proper handling, storage, and display of textiles. Its outreach educational program specifically targets small museums that need advice on preventative measures in caring for textile collections.

New York State Conservation Consultancy

In Elmsford, New York, The Consultancy was formed to provide expert conservation advice on the care of collections in smaller museums, historical societies, and other nonprofit organizations in New York. It offers three services: conservation information, surveys, and seminars on conservation education.

The Consultancy's conservation information services, which are free of charge, include issuing advice on the care of collections and making referrals to conservators and suppliers of conservation materials. Bulletins on conservation issues relevant to historic house museums are also available. These are obtainable for a nominal charge to any interested museum staff or individual. Write to

New York State Conservation Consultancy
c/o Lower Hudson Conference
2199 Saw Mill River Road
Elmsford, New York 10523

The Consultancy will also provide, free of charge, surveys conducted by conservation specialists on caring for historical collections. Five types of surveys are offered: a **general survey,** or overall assessment of the collection; an **environment survey,** which focuses on the climatic conditions affecting collections; a **storage survey,** in which storage conditions are assessed; an **exhibit survey,** which focuses on general exhibit practices or on the specific needs of a collection on exhibit; and a **treatment survey,** in which condition reports are made on specific collection or objects. After a survey is completed, a written report and recommendations for improvements are made. The Consultancy also offers professional-level seminars—given in various locations in New York state—on conservation relating to care of collections.

Many other regional conservation organizations can provide artifact treatment for a fee (see Appendix).

Conservation and Collections Care Center at Peebles Island

A staff of five conservators that treats objects belonging to New York's historic park sites (of which there are thirty-four) works at this facility near Albany, New York.

The Harpers Ferry Conservation Laboratory

Run by and for the National Park Service, this facility employs conservators who work with site managers who direct the 337 park sites. Conservators not only treat objects, but also assist site managers in collections maintenance and management.

Publications that Help the Historic House Curator

It is essential that every historic house museum keep a library of books and periodicals on museum topics for the professional development of the staff and for reference. The American Association of Museums and the American Association for State and Local History each issue catalogs listing books for museum professionals. Both organizations provide publications catalogs to members several times a year. Many state and local historical societies publish books that are pertinent to historic houses. Request recent catalogs from historical societies in your region. Periodicals are important in keeping museum professionals abreast of current trends and issues and in finding solutions to common problems. In addition AASLH offers a vast number of technical leaflets, reports, and audiovisual presentations on topics related to museum management, restoration, education, public relations, security, furnishings, insurance, housekeeping, building construction, house technology, and other relevant topics.

Books

As a foundation, the books listed below are suggested to cover the primary topics of concern to curators of house museums. These books offer valuable and practical information, and they should become well worn within a short time. Each is available in one of the above-mentioned catalogs.

- William Alderson and Shirley Payne Low, *Interpretation of Historic Sites* (Nashville, Tenn.: American Association for State and Local History, 1976), is an essential resource that offers ideas for developing and conducting interpretative programs at historic sites. The authors are well acquainted with a variety of levels of budgets for historic house museums and offer helpful advice on developing a strong interpretative program appropriate for the museum.
- Edward P. Alexander, *Museums in Motion* (Nashville, Tenn.: American Association for State and Local History, 1979), is a general work on the functions of museums in this country. It includes a helpful history of the museum profession; it defines the roles of different types of museums and the ways in which museums function.
- American Association of Museums, *Museum Ethics,* 2d ed. (Washington, D.C.: American Association of Museums, 1991), is the official report on the ethical principles to be applied to all areas of museum operations. This small book is essential reading for all museum staff, volunteers, and trustees.
- American Association of Museums, *Museums for a New Century* (Washington, D.C.: American Association of Museums, 1984), offers museum professionals' examinations of the major issues museums face and recommendations of how to deal with these challenges.
- Dorothy Dudley, Irma Bezold Wilkinson, et al., *Museum Registration Methods* (Washington, D.C.: American Association of Mu-

seums, 1979), is a standard manual for registering, managing, storing, and caring for museum collections.

- Kathleen Brown Fletcher, *The Nine Keys to Successful Volunteer Programs* (Rockville, Md.: Taft Group, 1987), discusses how to establish and manage a successful volunteer program.

- Carl E. Guthe, *The Management of Small History Museums* (Nashville, Tenn.: American Association for State and Local History, 1988), is a time-honored work. It offers advice on defining the museum's purpose, governance, funding, collections, and interpretation. Use it as a guide in managing the historic house museum.

- A. Bruce MacLeish, *The Care of Antiques and Historical Collections*, 2d ed. (Nashville, Tenn.: American Association for State and Local History, 1985), describes, in clear terms, conservation strategies in caring for and preserving historic objects. It includes particularly useful information on preventive measures in preserving collections and on improving standards for storing collections.

- Arminta Neal, *Exhibits for the Small Museum* (Nashville, Tenn.: American Association for State and Local History, 1976), is a classic book that offers advice on creating effective exhibits while coping with small budgets and limited resources.

- *The Secretary of the Interior's Standards for Historic Preservation Projects and Guidelines for Applying the Standards* (Washington, D.C.: Department of the Interior, 1979), is a guide for properties eligible for or already on the National Register of Historic Places. It defines recommended preservation treatments and those that are not, as they apply to historic properties. Available through the Government Printing Office in Washington, D.C., *Museum Trusteeship* (Washington, D.C.: American Association of Museums, 1981), is a standard handbook on governance in museums. It covers such important topics as the legal and ethical accountability of the board of trustees, structure and operations of the board, relationships between board members, directors, and staff, and policy-making in the museum. This book should be carefully read by trustees and museum staff.

Periodicals

The major journals in the American museum profession are *Museum News, History News, Curator,* and the *Museologist.* Also important are the National Trust periodicals: *Preservation Forum, Historic Preservation,* and *Preservation News.*

The Old-House Journal, published since 1973, is also important for those who manage historic houses. It is a popular guide with practical information on general preservation and maintenance of houses built before 1914. *The Old-House Journal Catalog,* published annually, is useful for locating companies that sell architectural materials needed for restoration, as well as services required for this work. The catalog can be found in most bookstores. For a subscription to *The Old-House Journal,* write to

>Old-House Journal Corporation
>2 Main Street
>Gloucester, Massachusetts 01930

Many other periodicals are available that are of use to the historic house curator. Some journals, such as *American Quarterly, Journal of Interdisciplinary History, Nineteenth Century, Social Education,* and *Journal of American Culture,* often carry articles that explore life during different periods in American history. Other articles discuss the cultural and social importance of material objects used in historic houses. Periodicals such as *Journal of Garden History* and *Landscape* discuss such topics as historic landscapes and their meaning and changes through time. Several journals deal with architectural preservation, such as *American Preservation* and *Technology and Conservation,* and *American Architecture* and *Journal of the Society of Architectural Historians* carry articles on the significance and development of U.S. architecture. *The Decorative Arts Trust Newsletter* deals with the furnishings commonly found in historic houses and museum collections and discusses their influences and importance.

Education and Professional Development for Museum Staff

Many state historical societies, state museums, and museum associations offer outreach programs, workshops, and seminars on topics relevant to museums. State historical commissions, historic preservation organizations, historic preservation offices, arts organizations, and state and regional humanities councils also sponsor conferences, lectures, classes, and seminars that are of interest to the staffs of historic house museums. Library associations are another source for courses and workshops on topics dealing with archival preservation. These organizations can be located through the telephone directory.

The simplest way to discover what educational events are being offered is to ask professionals at museums in the area. It is important to know the local museums and to get acquainted with the staff of other historic house museums. They may be able to answer questions on puzzling problems and can serve as moral support since they are often faced with challenges similar to your own.

Training Through Museum Organization

In addition to training sessions for museum professionals, volunteers, and trustees offered by the American Association for State and Local History and the American Association of Museums, some larger museums offer training in various aspects of museum work, ranging from American material culture to collections management. Among these are the Smithsonian Institution in Washington, D.C., Colonial Williamsburg in Virginia, the Winterthur Museum in Delaware, Historic Deerfield in Michigan, and the National Trust for Historic Preservation. The National Park Service also offers a few training courses.

Courses in Museum Studies

Various universities and colleges around the nation offer degree programs in museology (museum studies), architecture, archaeology, landscape architecture, museum conservation, and historic preservation studies. Some universities run graduate-level degree programs in museum studies, such as New York University, which offers an intensive, interdisciplinary program, and the University of Nebraska–Lincoln, which offers a broad-based program for those interested in a career in museums. Other universities offer a variety of courses in museum studies through art history, anthropology and history departments.

The **Cooperstown Graduate Program in History Museum Studies** is cosponsored by the State University of New York at Oneonta and the New York State Historical Association. Founded in 1964, the program awards a master's degree in history museum studies to those who complete either the regular track or the continuing education track. Either course is designed to train generalists, providing a foundation in all aspects of museum work. The curriculum emphasizes museum studies, including theory and procedures, ethics and professional standards, administration, collections management, education, and research. Both practical and professional skills necessary to museum work are taught. For more information about the Cooperstown Graduate Program write to

> CGP
> P.O. Box 800
> Cooperstown, New York 13326

The Center for Historic Preservation at Middle Tennessee State University in Murfreesboro offers both undergraduate- and graduate-level programs for anyone interested in historic preservation studies. At the undergraduate level, the historic preservation program prepares students for careers in preservation, planning and administration, and historic site interpretation and management, combining theory with practical experience. The graduate program at MTSU offers the M.A. and D.A. degrees in history with emphasis in historic preservation. For information write to

> Center for Historic Preservation
> Box 80
> Middle Tennessee State University
> Murfreesboro, Tennessee 37132

Senior Museum Professionals

The Museum Management Institute (MMI), designed for senior museum professionals, offers a four-week program every summer, geared to critical management issues. Topics include negotiation, conflict resolution, resource allocation, financial analysis, marketing, the politics of organizations, ethics, legal issues, intergroup dynamics, organizational change, and strategic vision. The MMI is sponsored by the Getty Trust, the Art Museum Association of America, and the University of California at Berkeley. MMI is taught at the University of California, Berkeley. For information write to

> Museum Management Institute
> 2510 Channing Way
> Suite 4
> Berkeley, California 94704

The **Williamsburg Seminar on Historical Administration** is a four-week course, held annually, designed for professionals in preservation management. It explores all facets of historical administration and is a must for directors, curators, and managers of historic museums. The seminar is jointly sponsored by the American Association for State and Local History, the American Association of Museums, Colonial Williamsburg, and the National Trust for Historic Preservation. This annual course is held in Williamsburg, Virginia.

The **Winedale Museum Seminar,** sponsored by the Texas Historical Commission and the Winedale Historical Center, University of Texas, is a twelve-day course geared to middle- to upper-level museum professionals or to experienced volunteers. Sessions cover such topics as grant writing, fund-raising, financial planning, trustee relations and board development, staff relations, volunteer management, marketing, ethics, and museum politics. Classes consist of lectures, discussions, group problem-solving, practical exercises, participant presentations and hands-on activities. Field trips to area museums are included. The seminar is usually held twice a year, depending on funding, and is held in Round Top, Texas. Contact

> Texas Historical Commission
> P.O. Box 12276
> Austin, Texas 78711

The **Museum Management Program,** a one-week course held annually during the first week of July at the University of Colorado Conference Center in Boulder, is a general program geared to senior managers from all types of museums. The topics vary somewhat from year to year, but the focus is on critical issues in museum management such as the handling staff needs, working with advisory committees, trustee selection, developing new revenues, influencing communities and local government, and taking positions on sensitive issues in the field. For information contact

> Office of Conference Services
> University of Colorado
> Campus Box 153
> Boulder, Colorado 80309–0153

NOTE

1. American Association of Museums, *Museums for a New Century* (Washington, D.C.: American Assocsiation of Museum, 1984), p. 75.

4

//

Collections: The Essence
of the Museum

In planning for the growth of its collections, we urge each museum to set, clear, rational and appropriate goals for the contribution it can make to the stewardship of our cultural and natural heritage. It is important that every museum collect both carefully and purposefully. Each museum must exercise care by collecting within its capacity to house and preserve the objects, artifacts and specimens in its stewardship; each must collect purposefully by continuing its own traditions of quality and diversity. A periodic review of the collections policy will ensure that it is in keeping with current professional standards and the purposes of the institution.

American Association of Museums, *Museums for a New Century*

THE COLLECTION AND preservation of objects that represent our cultural past are generally agreed to be a museum's most important functions. It is the collection—the objects exhibited and stored—that is the very essence of the historic house museum.

Objects help to flesh out the stories that make up our world. Objects are what draw us to museums: they teach us about our past and help us understand the present. Objects are powerful. They have the ability to strike chords in our subconscious and to provoke memories. The sight of an old textbook used by a student or the odor of kerosene burning in an oil lamp can draw out past experiences or create new ones.

Objects can stir our senses. The impact of what we see, hear, touch, and smell in an old house cannot be repeated in a photo-

Trunk brought by Swedish immigrants to "Amerika" containing utilitarian objects. Artifacts such as these make up collections contained in historic house museums. (Photograph by Jerry Taube, courtesy of the American Swedish Institute)

graph or on film. It is the touch of the cool, smooth stone facade, the smell of the leather furnishings and polished wood, the hum of the old ceiling fan in the master bedroom, or the carved woodwork in the grand hall that make up the experience.

It is the experience of objects and their environment that visitors seek—and it is museum manager's job is to collect the proper objects to help create that experience. Along with the thrill of collecting materials for the museum, however, comes a serious re-

sponsibility: collections must be maintained, preserved, documented, and secured. If the collection is not well managed, the
museum has failed to carry out a primary function.

Management of Collections

Historic house museums most commonly house utilitarian objects—tools, household articles, furniture, china and glassware, and
other furnishings. Many have examples of period costumes and
archival materials—books, letters, diaries, and photographs. Some
own valuable paintings, prints, or tapestries. Much of this material
is organic and can deteriorate easily in uncontrolled environments.
Yet all too often staff and volunteers are inadequately trained in
managing collections or have little time to devote to their care—
they may be struggling simply to keep the programs running and
the roof repaired. Nevertheless, museums must make a commitment to protect and preserve their holdings in order to assure the
museum's future.

Is it possible to collect significant objects of material culture and
to care for them appropriately? Can the museum afford a salary
for professionals and provide adequate training for volunteers? Does
the museum fully understand that, in accepting objects for its collection, it also commits to their preservation? Should the trustees,
in good conscience, accept objects that could deteriorate in a museum environment, despite the care given them?

These questions are not easy to answer. Lack of community
support, financial backing, or commitment to excellence may in-
hibit a museum from properly caring for its collection. If a museum cannot maintain basic preservation standards, its collection
should be placed in another institution where the proper care can
be provided. However, once a museum has made a commitment to
maintain the collection several fundamental steps must be followed. The most important is to write a **collections management
policy.** The most basic document used in administering collections,
the policy often is required for grant applications and may be re-
quested by potential donors who wish to determine if the aims of
the museum are serious.

This document explains, in exacting detail, the purpose of the
museum, its collecting goals, and its procedures for acquiring and
disposing of objects, handling loans (both incoming and outgoing)
and insurance. It should be precise yet flexible enough to handle

Collection of "Santos" and other religious artifacts at Martinez Hacienda, Taos, New Mexico. (Photograph courtesy of Kit Carson Historic Museums)

the unexpected opportunities that may arise.[1] While the policy should be written by those who work most closely with the collections, it should be accessible to, and respected by, all staff members and trustees.

A typical collections management policy covers the following points:

• The museum's purpose and what it hopes to contribute to the public through its collections. The type of collection and its geographical or chronological confines should be defined: are the objects to represent the general time period of the historic house or are they only to include original material, furnishings that once belonged to the house?

- Methods for acquiring items Acquisition may be defined as the "discovery, preliminary evaluation, negotiation for, taking complete custody of, documenting title to, and acknowledging receipt of materials and objects; or negotiating for and recording information concerning borrowed objects."[2] The policy must include specific instructions on how objects proposed for the collection are accepted and documented, and the legal method and documents required for the transfer of title from previous owners to the museum.

- The criteria for acquiring objects. The standards an object must meet before it can be considered for the museum's collection. A thorough history of the object is essential—its owner, function, origin, maker, or manufacturer and any other pertinent information.

- Guidelines for establishing an acquisitions committee to make recommendations to the curator and director in assessing the value of an object for a specific collection.

- Methods for deaccessioning or disposing of items. (Deaccessioning refers to removing an object permanently from a collection.) This section must be written clearly and explicitly. Explain why objects may be deaccessioned; for example, they are no longer relevant or serve the purpose of the museum (refer to charter purpose), or they are unstable or seriously deteriorated and cannot be preserved by the museum. Describe how to handle the object after it has been deaccessioned. This part of the policy is very important, given the delicate nature of disposing of objects that might have been donated by members of the community. Some accepted methods of disposition are (1) donating the object to another museum or tax-exempt cultural institution, (2) selling the object, with proceeds going to an acquisitions fund, (3) transferring the object to an "educational collection" (one that can be used and touched by museum visitors), and (4) destroying the object if it is in total disrepair.

  Include a statement on ethical considerations; that is, the museum will not sell or give deaccessioned objects to museum staff, volunteers, trustees, or their immediate families or representatives. A statement on public disclosure of deaccessioned objects is also important.

- Procedures for handling incoming and outgoing loans. Museum objects should be loaned only after approval by the director and curator and only after the object's safety during transport and exhibition are assured. The staff member responsible for monitoring the loans should also be identified in the policy.

LOAN PROCEDURE

1. The museum requesting a loan completes a facilities report, which includes details concerning its security and climate control systems, methods of transport and handling, and insurance.

2. A loan agreed upon, the curator completes a **loan form** listing the borrower's responsibilities and prepares a **condition report** disclosing the condition of the object before it leaves the museum.

3. The borrowing institution issues a **Certificate of Insurance** and the object is released.

4. On receipt of the object, the borrowing museum checks the condition report and reports any changes that might have occurred in transit.

- Procedures for inventories. A schedule should be established for taking inventory of the museum's collection.
- Procedures for insurance coverage. Dealing with lost or damaged objects and loans to other museums and keeping the insurance company apprised of new donations. Procedures for the appraisal of collections and how often it should be done.

The guidelines provided above are just that, a guide. They are but one pattern of a collections management policy. Your policy should be tailored specifically to the needs of your museum. When it is time to write the policy it may be helpful to look at policies from several other well-run historic houses or small museums.

The collections management policy is a tool that should be used by everyone.

Code of Ethics

All museums need to establish principles to guide directors, curators, staff, volunteers, and members of the governing body. In 1991, the American Association of Museums revised the handbook on museum ethics and added that all nonprofit museum members of

AAM are to subscribe to the code as a condition of membership. (This code of ethics—because of complex issues—will not be finalized until 1993.) The association also states that by January 1, 1997, each nonprofit member must have its own written code of ethics: although the standard code of ethics is in place, each museum is unique and requires a tailor-made policy specifying standards for professional behavior and proper actions. This policy may be written as a separate document or incorporated in the collections management policy. There are a number of questions to consider in setting down the policy.

What are the museum's responsibilities in managing and conserving the collections? Who will use collections—curatorial staff, museum interpreters, the public? How will the museum acquire objects and dispose of them?

What are the guidelines for curators who collect in the same areas they curate? In the past, art museums encouraged their curators to build personal collections in the belief this practice would enhance the curators' knowledge and understanding. Today most museums restrict personal collecting because of a potential conflict of interest. In 1986, the International Council of Museums (ICOM), composed a general code for museum professionals, citing the dilemma of "personal collecting, and the basic obligation not to complete with one's institution for objects, and the requirement to provide a personal inventory to the museum."[3] The ethics code established by the Curators' Committee of the American Association of Museums also requires curators to provide inventories of their private collections, offering their institutions the opportunity to acquire objects before adding them to their personal collections. In May 1991, an AAM task force hammered out a new code of ethics containing more stringent rules on personal collecting.

Personal collecting is one of the most complex issues of museum ethics, and not everyone agrees on policy. The important consideration here is to define clear guidelines—in accordance with the AAM code of ethics—for your museum and to set them in writing. For guidelines, refer to the American Association of Museums, *Museum Ethics;* the Association of Art Museum Directors regulations; and the Curators' Committee Ethics Code (an AAM committee), copies available through AAM.

How does the museum appraise objects? This procedure is well defined for museums; it is unacceptable for staff members to provide tax appraisals for donations. To avoid conflict of interest, prospective donors should hire and pay for an independent, professional appraiser who will prepare a written valuation.

What policies will the institution establish regarding gifts, discounts (on personal purchases from suppliers to the museum), and dispensation of valuable items that are available because of a staff member's association with the museum? The AAM Code of Ethics strictly states that no employee may accept gifts unless they are of "trifling value" or discounts unless they are regularly offered to the general public.

What are the policies on outside employment and consulting?

How does the institution deal with sacred objects and other sensitive materials that the collection may include or may be offered to the museum? How will it handle potential donation that have been imported illegally, collected unscrupulously, or stolen?

What will be the director's responsibilities to the museum? What principles will guide the board's relation to the director, and the director's to the staff? How should the staff communicate with the members of the museum?

In addition to the collections management policy and the code of ethics, a **personnel manual** outlining specific policies of the museum is essential. Each employee should have a copy, as well as a detailed, up-to-date job description of each position in the museum.

Museums' Methods of Collecting

Museum collections grow in a number of ways: by gifts from the public made to the museum, by purchases sought by the curator, or by transfers, exchanges, or gifts from other educational institutions.[4]

The most prudent type of collecting is that which is done actively. The curator identifies the gaps that exist in the current collections or defines new categories to be represented. Objects are sought and collected that fill those categories. Collecting must also be done systematically with a definite plan appropriate to the mission of the museum and in harmony with the museum collection policy. Good collecting is a recognition of an institution's limitations and boundaries and is evaluated regularly to ensure its appropriateness to the mission of the museum.

Unfortunately, the most common method of acquiring objects

in small museums, passive collecting, is the least beneficial. Passive collecting takes place when a curator accepts all objects presented to the museum by the public, regardless of their significance, relevance to the collection, or provenance (their origin, maker, cultural affiliation, or source). This, in essence, is allowing the public to decide what objects the museum will hold, care for, and display. It is difficult to collect actively because it requires money, and often there are little or no funds from which to draw. Consequently, many historic house museums have become "public attics"—places where well-meaning people drop off antiques, books, photographs, vintage clothing, and other items they cannot bear to throw away. Or, with the thought that the family name will appear on an exhibit label, they contribute bags full of "important" historic objects from great Aunt Clara's estate. Perhaps a trustee offers to the museum the very spinning wheel that grandmother brought with her when she came to America in 1872. Currently, in the museum's collection there are twelve spinning wheels in good condition, all dating from the same time period and the same geographic region as the one being offered, presenting a difficult decision.

To circumvent such acts of "good will"—and to be more purposeful in collecting—a curator will need a strong sense of responsibility and purpose. The decision to accept an object should be based on its characteristics and not on who the donor is. No matter how well meaning or powerful the donor may be, ensure that the object is germane to the museum's purpose and that there is a reasonable chance that it will be used. If a proffered object does not fit the museum's collecting philosophy, refer the donor to another, more appropriate museum. A word of warning about donations given with stipulations.

When an object is accepted, it must be free of restraints to ensure that it may be used appropriately and properly cared for. Endless display of an artifact is not stimulating to museum audiences nor is it good for the object. The rule is never accept conditional gifts, no matter how good they appear. It is often difficult for a curator to stand firm against a distinguished donor who offers a seemingly valuable collection—with strings. Accepting such a gift can only burden the museum by allowing the donor to maintain control. The museum's scope could change, and there should not be donor's restrictions preventing the curator from giving the object to a more appropriate museum.

Long-term loans can be another burden to a museum. Often curators accept such loans because they believe that eventually the objects will be given to the museum. This thinking is erroneous! If a museum appears eager and willing to store and care for a privately owned collection, owners will often avoid donating it, either because of the effort involved or because they have no intention of actually parting with it. Unfortunately, curators are lulled into thinking of the lent objects as the museum's own property. After years of "curating" long-term loans, a museum may be no closer to owning a collection than the day it arrived. A family or an institution, if it can prove ownership (and it usually can), can reclaim its possession and the museum is obligated to return it.

Since curators are responsible for the care of objects accepted for the collection, and caring for objects is an expensive undertaking, discrimination in collecting is essential. Do not accept everything that is offered! It is also helpful to know what other institutions are collecting; by keeping in touch with other museums in the area, unnecessary duplication can be avoided.

Making Judgments in Collecting

Several basic questions need to be asked when deciding whether to accept an object.

- Is the object relevant to the purpose and priority of the museum?
- What is the quality of the object? Is it a rare piece? Does the price fit the acquisitions budget?
- How important is the object? Is it important to the experience of the historic house? Does it explain a process or a particular tradition specific to the museum?
- Is the object well documented? Who made it, who used it, and where did it come from? Without this information, an object loses its cultural and historical context, and consequently its integrity. Gone are the days that an article has value simply because it is beautiful. Museum professionals need to be selective in acquiring objects, and select those with known provenance.
- Is there room for the object in storage? Is it too big or too fragile to store properly?
- Can the museum properly care for the object, either in storage or on display? If not, another institution should be sought to serve as steward of the object.

- Can the object be exhibited or studied without the expense of special conservation work or cleaning? If not, are these resources available to the museum?
- Will the object be duplicated in the collection, and, if so, is this acceptable? Is the museum collecting a wide range of the same object for a particular reason?

These questions may be difficult for one curator to answer. Many museums have an **acquisitions committee** to assist curators in assessing the significance and usefulness of an object in relation to the museum's goals. The committee may be made up of professionals from other museums, board members, educators, historians, collectors, or anyone who has an understanding of the museum's mission and collecting goals. Acquisition committees are helpful in making suggestions; however, the final decision of whether to acquire materials for the museum rests in the hands of the director after a recommendation has been made by the curator.

Reevaluating Collecting Strategies

Museums periodically need to reevaluate their collecting to ensure continued development. This can be done by studying the existing collection and evaluating its strengths and weaknesses. Serious questions must be asked: Does the collection support the mission of the museum? Are there gaps and if so, what objects should be added to make the collection more comprehensive? Does the collection fulfill the museum's goals as a resource for research? Does it provide adequate materials for exhibition and interpretation? What does the assemblage communicate to the public?

Collecting Strategies

Collecting strategies can take many forms and directions, each plan will be unique to the individual museum. An essential part of the strategy is to keep the museum's collecting goals firmly in mind. These goals and the plan to accomplish them should be included in the long-range plan.

A common strategy for museums whose mission is to document the life of a founding family is to collect only those objects that once belonged to the family. This approach is logical, of course, but can be restrictive, conveying little about the family in a broader societal context. One way to broaden this focus is to collect material about the daily lives of the family and the people connected with the house. For example, questions might be asked about children in the family—how they related to the domestic help, schoolmates, and friends. How did they view their social position and how did their life-style compare with and contrast to that of other children in the area? The lives of workmen, neighbors, and the local religious figures might also be examined within the context of the house. A sampling of their personal objects as well would shed light on a wide range of life-styles common to a period.

If past owners of the house employed servants, information might be sought about the social structure that existed between servants themselves. What did they wear while they worked? How did they dress on their days off? How did they entertain themselves? What did they write to their friends and families about their experiences while living with the wealthy family?

Where and how does the curator go about collecting such materials and information? Facts might be found in such records as postcards, letters, diaries, and photographs. Perhaps even some of the clothing and personal effects of the family's servants have been kept by descendants who still live in the locality. Oral histories can provide details about relationships, attitudes, prejudices, personal habits, and life-styles in general. Information can also be gleaned from a study of the spatial arrangements of the house itself and the furnishings and objects within it. The size of rooms and their location in the house in relation to other rooms offer insight into people's values and their views, even their "placement" within the hierarchical structure of the household.

Documenting Objects

Museums are "legally and ethically obligated to assemble certain basic information about their collections and to maintain it according to accepted professional standards."[5] Documenting fleshes out objects and provides a "real" sense of the qualities that each possesses. It is a way of gaining knowledge about past life-styles and folkways that are no longer a part of contemporary culture. Without an idea of the history of an object, a museum is unable to tell its entire story. This is an area where a museum, as a repository of past information, cannot afford to be negligent.

The details about an object can often be obtained by asking the donor or previous owner some basic questions. Who was the original owner? Where and how was the object made? Who designed it? When was it made and how long was it used? Is it still used? What replaced it? Who designed it? Has it been modified or altered in any way?

Registering Collections

Procuring information about objects is only the first step. Once data about an object are collected, the object must be registered—that is, organized and stored in the museum's filing system.

Registration is a complex but absolutely necessary process. By registering a porcelain tureen, a woven bed coverlet, or a flintlock musket into a collection, one is, in essence, creating a written record of the object's existence, previous owners, physical description, condition, location in the museum, and what it means or has meant to people.

All too often, small museums struggle with large backlogs of unprocessed acquisitions, most of which have no accompanying historical information. Unprocessed materials are a great weight on museums and remain so until they have been cataloged or, if necessary and appropriate, deaccessioned. A museum cannot deaccession an object, before the curator verifies ownership.

Objects may be mismarked, marked impermanently with tape or stickers that easily fall off, or are not fully cataloged. Donor cards may be missing, or historical information may not have been recorded. New curators frequently inherit incomplete and disorganized records because in the past no trained personnel were available to register incoming gifts or well-meaning curators kept mental records of acquisitions instead of in written documents, or perhaps the task was simply ignored.

After an object has been accepted into the museum's collection, the registration process begins. Each is carefully documented and properly marked, and records are begun. Computerized or standard filing systems may be used. Many books have been written about appropriate museum methods of registration. One of the most widely used is *Museum Registration Methods* by Dorothy Dudley and Irma Bezold Wilkinson.

CATALOGING OBJECTS

Let's follow an object through the typical steps taken when an object comes to a museum for possible acquisition.

1. The staff issues a **temporary deposit receipt** form. This form documents the object being left in the temporary care of the museum. It should contain the owner's name, address, and telephone number, the date received, and a short description of the object. The form should also note whether the object is to be considered for purchase or as a gift. One copy is given to the lender, and one is retained for the museum's files.

2. If the object is made from an organic material such as wood, cloth, leather, or basket fiber, isolate it from the collections until the curator has determined whether an insect infestation, a mold, or an inherent defect exists. Nonorganic materials, such as ceramics, metals and glass, ordinarily do not have to be isolated.

3. If the object is donated a **deed of gift** form or **form of acceptance** is drawn up. This extremely important document, the legal form for transfer of ownership, must be carefully completed for every museum accession. It contains the accession number of the artifact and acknowledgment that the museum has accepted the gift and is signed and dated by the donor and countersigned by the curator. The original document is kept in an accession file folder, which is begun with each new accession, and a copy is given to the donor. If preparation of the document is neglected, and questions of ownership arise, the legal repercussions can be serious.

4. If an object is purchased a bill of sale or deed must be obtained. This proof of purchase document must be kept in the accession file, along with any other documents about the object's authenticity, value, and history. A record of who sold the object, where it was sold, and the date of the transaction must also be kept.

5. The deed of gift is returned to the museum and the object is recorded in the **accessions register,** usually a bound ledger. Entries should be made in permanent ink and should include the current date, the accession number, a brief description of the artifact, and the source and related data.

The accessions register serves as a sequential record for all objects that have been accepted for the museum's collections, and can be reviewed quickly without going through each individual catalog card. The pages of this ledger should be photocopied and kept in a safety deposit box off the premises as a permanent record of museum acquisitions.

6. Compilation of data begins. The curator gathers as much information as possible about the object. A good place to start is with the donor or previous owner, whose oral history might answer questions of origin, date made, previous ownership, and function. The curator will also search for historic and recent photographs, drawings, or blueprints, consulting reference books and catalogs and conferring with specialists. All of this information, in transcript form, is placed in the **accession file.**

7. The object is then assigned an **object number,** which consists of three units and usually looks like this: 92:01:01. The first two units are the **accession number.** The first unit refers to the year; the second, to the sequence in that year's acquisitions. A third unit is the *catalog number,* which refers to the number of objects in the accession. For example, the first acquisition in the calendar year 1992 might be a gift of three handwoven rugs. The first rug would be assigned the number 92:01:01. The first number indicates that the rug was given in the year 1992. The next, 01, means that it is part of the first group of objects accepted by the museum that year. The last, 01, indicates that it is the first object within a given group. The next rug in the group would be assigned the number 92:01:02; the third rug, 92:01:03.

After the object is removed from isolation, work can begin on its permanent museum record. This is usually started by compiling a **catalog worksheet,** which should contain the following information:

- Object number. (The number should be written on the object.)
- Classification or category. Is it clothing, a tool, a household article, archival material, art, a toy, a weapon? (Refer to Robert G. Chenall's *Nomenclature for Classifying Man-Made Objects.*)
- Date received. When was the object received or purchased?
- Date of legal transfer and name of donor. Who gave it? When was the deed of gift signed?

- Origin and age. Where did it come from? Who used it? How old is it?
- Description. Detailed description of the color, shape, design, material, function, medium, and what is known about the artist or maker.
- Dimensions. Detailed measurements of the object in centimeters—its length, width, and height or diameter and circumference, as appropriate.
- Condition. Its overall state. Establish a guide for determining different stages of deterioration and be consistent in the descriptions.
- Storage location. The location of the object.
- Exhibition history. A record of when, where, and how long was the object exhibited.
- Comments. Any additional observations about the object.
- References. List references to publications concerning the object or like objects.

After the worksheet has been completed, the information should be entered on a 4×6-inch **catalog card.** The card should be typed in triplicate (for smaller museums), with one card filed numerically by object number, one by subject (category), and a third (called the curator's card) in a safe location, off the premises, such as a bank vault. If a computer system is in place, information from the catalog worksheet can be entered into the program.

A 4×6-inch **source card** for donations, purchases, and exchanges should also be kept. Used to determine previous acquisitions from an individual or organization, the source card contains the name, address, and telephone number of the source, accession number or numbers, and is filed alphabetically by the last name of the source. Additional objects from the same source are recorded on the original card. If the museum is computerized and the program has a constituent function, donor information can be entered directly into this file.

MARKING NUMBERS ON OBJECTS

Inscribing numbers on museum objects legibly and with permanent ink ensures that they can be identified and matched with their specific documentation. In the past, numbers often were affixed to objects with adhesive tape or sticky labels, or written directly on the object with nonpermanent inks. But with time, numbers rubbed or peeled off, leaving only questions about an object's identity.

The most common method of marking objects today is with india ink, using a crowquill pen. Crowquills, which are well suited for writing on a variety of surfaces, can be purchased at any stationery or art-supply store. Several types of india ink are recommended by museum conservators as safe and noncorrosive. The preferred brands are Rotring 17 Black, Hunt Speedball Super Black India, Pelikan 17 Black or 50 Special Black, and Higgins T–100.[7]

When marking an artifact, locate the smoothest part of its surface, making sure to avoid areas that may wear due to contact. (For example, a number on the flat bottom of a vase may wear away eventually due to continual abrasion from setting it down.) Then place a coat of clear nail polish on the spot where the number is to be written and write the accession number small enough that it will not to be unsightly but large enough to read; then seal with another coat of clear nail polish. The number will remain permanently. When it is no longer needed, however, the base coat, along with the number, can be removed with an acetone solution.

When marking a dark-colored artifact, first coat a small area with white acrylic paint to create a light background so that the number can be seen easily. After the paint has dried, write the catalog numbers and cover with clear nail polish.

When marking clothing and textiles, do not write directly on the fabric. Instead, use a 1-inch strip of tightly woven, 100 percent cotton twill tape marked with a permanent black ink pen and sew it onto the garment. (For standards for marking locations, see Dudley and Wilkenson's *Museum Registration Methods*.)

Objects too miniscule to mark should be tagged with an acid-free paper label and stored in a box or an inert (safe, because the materials do not react with their surrounding) plastic bag with a strong closure so they will not be lost. Write accession numbers directly on top of the boxes. If an object is too fragile for a tag, attach the tag to the bag instead.

PHOTOGRAPHING THE COLLECTION

It is essential that the museum commit a part of its budget to photographing its collection. The benefits far outweigh the relatively inexpensive costs of creating such an important visual record.

Black-and-white prints are preferred because they last longer than color prints and will not fade, causing image distortion. When preparing objects to be photographed, it is important to include the accession number in the shot. The number can be written with a black marker on a folded index card, or plastic numbers (available at stationery or book stores) can be placed next to the artifact. A metric ruler, too, should be placed near the object to indicate scale.

A contact sheet of images and a 3×5-inch print of each should be obtained. The small contact sheet images can be pasted on the corresponding catalog cards, providing a useful guide for locating the object in storage. The standard prints can be placed in the accession file as a permanent record. Negatives are filed in archival negative sleeves held in a three-ring binder and organized numerically by accession number.

The object that has now been documented, isolated, described, measured, marked, and photographed may be placed in protective storage or on display.

After an object is cataloged, how can it be retrieved? Often museums keep a **location file** with index cards containing the accession number and the object's location in storage. When the location is changed, pencil in the new location and date.

Some museums use a shorter method of marking object locations. Location codes are written in pencil in the right corner of the catalog cards filed by accession number. When the object's location is changed, the catalog card can easily be erased and the new one penciled in. If the museum has computerized records the location code can be managed by the system.

Computerization of Museum Collections

Needs Assessment

With the increasing affordability of computer hardware and software, electronic filing of collection records is a realistic tool for curators who are bogged down with outdated manual record-keeping. Before diving into the sometimes confusing world of computers, however, the staff needs to decide what role a computer system should play in its museum's functions. The staff should conduct a needs assessment, which is made up of a number of tasks.

- Examine the manual system in place and understand its limitations.
- Define the basic needs of the museum: Will the museum want a full collections management system offering many functions or a simple and less costly data retrieval system?
- Determine whether other departments, such as membership and accounting are to be on the same system. Would separate systems be more appropriate? Should the museum start with a small project, at first computerizing one area only? The choices made have long-term effects. Have discussions with the staff in order to understand everyone's expectations.
- Decide who will oversee the technical functioning of the system. This person has an integral role and must be able to converse with the computer professional.
- Find out the length of time required to install the system and put it on-line.
- Estimate the extent of the system needed. Will the museum use a personal computer with an existing software such as Data Base IV or install a museum-based system such as ARGUS or REGIS? Should a system programmer be hired to design a custom system?
- Explore the systems similar museums are using; they may be able to offer insights into problems and successes.
- Get cost estimates and, after careful examination, decide if the project is worth undertaking.

Obtaining Information

Many publications relate directly to computer use in museums. They are listed in the catalogs provided by the American Association for State and Local History and the American Association of Museums. Workshops and conferences on museum computerization are offered frequently at regional museum conferences and state museum association workshops. Help is also available from vendors. They will send printed information about their systems or will visit, offer demonstrations, and give estimates on systems that they believe are most likely to fit the museum's needs. Be careful to protect your museum, however; investigate each computer system and its vendor carefully. Make sure that the vendor provides long-term technical support for the computer system. Have key staff observe software demonstrations and, if the software seems viable, review it again.

Realistic Expectations

The process of choosing a computer system is time consuming and painstaking. By understanding the steps required to get the system up and running, the staff will have realistic expectations about how long and the amount of energy that job will take.

NOTES

1. Marie C. Malaro, "Collections Management Policies," *Museum News* 58, no. 2 (1979): 59.

2. Quoted from the American Swedish Institute's Museum Collection Policy.

3. Allan D. Ullberg and Robert C. Lind, "Personal Collecting: Proceed with Caution," *Museum News* 69, no. 5 (1990): 33.

4. G. Ellis Burcaw, *Introduction to Museum Work,* 2d ed. (Nashville: Tenn.: American Association for State and Local History, 1983), p. 50.

5. American Association of Museums, *Museums for a New Century* (Washington, D.C.: American Association of Museums, 1984), p. 46.

6. Stephen L. Williams and Catharine A. Hawks, "Inks for Documentation in Vertebrate Research Collections," *Curator* 29, no. 2 (1986): 93–108.

5

///

Storage and Preservation
of the Museum's Collections

Collections maintenance, collections management and conservation are among the most demanding functions for all museums; they are also the least visible to those outside the museum.
American Association of Museums, *Caring for Collections*

CURATORS OF HISTORIC houses often find themselves with more objects than places to store them, and finding storage space is one of
their most challenging responsibilities. It is important to use existing areas in the most efficient and economical manner possible,
while applying proper museum storage techniques. The main criteria for storage areas are that they must be clean, well organized,
safe from pests and thieves, and provide a stable environment.

Although the safety of objects is paramount, they must also be
stored so that they are easily accessible. Collections often are retrieved for examination, inventory, research, condition assessment,
and preparation for exhibition. When objects cannot be reached or
even seen, they will probably be neglected and could deteriorate.

Access should not be too easy, though. It is not uncommon to
find the collections used improperly because they are open to virtually anyone in need of an object for a museum function: ceramic
vases are used to hold flower arrangements, antique silver tea services for serving guests, period chairs for seating at events.

Safe Storage Techniques

In historic houses, it is often necessary to use less than ideal areas
for storage. After all, the structure was constructed for a family's

use, not to house a museum. It is necessary, therefore, to be resourceful, to rely on one's own imagination and creativity. Ingenious methods for storing collections can be found in the most unlikely locations. When considering storage areas, ask the following questions:

- Are the light levels appropriate? Can the area be darkened for storage of light-sensitive objects? Can windows be modified by applying ultraviolet inhibiting film or blocked to screen out all natural light?
- Is the area large enough to hold artifacts safely? Can they be stored without stacking or overcrowding?
- Can the areas with wood surfaces—closets, shelves, or drawers—be modified to prevent wood acids from damaging objects?
- Can objects be easily found and retrieved?
- Can the temperature and humidity be controlled in the space, and can air circulate freely?
- Can dehumidifiers and humidifiers be installed and accessed easily? Can relative humidity tests be taken in and around the storage area?
- Is the area protected against fire? Are there smoke detectors and heat sensor devices?
- Can the area be monitored and cleaned frequently?
- Have all chemicals—such as alcohol, acetone, household cleaners—been removed from the storage area?
- Can the area be locked? Can it be restricted from those who are not trained in handling objects?

Storage Equipment

Museums usually store objects on open shelving units, in closed-door cabinets, in flat storage (such as drawers), and in acid-free boxes and bags of various sizes and shapes. Single-layer textiles are commonly rolled on tubes that are suspended from the ceiling. Paintings are often placed in padded slots or hung on panels. Clothing is padded with acid-free paper and hung on padded hangers or, if particularly delicate, stored in flat boxes.

METAL STORAGE UNITS

Museums often use open metal shelves (aluminum or steel coated with a baked enamel paint) to hold objects. If properly constructed, they are lighter and stronger than wood shelving and do not pose a fire hazard. However, if metal shelves are used in an unconditioned environment, they may corrode, subsequently damaging objects. In the past such shelving was thought to be harmless, but recently it has been found that aluminum, if not anodized, will emit damaging peroxides as it oxidizes. Metal shelves must be made either of enameled steel or of anodized aluminum.

Metal units should bear only the amount of weight for which they are designed. An overloaded unit, one that bends or sways from its load, is dangerous both to the staff and the objects. The bottom shelf should be elevated several inches above the floor, should water enter the area. Cover sharp edges or protruding bolts or screws that could damage an object being put in or taken out of the unit. Place padding—polyethylene liners, unbleached muslin, or heavy acid-free paper—on the shelves as support for the objects.

Larger museums may have the funds and space for closed-door steel cabinets. These cases are quite versatile, with adjusting drawers and shelves, and they keep out insects, rodents, light, and dirt. Acid-free cardboard trays frequently are used in the cabinet drawers to hold smaller objects and to prevent them from rolling around and striking one another.

WOOD STORAGE UNITS

Wood is the least desirable material for storage of artifacts; however, because it is inexpensive, readily available and can be easily constructed into storage units, it is commonly used in historic house museums. Historic houses often come equipped with antique, built-in wooden drawers and bookcases—in bedrooms, dressing areas, kitchens, pantries, and workrooms. *A word of warning about using new wood:* it will release acids, as well as alcohols, and if organic materials such as textiles and clothing come in contact with new wood, the fibers may weaken, discolor, or become brittle. The rate at which acids are released depends on the type of wood, how it was seasoned, and how much moisture it contains. (Hardwoods contain more free acids than softwoods such as pine or even high-grade plywood.) Antique wooden drawers and bookcases will also emit acids—especially where temperatures are high and relative humidity is above 80 percent—even if the wood has had years to "off-gas." Another drawback to using wood for storage is that it poses a fire hazard.

Using New Wood for Storage   If wood must be used for constructing storage units, it is important to use a high-grade **exterior plywood.** Exterior plywood is safer than the interior grades because the thin wood sheets of which it is made are bonded with phenol-formaldehyde—a resin that remains stable as it ages. Interior plywood, on the other hand, is often made with the unstable adhesive urea-formaldehyde, dangerous because it breaks down easily, emitting formaldehyde. Exterior plywood also releases fewer acids than most hardwoods.[1]

Treating Wood Storage Units   Wood must be treated to be made relatively safe for holding artifacts. Museum conservators recommend several methods for treating raw or antique woods.

- Cover raw or antique woods with a laminated film. This film is waterproof and vapor proof and consists of three layers: one of polyethylene, one of aluminum, and one of polypropylene. It is an effective barrier used on wooden shelves, in drawers, and on wooden rods for storing textiles and costumes. The film comes in rolls and is easy to work with; it can be cut to size and heat welded with a hot-air gun. After the film has been applied to the entire surface (both sides and edges) of the raw wood, a layer of un-bleached, washed muslin should be placed over it for softness. (The specifications of the film are MIL–B–131H, Type 1, Class 1. It is available through Bell Fibre Products Corporation, Columbus, Georgia.)
- Coat the wood with a non-oil modified urethane or latex urethane acrylic such as Benjamin Moore's product #416 (either is acceptable). After the surfaces have been coated, they should be lined with aluminum sheets or heavy aluminum foil to serve as a barrier against acids that damage objects. As added protection, cover the shelves with cotton muslin, especially when storing sensitive organic materials.[2]
- Line raw wood shelving with a calcium-carbonate matte board (obtainable through any conservation supply company), or coat it with paint containing calcium carbonate, mica, or aluminum flakes.[3] Calcium carbonate acts as a buffer against acid migration and will absorb acid gases.[4] Mica or aluminum flakes also provide effec-

tive barriers against wood acids.[5] These paints can be purchased in any paint stores.

A great deal of effort goes into preparing museum objects for storage. Costumes and accessories are stuffed with tissue paper to fill out creases, textiles are padded at the folds, and documents are boxed. But safe materials must be used; ordinary papers, boxes and cardboard cartons contain dangerously high levels of acids and lignin, a substance that occurs naturally in woods and will hasten deterioration of organic materials. Objects stored in them or around them become damaged by the "burning" effects of the chemicals. Fortunately, safe supplies are available.

Acid-free, lignin-free paper can be used in many ways—for padding costumes, wrapping organic materials, stuffing leather and hide, interleaving documents, and covering cardboard tubes to prevent acid migration when rolling textiles. Acid-free paper comes in various thicknesses, from thin tissue to heavy sheets and even corrugated cardboard. Interleaving paper is lightweight and can safely be used to protect surfaces of prints, documents, manuscripts, and works of art on paper from grit, dust, and abrasion. Acid-free paper may be purchased through the major conservation companies.

Acid-free, lignin-free containers, boxes, and trays are used by museums to store a wide variety of artifacts, from documents and photographs to costumes and textiles. Archival-quality boxes protect objects from acids, dust, dirt, fingerprints, abrasion, and chemical deterioration. Boxes come in many shapes and sizes and are readily available through most conservation supply companies. Protective boxes or papers and packing materials must be lignin free, as well as acid free. Lignin, which occurs naturally in wood, will hasten deterioration of organic materials, such as paper, by exuding acids and peroxides.

Storage boxes are essential conservation supplies, but they tend to be expensive, especially for small museums with limited budgets. Instead of buying them, curators can reduce costs by making boxes by hand, using acid- and lignin-free boxboard and linen tape. Both products are available through conservation companies. Boxboard can be cut to the appropriate size and assembled into any shape with linen tape. To construct smaller, more flexible boxes, a lightweight board or heavy paper can be used and folded to the desired

Custom-made costume and textile storage solves problems of overcrowding. With ingenuity and creativity, safe storage can be obtained at a relatively low cost. Shown here is the textile storage room at Shadows-on-the-Teche, New Iberia, Louisiana. (Photograph courtesy of the National Trust for Historic Preservation)

shape. Lids for the boxes can be made using the same folding process.

Polyethylene storage bags are indispensable for storing collections. Polyethylene is a safe, inert material and is strong, durable, and transparent. Bags can be purchased through conservation supply companies or scientific product suppliers in a variety of sizes. Some include a zipper-locking seam for easy closure and have a white patch on the bag for labeling contents. A good standard weight for museum objects is a 4-millimeter thickness. Bags purchased from grocery or hardware stores are not suitable. They are made from or are coated with materials that are unsuitable for museum storage.

Polyethylene foam is an inert plastic that can be purchased in different densities and thicknesses, in sheets or rolls, from local packaging and shipping companies. It is especially useful for lining exhibit and storage cases and drawers because it prevents objects from rolling around and striking each other. It can also be used as padding between artifacts and for wrapping materials for transport. As a background for detection of insect frass, which may indicate a live infestation, it serves an extra purpose.

Archival polyester (Mylar) is a safe, transparent, flexible plastic frequently used in museum storage to encapsulate documents, photographs, maps, newspapers, postcards, or other flat objects. It is also commonly used to cover rolled textiles and artifacts in open storage, or as a lining in antique wooden drawers. Polyester can be purchased in sheets or rolls through archival- and art-supply companies.

Unbleached, undyed cotton muslin that has been washed to eliminate all sizing is a safe and inexpensive protective covering for objects. It can be made into bags for storing artifacts, covers for padded hangers, or liners for shelves, drawers, and cardboard tubes to help protect artifacts from harmful acids. The cloth should be washed periodically, however, to remove the acids that eventually will migrate through its fibers.

UNSAFE STORAGE CONTAINERS AND MATERIALS

Many materials are unsafe for use with museum collections. If you are uncertain about a material *do not use it* until it has been tested by a conservator. Sticky substances—such as wax, silicone rubber adhesives, and tape—should never be used. The adhesive on all types of tape, including masking tape and transparent tape, is dangerous, and attempts to remove it can scar and damage objects. Other common items that should not be used are staples, safety and straight pins, nails, tacks, and screws. They can rust or corrode and stain objects. Even rustproof staples, pins, or nails can break textile fibers or mar the surface of other materials such as wood, ivory, or bone.

Caring for and Storing Museum Materials

When storing museum collections, it is common to separate them into categories according to the materials from which they are made.

Often there is a storage area for glass and ceramics, one for wooden objects, one for tools and larger artifacts, one for textiles and clothing, and specialized spaces for paintings, prints, and sculpture. Some museums store all their collections in one area, such as the basement, carriage house, or attic. Others use closets and drawers, or smaller rooms that once served as servants' quarters, or upper-story bedrooms.

Regardless of where storage areas are located, it is imperative that each category of artifact receive special consideration with regard to its condition and composition.

Glass and Ceramics

Glass and ceramic materials are fragile and need special care in storage. Open shelving, either metal or wood, can be used, preferably with a lip or rim along the edges for safety. Shelves can be lined with felt (felt should be used only with glass) or with polyethylene foam, forming a soft foundation. A padded surface will prevent abrasion of etched glass surfaces that may contain information about the maker. (Never slide glass across any surface.) Also, any chips or fragments that may break loose from the glass and ceramic artifacts can be found easily and removed from a felt or foam surface. Labels with catalog numbers placed on the edges of the shelves will allow the effortless location and retrieval of artifacts without unnecessary handling.

Drawers lined with polyethylene foam can also be used to store glassware. Place a ½-inch layer of foam on the bottom of the drawer; on top of this place another layer of foam with cut-out shapes of the objects to be stored; they can then be nested into these shapes, preventing jarring and breakage when the drawer is opened.[6] Label the outside of the drawers with the contents to avoid having to open the drawers unnecessarily.

Ceramics should not be stacked. If this is unavoidable, however, use layers of polyethylene foam between each piece to avoid contact.

Most glass is stable and can tolerate higher relative humidities than organic materials. However, some glass (especially that which has been improperly made) is susceptible to moisture and will soak it up, a condition known as **crizzling.** Crizzling can leave a fine surface network of crazing (a surface of minute cracks) on the glass vessel. Such glass should be stored in areas with a relative humidity of about 40 to 50 percent. Use silica gel as a desiccant to control excessive humidity in these areas. Silica gel can be purchased from any conservation supply company.

It may be necessary to clean glass and ceramic objects before placing them in storage. Two plastic tubs should be used for washing: one with clear water, and the other with a solution of water and a small amount of mild soap. (Orvus, a conservation product, or Lux liquid or Woolite are good, gentle soaps.) Wash objects gently in the soapy mixture and rinse them in the clear water tub. Dry the objects thoroughly with a clean, dry cloth before placing them in storage. Careful drying will deter surface deterioration and pitting. (To prevent condensation inside bottles and decanters store them with their stoppers and tops off.)[7] Do not immerse in water any low-fired or painted ceramics. Glass or ceramic objects that have been repaired should not be submerged in water; they may come apart. Such objects should be dusted with a soft dry or slightly damp cloth to attract surface dust.

If a glass container is heavily soiled, place soap-saturated cotton balls inside the vessel and gently agitate it until the stain has been removed. Rinse and dry the vessel completely before placing it on the shelf. Sturdy vessels that are extremely soiled can be cleaned by soaking them overnight in a solution of soap, water softener (such as Calgon), and water. Some conservators recommend inserting a handful of uncooked rice in the vessel and gently swirling it around after this procedure.[8] This should help to eliminate any remaining soil or deposits.

When carrying glass objects to storage, be sure to place them in an adequately padded carrying box. Place padding between fragile pieces in the box as well. When removing an object, never place stress on protruding parts—picking up a teapot spout, for example, or handle. Cotton gloves with polypropolene grips are helpful when handling glass or ceramics. These can be found at hardware or garden stores.

Costumes and Textiles

Many historic house museums own collections of period costumes and textiles. The typical items represented may have belonged to the original owners or have been collected from different periods. Whatever the period, however, it is likely that many of the gar-

Even closets and cramped spaces can be converted to usable storage areas. Here, banks of cabinets have been inexpensively constructed with the help of experienced volunteers. Note that shelves have been lined with soft felt to prevent glass from abrading, that they have a lip in front, and that they are labeled with each object's accession number to provide for easy access and to prevent the needless handling of these fragile objects. (Photograph courtesy of the American Swedish Institute)

ments and textiles have deteriorated seriously, weakened by age, neglect, or improper care.

General Concerns

Most costumes and textiles are very fragile and, if possible, should be stored separately in a cool area with temperatures below 70 degrees Fahrenheit and a relative humidity between 45 and 55 percent. Too much moisture in the air will cause the growth of mold

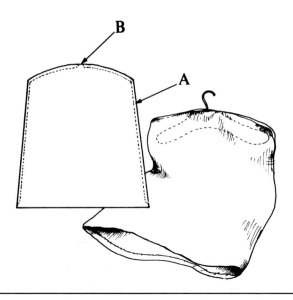

Open dust covers can be easily made with the help of volunteers. (A) 5-centimeter seam; (B) 2.5-centimeter opening for hook of hanger. (Reproduced with permission of the Canadian Conservation Institute)

and mildew; too little will desiccate the fibers. Humidity control may be difficult or impossible for museums having no environmental controls. Portable humidifiers or dehumidifiers will aid in a problematic environment.

Storage areas should be as dust- and dirt-free as possible—airborne particles can damage fibers and the structure of fabrics. It may be necessary to filter the incoming air in the museum to achieve this. Prudent housekeeping will also greatly increase the life of fabrics. Drape textiles with washed muslin, polyethylene plastic or a polyester, such as Mylar, and use protective dust covers for individual costumes.

Pests are the enemies of the more vulnerable textiles, such as wool and the fur and feathers that often embellish costumes. Given the opportunity, rodents will nest in any fabric, and insects will thrive on wools, fur, and hides. Frequent monitoring of storage areas and isolation of objects before they are integrated into the collection are essential.

When working with garments, the staff should wear white cotton gloves to prevent soiling from natural oils in the skin. Pencils are the only writing implements that should be used around fabrics. Marks from pens and markers usually cannot be removed. Always keep sharp objects such as scissors and needles in a box or basket well away from fabrics.

Costumes

PREPARATION FOR STORAGE

Before costumes are placed in storage, they must be scrutinized and carefully prepared. All pins and remnants of glue-on labels or tape must be removed from the garments. Pins, if not carefully

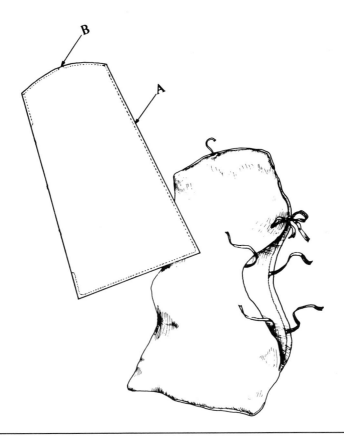

Closed dust covers can protect garments from soiling. (A) 5-centimeter seam; (B) 2.5-centimeter opening for hook of hanger. (Reproduced with permission of the Canadian Conservation Institute)

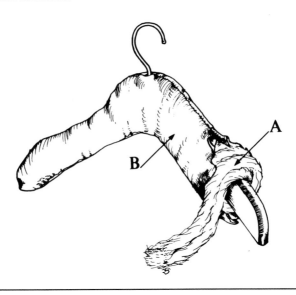

Bare wood and wire hangers are not safe for holding costumes. Wood hangers must be padded and covered with muslin before they can be safely used. (A) Polyester or cotton quilt batting; (B) cotton muslin cover. (Reproduced with permission of the Canadian Conservation Institute)

placed between threads, can cut the fabric, and pins that are not rustproof can leave irreversible stains. Adhesives from tapes can leave a sticky residue that scars a garment and breaks fibers when it is removed.

If clothing is soiled, try to remove the surface dirt to prevent further deterioration. This can be done by using a hand vacuum with slow-action suction. A screen placed over the mouth of the vacuum will prevent loose fibers from being sucked into the instrument. Do not apply the vacuum brush directly to the costume or fabric and do not apply pressure.

Wet cleaning a costume is controversial and should only be done by a conservator or under instructions of a trained professional. Never wash garments in a washing machine! Even on a gentle cycle, costumes can be damaged by the agitation of a machine. Dry cleaning should be avoided as well; the chemicals used in the process may damage fragile costumes or leave a residue that will deteriorate fibers.

A basic technique used by many museums in preparing costumes for storage is to pad them to help remove stress and strain from seams. Crumpled acid-free tissue paper placed into sleeves, shoulder seams, and folds will assist in evenly distributing weight while the costumes hang in storage or rest in boxes or drawers. After garments have been adequately padded they should be placed on specially prepared padded hangers, not bare or varnished wood, wire or plastic hangers. Wood hangers contain harmful acids that will migrate into the fabric. Wire or plastic hangers are not strong enough to hold garments properly; consequently, too much stress is placed on the shoulder seams. Also, wire hangers might rust.

Padded hangers are easy to make. Place padding (fiberfill or cotton or polyester batting) over the frame, cushioning sharp edges. Add extra padding in the shoulder area for additional support. Patterns can be made and followed for each type of hanger. Al-

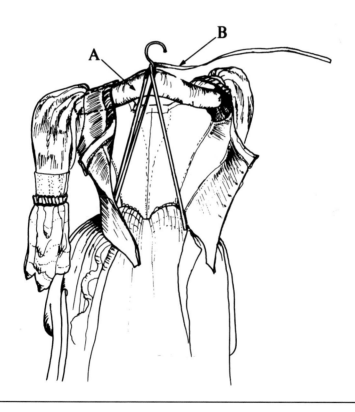

For additional support, tapes can be attached to the waistband of a garment and placed around the hook of the hanger. (Reproduced with permission of the Canadian Conservation Institute)

though making the hangers is simple, the task is labor intensive. Volunteers might be a good source of labor to assist with the project, perhaps a local weavers' guild or sewing club.

Dust covers can be made easily from unbleached, washed all-cotton muslin stitched on three sides, leaving the bottom open to pull down over the garment and a slit in the top for the hanger. In an other version, the top, bottom, and one side seam are sewed, the other is left open. Tapes sewn to each side of the open seam permit the bag to be tied closed. Plastic dry-cleaning bags should never be used for covering garments. Proper storage requires air to circulate around garments, and plastic bags will not allow for this essential airflow.

Because of space limitations, garments must often be prepared for storage and exhibition in the same area in which they are stored. A large padded table is essential. Place fiberfill or polyester or cotton batting on the table top and finish it by stretching cotton muslin over the top, securing it to the underside. The edges must also be padded and covered to prevent snags.

STORING ACCESSORIES

Store costume accessories such as hats, gloves, beaded bags, and lunettes in padded and muslin-lined drawers or acid-free, lignin-free boxes. Drawers and boxes should be labeled on the outside to facilitate retrieval and prevent unnecessary handling.

Larger costume accessories, such as scarves and shawls, should be rolled on cardboard tubes covered either with acid-free, lignin-free paper or polyester (Mylar).

Canes and parasols can be kept in a vertical, circular stand with individual holes for each or placed horizontally on a pegboard with plastic-covered hooks. Each artifact should be tagged with its accession number and any pertinent information on an acid-free, lignin-free paper tag.

Textiles and Floor Coverings

Textiles are ubiquitous in historic house collections. Fine linens were carefully stored and saved, often in trunks kept in unused areas of the house. Everyday textiles—such as bed coverlets, quilts, draperies, and woven floor coverings—were also saved. Today in many historic houses, such antique fabrics are still in place. Whether in storage or on display, all historic fabrics must be treated with special care.

GENERAL CARE

Historic fabrics should be handled as little as possible. If it is necessary to handle them, it should be done carefully to prevent stress on the fibers and breakage. The effects can be disastrous when untrained staff handle fragile textiles carelessly. Fabrics with severe dry rot may literally fall apart in one's hands.

Walking on historic rugs should be avoided. Direct all traffic to special runners placed over the rugs. These "museum" runners can be specially woven with an uncut loop wool pile with a cotton binding to prevent raveling. *No backing* should be applied. The runner should be at least 40 inches wide to accommodate wheelchairs and strollers. The Henry Francis du Pont Wintherthur Museum has tested the museum runners for more than a decade and has found them satisfactory in reducing abrasion caused by foot traffic. Special orders for runners can be placed at area carpet-weaving mills. It is recommended that the museum staff who must walk on the rugs from time to time wear low-heeled shoes or even just cotton socks, which will not catch or tear fibers.

Special care must also be taken with historic draperies. If shades cover the windows, pull them down gently; a forceful pull will abrade the sides of the draperies. Apply the same rules to antique bedcovers and all other historic textiles; handle them with care and protect them from light, dust, and fluctuating humidity.

PREPARATION FOR STORAGE

The first step in preparing textiles for storage is assessing and recording their condition. If they are soiled, they should be carefully vacuumed.

Since textiles are especially vulnerable to light degradation, it is essential to store them in a dark environment. Improper light levels will cause fading and fiber breakdown.

Textiles are hygroscopic and will acclimatize to a wetter or drier environment. Ideally, however, they should be kept in a cool areas with temperatures below 70°F and a relative humidity between 45 and 55 percent. In historic houses where it is not possible to maintain the desired level of humidity, it is important to try to maintain a constant relative humidity.

Giving textiles adequate support is a paramount goal when storing, exhibiting, or handling them. Do not place undue stress on fibers by allowing them to carry too much of an object's weight. When moving a textile, be sure not to pull or stretch it, and use acid-free ragboard or textile boxes to support the weight.

To increase the life of textiles, they should be stored unfolded. When cloth is folded, especially aged and fragile cloth, the fibers tend to break along the crease line. If folding is necessary, fold along seams or in the stronger areas of the fabric and do not fold along previous fold lines. Using acid-free, lignin-free paper, pad out the fold lines to prevent sharp creases. Check the textiles periodically and refold them along different lines.

If space allows, small textiles should be stored flat, in drawers or on shelves. If possible, they should not be stacked. The weight of layers might crush those on the bottom or cause creases and fiber breakage. Make certain the fabrics do not touch wooden surfaces, and place acid-free, lignin-free paper underneath and on top of the stored items to protect them from dust.

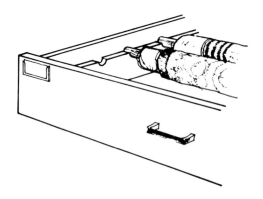

Storing textiles in drawers with an inserted bracket with cut grooves. Grooves hold the wooden dowel, allowing the textiles to hang in suspension. (Reproduced with permission of the Canadian Conservation Institute)

Rolling Textiles for Storage   It is often impractical to store large textiles flat. An acceptable alternative is to roll the fabric, single-layer, on a cardboard tube covered with acid-free, lignin-free paper or polyester. The tube is hung on hooks and chains that are suspended from a ceiling or placed in a custom-made rack. Multilayer textiles such as quilts, however, must be folded with acid-free, lignin-free tissue paper, padding each fold to remove stress from the folded fibers and stored in an acid-free, lignin-free box. (Quilts must be refolded periodically, too.)

Acid-free tubes can be purchased from conservation suppliers around the country but often are too expensive for smaller museums. Rollers that are not acid free can be procured at little or no cost at all and, when prepared properly, are suitable for rolling textiles. Mailing tubes, fabric rolls, carpet and linoleum rollers, even paper towel tubes can be altered as follows to hold textiles safely.

1. Select a tube with an appropriate diameter for the textile to be rolled. Too small a diameter can place stress on the fabric by crushing its interior. The aim is to bend the fabric gently, placing a minimum of strain on the structure of the weave and the threads.[9] In order to enlarge the tube's diameter, it is acceptable to cover it with plastic bubble cushioning materials (bubble wrap).[10]

2. Cut the tube to fit the textile, allowing about an inch on either side, and cover it with polyethylene sheeting or polyester (Mylar). Tuck in the excess on either end, and roll the tube in unbuffered (having no added buffer such as calcium carbonate), acid-free, lignin-free tissue paper, or in washed cotton muslin. Tuck in these ends as well.

3. Lay the fabric flat on a table, removing all creases by smoothing them out with a cotton-gloved hand. Use another piece of acid-free tissue paper as interleaving for added protection. Roll the fabric with the right side inward, keeping the warp perpendicular to the tube. Do not strain the object by pulling on it or applying uneven tension while rolling. Pile carpets or embroidered pieces should be rolled with the right side out. Roll only one textile per tube.

4. After the roll is complete, cover it with clear polyethylene plastic to protect it from dust. Do not tuck this layer into the tube ends; closing it prevents air from circulating

around the fabric. Secure the plastic by tying loosely with strips of cotton muslin or with white cotton tapes.

5. Attach an acid-free, lignin-free paper tag to the tie with the textile's object number and brief description of the object.

6. Insert a wooden dowel or metal rod in the tube and suspend it from hooks. Do not store the tube flat, the weight of the textile presses down on itself, placing strain on the fabric.[11]

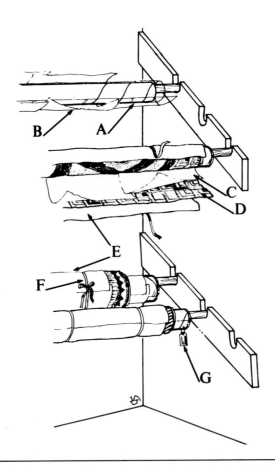

Cupboards and small closets can be modified for textile storage by inserting a bracket system. (A) Mylar covering cardboard tubes; (B) acid-free tissue over Mylar; (C) interleaving of neutral pH tissue; (D) textile with pile on outside; (E) unbleached cotton muslin cover; (F) cotton tape; (G) identification tag. (Reproduced with permission of the Canadian Conservation Institute)

Storing Rolled Textiles There are a number of methods for storing rolled textiles; the type that you choose will depend on the size of your storage areas and the size and number of the rolled pieces in your collection. For smaller collections it may be more efficient to use a bracket storage system set into a cupboard or drawers. Brackets are simply boards with a rounded notch to hold the rod. To retrieve the tube the rod is merely lifted out of the notch.

Another method of suspending textiles on rods is to hang them on chains affixed to a ceiling track. Tubes holding the textiles can be slipped over large wooden rods or steel poles. This technique works well with large rugs and heavy textiles, but may also be used for smaller textiles with several cardboard tubes placed adjacent to

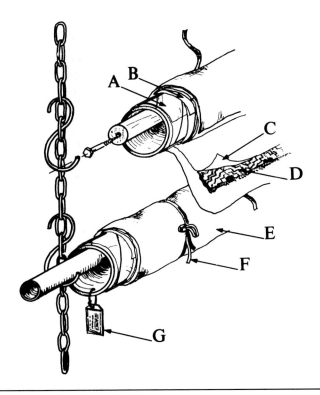

Suspended storage can be made with materials found at a local building supply store. (A) Mylar covering cardboard tube; (B) acid-free tissue over Mylar; (C) interleaving of neutral pH tissue; (D) textile with pile on outside; (E) unbleached cotton muslin cover; (F) cotton tape; (G) identification tag. (Reproduced with permission of the Canadian Conservation Institute)

each other on each rod. Suggestions for constructing and using this system:

1. Make certain the ceiling can sustain the weight of the system, especially if you plan to hang heavy rugs.
2. Garage-door tracks are inexpensive and can be installed easily. Install the two tracks on the ceiling, each running parallel and spaced as far apart as required (usually 8 or 12 feet apart). This distance corresponds to the standard size of wood closet rods or steel tubes.
3. Insert steel trolleys (part of the garage-door system) in the tracks and attach steel chains to them. (Chains can be found at hardware stores or builder's supply companies.)
4. Attach large S-hooks or U-bolts with wing nuts to the chains at various heights.
5. Place the rolled textile on the hooks or through U-bolts.

To retrieve a rolled textile, remove one side of the rod from the hook or bolt and slip the tube off.

Archival Materials

Even if a museum has no formal library or archives, it probably has some historic letters, personal notes, house blueprints, photographs, postcards, journals, or other archival material. Since much of our information about historic houses and the families that lived in them is drawn from such documents and photographs, it is essential to preserve them with great care.

The first step in preserving documents is to assess them for their importance and relevance to the museum's collection. Documents that are not pertinent should be given to the state historical society or a county society where they can be better used by the public. Those that remain will need special stabilizing treatments and customized storage. Some will require the skills of a paper conservator, but there are specific treatments that the staff can perform to arrest the decay and deterioration that is a natural part of the aging of paper.

Acids are inherent in most papers and play a major role in their destruction. The amount of acidity depends on the way the manufacturing process and composition of the paper. For example, newspaper, meant to be short-lived, is made from an extremely acidic low-quality wood-pulp core and is self-destructive. However, most paper can be deacidified by using aqueous (wet) or nonaqueous (nonwetting) conservation techniques. A trained archivist must be consulted before deacidification is attempted.

Commonly, papers are stored in, or come in contact with, other acidic materials. Brown craft envelopes (often used for storing negatives), white commercial envelopes, manila folders, and often the mount and matte board used to store papers and photographs are highly acidic and damaging to paper. Documents and photographs should be removed from their mounts, however, *only* if they are loose and easily removed; efforts at removal may actually destroy the object itself because with the passage of time a mount can actually meld onto a photograph or document.

Like other organic materials, documents and photographs must be kept in dark areas and not exposed to ultraviolet light for extended periods. Like fabrics, paper will yellow and become brittle with age, and inks will fade from prolonged exposure to light. By following the environmental standards set for costume and textile care (relative humidity levels of 45 to 55 percent and temperatures at below 70°F) and by filtering the air in archival storage areas, the rate of decay will greatly decrease.

Documents should be stored flat and, if possible, not folded. Photographs must never be folded because folding creates permanent cracks.

When working with documents, wear white cotton gloves or, if gloves are not used, wash hands that come in contact with paper items to prevent oils and grime from soiling documents. Do not use pressure-sensitive tapes, commercial glues, pastes, or rubber cement. These substances contain acids and will stain paper and hasten its deterioration. Never fasten papers or photographs with metal paper clips, staples, or pins; they will perforate and stain paper. If mending is necessary, it is acceptable to use wheat-starch paste.

To clean paper use Pink Pearl erasers or powdered eraser pads, such as Opaline and Scum X. These cleaners must be used carefully and only in areas void of inks or designs. Clean surfaces carefully to remove eraser dust. Do not use these cleaners on the surfaces of photographs.

Documents

Documents being prepared for storage can be protected in a variety of ways from dust and dirt, acidic materials, and deterioration caused by handling. One procedure, commonly used because of its simplicity, is encapsulation, in which a document is placed between sheets of transparent polyester film and sealed inside the film with a special double-coated tape on three or four sides. Because the enclosure is transparent, the document can easily be studied. Materials required for this method are easily obtained from conservation supply companies, and the work can be accomplished with the help of volunteers.

Archival folders and envelopes that are lignin free, buffered with calcium carbonate, and have a pH of 8.5 come in a variety of sizes and are appropriate for preserving and storing documents. Acid-free file boxes can also be used to store documents.

Photographs

For the preservation and storage of photographs, acid- and lignin-free nonbuffered envelopes and boxes should be used. Many museums mat photographs with museum-quality matte board and store them, between interleaving tissue, in acid-free portfolio boxes. Photographs can also be encapsulated with polyester film or placed in polyester sleeves (available at conservation supply companies).

Negatives must be kept in acid- and lignin-free envelopes with no glue and no abrasive surfaces (to prevent scratching) or in polyethylene envelopes. *Never* use glassine envelopes, vinyl or PVC (polyvinyl chloride) plastic enclosures, acidic envelopes, or cardboard boxes. (Many curators find the archival collections in historic house museums stored in these materials.) Polyethylene sheets with pockets for storing negatives are also acceptable. After the negatives are enclosed the sheets should be stored in acid-free file boxes.

To prolong the life of framed historic photographs, prevent them from coming in direct contact with the surface of the glass by wedging acid-free paper along the edges. Photographs coming in contact with glass will eventually stick to the surface and be impossible to remove.

At many house museums original photographs of the family who once lived there often are displayed. This is unfortunate because exposure to light and high temperature and humidity can destroy the prints. A rule of thumb is to have negatives made from original photographs. Duplicate prints can be produced from the copies and the original photographs stored. The process is inexpensive and preserves the original photograph while allowing visitors to enjoy the historic image.[12]

Other archival materials—such as journals, postcards, magazines, sheet music, and newspapers—can be safely stored in flat storage boxes made from acid- and lignin-free board. All items stored together should be interleaved with acid-free paper to prevent acid from migrating from one document to another.

Paintings and Prints

Paintings and works of art on paper are routinely found in collections of historic houses. Works of art, often the most precious possessions of homeowners, were displayed prominently to show the wealth of the owners. In large houses, galleries designed for an owner's entire artistic holdings were not uncommon.

Exhibiting and storing works of art are complicated matters and require much analysis and planning. While on exhibit, they must be protected from the impulsive visitor who simply cannot resist reaching out and straightening a frame that has listed or touching a particularly moving scene. Paintings and prints must be displayed only in places where they will not be harmed by light, heat, or humidity, eaten by insects, or stolen. Curators of house museums must work to create a safe environment, at the same time trying to create an authentic "homelike" ambience.

Protecting Paintings and Prints While on Display

To reduce risks, paintings and prints should be displayed in areas where visitors are not likely to bump into them or scrape them with their shoulders or bags. Keep stairways and narrow corridors free of artwork. Place chairs, tables, or stands beneath paintings to reduce the temptation to touch. Another deterrent, if space allows, is a projecting rail installed beneath the artwork, creating a space between the visitor and the work. (Rails are less conspicuous if they are placed toward the bottom of the wall.)

Position trained volunteers or professional guards strategically around the house, and instruct them to ask guests not to touch or to take care not to bump against artwork (or other furnishings) in the house. Guards must be outspoken when protecting the building and its collections; they are an important line of defense in preventing innocent "touches" from causing serious damage.

Carefully calculate the possible hazards of a location before hanging a painting or print. Never position one above warm-air registers or radiators or too close to heat-producing light fixtures, such as picture lights, spotlights, or incandescent bulbs. Avoid outside walls where temperatures fluctuate, and guard against areas that are damp or where circulation is poor. These conditions cause mold to grow on paintings and "foxing" on works on paper. Never place paintings on a damp wall or one that has just been painted and has not had time to dry thoroughly. Avoid areas that are too dry as well. Either extreme is deleterious and can seriously damage precious works of art. (A desirable temperature for painting and prints is between 65° and 70°F and a relative humidity of 45 to 55 percent.)

Regularly inspect paintings while they are on exhibit or in storage, and document any signs of deterioration or damage. If a work of art has become unstable (i.e., canvas is buckling or there is loss of paint), contact a qualified conservator for instruction in handling it. Never attempt repair of paintings or prints; this is best left in the conservator's trained hands.

Handling Paintings and Prints

Do not touch the front or back of a painting or print with bare hands; the oils from fingers can cause damage. Instead, use clean white cotton gloves. If no gloves are available, be certain to wash hands thoroughly before, and several times during, the process of handling paintings. (Ornate frames, with irregular surfaces readily collect dust, and it is transferred to hands.) Do not allow tape, glue, or any kind of clip, staple, or other fastener to contact prints.

Never carry more than one painting or print at a time. Regardless of size, every painting must be supported by two hands, one on the bottom and the other along the side. This method more evenly distributes the stress on the frame and the painting itself. If carried by one side, the painting can easily pull away from the frame, or the frame can bend from the pressure. Large paintings should be carried by at least two people, each supporting each lower corner and side. Be careful to hold paintings at points where the frame is strong, not on, for example, fragile gesso decoration.

It is permissible to clean the frames of works of art by dusting with a soft, clean brush or vacuuming with a soft bristle attachment and low suction. Move all objects located beneath the artwork before dust removal begins to avoid transferring the dust to an object that may be even more difficult to clean. While working, make certain never to touch the frame or painting with the hard edges or handle of the brush. Vacuum any dust that has resettled onto the floor below.

When removing paintings from storage or when moving them from place to place, never rest them on hard surfaces. Place them on padded blocks, packing blankets, carpet scraps, or foam pads. Vibrations caused by mishandling can result in paint loss and cracking.

Storage Conditions

Never store unframed and framed paintings or prints together. Unframed works are susceptible to abrasions, scratches, perforations and loosened paint caused by vibrations. Protect artworks by wrapping them in a covering of acid-free, lignin-free paper and rigid cardboard (acid-free cardboard is preferred).

When storing paintings and prints, remove screw eyes and hanging wire to prevent damaging surfaces and frames.

Always use corrugated cardboard dividers between paintings (if the cardboard touches the surface of the paintings or prints, the cardboard must be acid free, if only the frames touch regular cardboard can be used). Cut cardboard panels larger than the paintings to afford maximum protection.

Prints are best stored in frames or matted and enclosed in specially designed, acid-free, lignin-free conservation boxes. Solander boxes, available through conservation supply companies, are commonly used. Unframed, unmatted prints must be stored flat, between sheets of acid-free, lignin-free paper.

If antique cabinets or chest of drawers are used to store works on paper, be careful to line drawers with acid-free, lignin-free paper, and change the paper every few years. Also, mark the outside of each drawer with tags listing the contents.

Regularly monitor for pests that feed on paper and paint, such as silverfish and cockroaches.

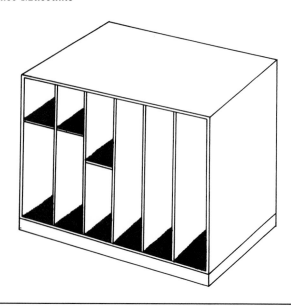

Storage rack for paintings, with vertical slots or bins. *(Reproduced with permission of the Canadian Conservation Institute)*

CREATING SAFE STORAGE FOR PAINTINGS

Sophisticated, commercial systems for storing paintings can be purchased and installed directly in suitable spaces, but few historic house museums can afford such systems or accommodate them because of their size. However, relatively inexpensive homemade storage racks can be constructed easily and fit into closets or small rooms within the museum.

A simple method that works well for small collections of paintings is a rectangular wooden rack containing a number of vertical slots or bins, some of which have been divided with shelves to hold smaller pictures. Typical dimensions for this rack are 6 to 7 feet high, 7 feet wide, and about 3 to 4 feet deep.[13] The actual size of the unit, of course, will depend on the space available. If a closet is used, it is possible to add an upper level to the rack if ceiling height and accessibility allow. Nonetheless, be cautious; it is difficult to safely retrieve paintings located well above one's head, and small spaces do not lend themselves to stepstools or ladders.

A high-grade, formaldehyde-free plywood can be used to make the rack, but the wood should first be treated by covering it with laminated film, paint with non-oil modified urethane or latex urethane acrylic, or paint containing calcium-carbonate, mica, or aluminum flakes (refer to description of wood storage).

The sides and bottom of the bins must be covered with a protective padding to prevent frames from chipping and splintering and to protect them from excessive vibration when moving paintings in and out of the slots. Carpet scraps, inexpensive and readily available, are a good cushioning material.

It may be helpful to label each bin with its contents. This will prevent the staff from having to remove and view each painting when retrieving a specific one.

It is important to note that bin storage should be used only when paintings are stable. Damaged or fragile pictures should be stored flat.

Hanging Storage Screens An inexpensive and space-efficient method of storing paintings is to hang them on large, vertical panels that slide on ceiling tracks. The unit for this function consists of large

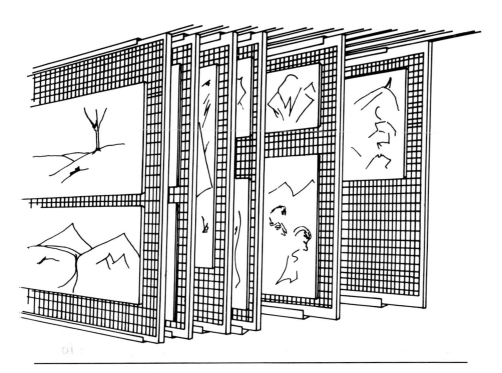

A track system can be easily installed for holding paintings of various sizes. (*Reproduced with permission of the Canadian Conservation Institute*)

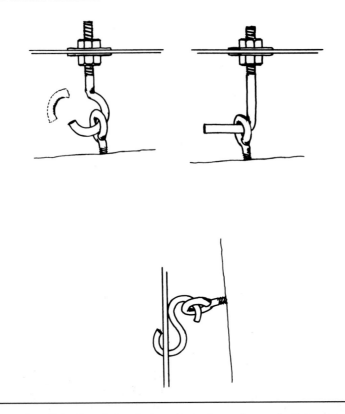

S-hooks work well for hanging paintings from the mesh panels. Other types of hooks also work well. *(Reproduced with permission of the Canadian Conservation Institute)*

panels, each a rectangular wood frame covered with rigid wire mesh. (The dimensions of the unit and number of the panels used will depend on the space available.) The panels are attached by interior door hangers to tracks secured to the ceiling. Paintings are hung from S-hooks positioned on the mesh and can be placed on both sides of the panels. Screw eyes on the backs of the frames are slipped onto the S-hooks, holding the paintings firmly in place.

The panels allow for easy access to the paintings because each panel can be pulled away from the other panels as needed for retrieval. As the collection grows, more tracks can be added to accommodate more artworks.

All materials needed for this system are readily available. The panels, mesh, and ceiling tracks, are available at most building-supply stores, and the S-hooks and screw eyes are common stock at hardware stores.

Stacking Paintings Against a Wall   As a rule, paintings should not be stacked against walls. If, however, no other method of storage is feasible, they should be placed front-to-front and back-to-back on padded blocks placed at right angles to the wall. The blocks not only elevate the paintings, but protect them from vibrations. For further protection, acid-free, lignin-free cardboard dividers should be placed between the paintings and on each end and drape muslin or polyethylene sheeting over paintings to prevent water damage or dust and dirt from collecting on them.

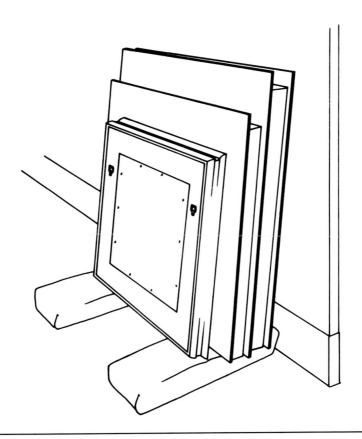

Wood blocks, padded with carpet remnants, can be used to store paintings temporarily. Always insert cardboard dividers between paintings when stacking them in this manner. (Reproduced with permission of the Canadian Conservation Institute)

Padded blocks are easy to make with 2×8-inch lengths of wood. They can be covered with carpet remnants or wrapped with fiber-fill and covered with muslin. The materials can be stapled or tacked to the bottom of the blocks. It is advisable to keep several pairs of blocks on hand, but stacking should be only a temporary means of storing paintings.

Wood

Wooden objects in historic house museum collections range in size and shape from small carved boxes to large elaborate furniture. It is useful to separate the wooden objects found in house museums into categories of large, medium, and small and to store them accordingly.

Large objects, such as furniture, can be stored by placing them directly on floor. If the artifact is flat bottomed, it should be raised on blocks or placed on a low platform to allow air to circulate around it.[14] Large pieces must not be stacked; stacking places stress on them and also poses a hazard to those who must lift or move the objects.

Medium-size objects are best stored on shallow metal shelving lined with polyethylene foam padding. Wood shelving units are also suitable after they have been painted with acid-inhibiting paints or covered with laminated film. The bottom shelf must be raised off the floor to protect objects from possible water damage, dust, and dirt. A muslin dust flap that can be rolled up or down can be attached to shelving. Or the objects themselves can be loosely draped with sheets of polyethylene. Store medium-size artifacts spaced so that they do not touch one another and avoid stacking them.

Small wooden objects should be kept in drawers, either in existing units or in metal storage drawers. These should be lined with polyethylene foam or unbleached, washed muslin. The lining will act as a dust barrier and provide a background for easy detection of insect activity. Tiny wooden artifacts can be stored in polyethylene bags or acid-free boxes to ensure that they do not roll into cracks or the corners of drawers.

Because wood is hygroscopic, it adjusts to its environment, absorbing water vapor under humid conditions and releasing water stored when the air is dry. This shrinking and swelling is known as

wood movement. When changes take place too quickly, wood will often crack and warp, veneers may detach, and finishes may checker. The preferred relative humidity for wood is between 40 and 55 percent. However, the actual relative humidity as it relates to wood is not as important as the speed with which changes in humidity occur. Wood does have a limited ability to adapt to either dry or moist environments as long as the transition is slow. When moving furniture or wooden artifacts from one area to another, check the environmental conditions in each area and their possible effects on the artifacts.

Air flow around wooden objects in storage is also paramount to their safety. Objects stored in unventilated, damp areas can develop mold, mildew, and fungus growths, which eventually will destroy wood fibers. If wooden objects must be stored in basements and other damp areas, monitor the area frequently and place fans at intervals to keep air circulating.

It may be necessary to clean wooden objects before storing them. Use a small bristle brush; a clean, dry, soft cloth; or a hand-held vacuum with a nozzle attachment (be sure that wooden surfaces are stable before using a vacuum). Highly finished surfaces can be cleaned with a slightly damp, clean cloth.

Finished wood surfaces may require wax to protect them. A thin coat of microcrystalline wax (which is translucent and moisture resistant) should be carefully applied once or twice a year.[15] This type of wax is available through conservation supply companies. Plain paste wax can also be used if applied lightly and thoroughly buffed.

Commercial furniture polishes should not be used because they often contain silicones that can accumulate on wood and become impossible to remove.[16] Other products to avoid are linseed oil and lemon oil. Linseed oil, with repeated application, can damage finishes and cause them to become tacky and attract dust, eventually even darkening the wood.[17] Lemon oil will also damage finishes by becoming tacky with prolonged use.

When moving wooden objects for any reason, place them in a padded carrying box or cart to avoid scratching and breaking. Pads should be placed between objects for further protection. Wooden objects can be fragile—pieces can come unglued or, because of shrinking, fall off. Lift wooden objects with two hands and always support the bottoms of smaller objects.

Metalwork

A detailed description of cleaning and polishing techniques for metal will be provided in Chapter 7, but the subject warrants comment here. The types of metalwork found in historic houses are varied. Some are gleaming and polished silver—candelabra, etched and decorated serving platters, elaborate desk accessories, or toilette services. Other metal artifacts have dull surfaces, such as utilitarian copper and brass pots, cooking utensils, and lanterns. Not all metal is intended to shine, and polishing would give an inaccurate interpretation of its original appearance.

Some metal objects will have a natural patina—a thin film, usually green, caused by oxidation. Metal may also be given an artificial patina by using acids instead of waiting for natural aging. Outdoor metal sculptures and statues sometimes painted to resemble marble and stone are other examples of applied film. Any patina, natural or applied, will preserve the metal with a protective cover and should never be removed.

Before attempting to "clean" a metal object, try to determine how it might have been used in its original setting. You may find that it always looked "aged," not polished and bright.

Storing Metal Objects

Metal objects can be stored according to size, either on metal shelves lined with thick felt or on wood shelves that have been covered with laminated film or painted with non-oil modified urethane or latex urethane acrylic. A thin padding of batting or polyester fill can placed on the shelves and covered with muslin cloth.

Relative humidity in the storage and exhibit areas should be kept below 60 percent to avoid corrosion of metals such as iron. If possible, metals should be stored apart from wood objects and other hygroscopic materials. Also, it is best to store metals on an inside wall, where there is less chance of moisture seeping through and causing rust or corrosion.

When placing metal artifacts in storage or moving them for any reason, always wear clean, white cotton gloves. Never allow bare skin to touch metal; oils from the hands will mark the surface and cause it to tarnish. Never overcrowd metal objects on the shelves, and never stack platters, plates, bowls, or similar artifacts. This practice may seriously scratch the surfaces.

When moving metal objects, place them in a padded carrying box or cart to avoid scratching or denting. Pads should be placed between objects for further protection.

Drape polyethylene sheets over stored metal objects to protect them from dirt and dust.

Cleaning Metal Objects

All metal artifacts must be cleaned with extreme care. Even a soft cloth can scratch and mar a metal surface. If an object is very dusty, go over it with a hand vacuum with a soft bristle attachment. This will pull the dirt from the piece instead of rubbing it across the surface. If the object is only lightly soiled, use a jeweler's brush to remove the dirt.

NOTES

1. Conservator Jim Horns, personal communication, September 1990. Pamela Hatchfield and Jane Carpenter treat formaldehyde and its harmfulness to museum objects in *Formaldehyde: How Great Is the Danger to Museum Collections?* (Boston: Center for Conservation and Technical Studies, Harvard University Art Museums, 1987). Copies are available through the Center for Conservation and Technical Studies, Harvard University Art Museums, 32 Quincy Street, Cambridge, Massachusetts 02138. (617) 495–2392.

2. Carolyn Rose, conservator, Anthropology Conservation Laboratory, Smithsonian Institution, personal communication, Summer 1990.

3. David Erhardt of the Smithsonian Institution's Conservation Analytical Laboratory suggested using calcium carbonate matte board or paint containing calcium carbonate on wood shelving to buffer objects from acids.

4. Information excerpted from a draft of an article by David Erhardt, submitted to *Restaurator,* as part of the proceedings of the National Archives and Records Administration Fifth Annual Preservation Conference, "Exhibits and Conservation: A Delicate Balance," p. 11.

5. Ibid.

6. Barbara Lang Rottenberg, *Care and Display of Glass Collections,* Technical Leaflet, no. 127 (Nashville, Tenn.: American Association for State and Local History, 1980), pp. 3–5.

7. Ibid., p. 5.

8. Ibid.

9. Mary Ann Butterfield and Lotus Stack, "An Ounce of Prevention," *Weaver's Journal* 10, no. 1(1985): 8.

10. Canadian Conservation Institute, *Rolled Storage for Textiles*, CCI Notes, vol. 13, no. 3 (Ottawa: Canadian Conservation, 1983), p. 1.

11. Butterfield and Stack, "Ounce of Prevention," p. 9.

12. Bonnie Wilson, curator of Sound and Visual Collections, Minnesota Historical Society, personal communication, October 12, 1990.

13. Canadian Conservation Institute, *Storage System for Paintings*, CCI Notes, vol. 10, no. 3 (Ottawa: Conservation Institute, 1986), p. 2.

14. R. L. Barclay, R. Eames, and A. Todd, *The Care of Wooden Objects*, Technical Bulletin, no. 8 (Ottawa: Canadian Conservation Institute, 1982), p. 8.

15. A. Bruce MacLeish, *The Care of Antiques and Historical Collections* (Nashville: Tenn.: American Association for State and Local History, 1972), p. 122.

16. Barclay, Eames, and Todd, *Care of Wooden Objects*, p. 12.

17. Ibid.

6

Preservation and Care
of the Historic House
Interior

The most difficult task is to maintain the right environment. It is a matter of compromising, of finding levels of temperature and humidity, for example which will suit the woodwork, although it would prefer to be more damp, and at the same time keeping paper happy, even though it would like to be drier.

David Winfield, Foreword, *The National Trust Manual of Housekeeping*

CONSERVATION, AS IT relates to historic house museums, means the preservation and maintenance of cultural materials as well as of the house itself. Many conditions—extremes in temperature and humidity, excessive light, pest infestations, corrosive pollutants, and careless handling—contribute to the deterioration and premature aging of historic artifacts.

In small museums setting the standards for conservation practices and seeing that they are carried out are the curator's responsibility. Yet the curator's role is one of a generalist, and frequently it is necessary to enlist the aid of a trained conservator when problems in the care of artifacts and structure arise. The conservator is a professional who can provide an understanding of the history, materials, and technology of objects and offer a diagnostic examination and analysis of their care. Today these specialists follow a holistic approach to treatment of objects and can advise on appropriate methods for long-term care, storage, handling, installation, environmental protection, and general maintenance of objects. They can also perform the treatment necessary for saving museum materials. If you do not know conservators in your area, contact a larger museum, the state historical society, or the American Institute for Conservation (AIC) for referrals. The AIC publishes an annual listing of qualified conservators in the United States as well as a free brochure, *Selecting and Working with a Conservator.*

Locating a conservator, however, may be easier than finding the funds to pay for his or her expertise. If the museum lacks sufficient funds for a conservator, it is recommended that a grant be sought. Conservation grants can be procured from the Institute of Museum Services (IMS), state historical societies, or from local corporations and foundations concerned with historic restoration (more detailed information is in Chapter 3).

The grants available to house museums provide for: (1) a review of the strengths and weaknesses of the museum's collections management and aids in establishing policies and procedures (MAP II), (2) general surveys by specialists of the overall condition of collections, upgrading the museum's storage facilities, improving the museum's environment and the architectural stability of the building (Conservation Assessment Program, and Conservation Project Support Program through IMS), and (3) treatment of objects in collections by conservation specialists (Conservation Project Support Program through IMS).

When seeking funds for conservation you may wish to apply for a series of conservation grants that begins with a general survey and a systematic long-range plan for upgrading storage facilities, improving the collection's environment overall, and treating artifacts in a methodical way. Or you may wish to hire a free-lance conservator to assess the conservation needs of the museum and to help train the in-house staff in preventive measures in collection's care.

Procuring a grant for conservation may take a long time, but it is worth the wait. Do not be tempted to allow an unqualified person to fill in until the professional arrives! The very objects that the museum is trying to save can be seriously damaged in the hands of an amateur. In the meantime, the curator and staff can become familiar with literature on preserving collections and historic structures. Such information will enable them to become proficient at recognizing conservation problems and areas that are in danger of deterioration. (A list of these sources is included under Chapter 6 in the references section at the end of this book.

Identifying Problems

Historic house museums are faced with many problems in protecting the structure and its collection. Often the environment is far from ideal. The indoor climate may be too cold in the winter months and far too hot in the summer. It is often difficult to control humidity, particularly when there is little ability to control temperature. Collections are stored in undesirable areas—attics, basements, or closets located on outside walls, where the temperature and humidity can vary greatly.

Sunlight streaming through windows and skylights damages rugs, bleaches wood-paneled walls, and fades and embrittles fabrics. Excessive light will also increase room temperature and consequently affect the relative humidity.

Unchecked, insects and rodents will devastate collections. Moths feed on and live in fabrics, dermestid beetles thrive in areas where dust has built up, and mice will happily create homes in and from valuable museum materials.

Atmospheric pollutants—soot particles, dust, acid compounds—are present everywhere. Museums located in metropolitan or industrial areas are more at risk because of the detrimental compounds emitted by automobile exhaust fumes and factory smoke. Unfortunately, most historic houses do not have air filtration systems to screen such harmful compounds from the air.

Objects are often irreversibly damaged as a result of handling by untrained staff or volunteers. Even staff or workers who are only indirectly involved with the museum's collection can wreak havoc in a historic house.

Controlling the Environment

Gaining control over the indoor environment is a major step in ensuring the longevity of a collection. The key factors are temperature and humidity. Historic house museums should strive for an optimal temperature range between 60° and 70°F and a relative humidity between 45 and 55 percent. The term *relative humidity* is one that is found frequently in museum literature. It is important to understand what it is, how it is measured, and how to acquire an acceptable level of relative humidity in your museum.

Air contains water vapor, ranging from almost none in the desert to complete saturation in a rainforest.[1] **Relative humidity** refers to the amount of water vapor in the atmosphere. Expressed as RH, relative humidity is the relationship between the absolute humidity (the amount of water vapor in a given volume of air) and the maximum amount of water vapor that a specific volume of air, at the same temperature and air pressure, is able to hold.[2] The ability of air to support and contain water vapor varies with the temperature.[3]

Because relative humidity and temperature are interrelated, the RH will decrease as the temperature increases; at the same time, the amount of water vapor that the air can hold will increase. Hot air, then, has a greater capacity for holding water than cold air. Consequently, when the temperature drops, so does the ability of the air to hold moisture.

Extremely high humidity, usually measured at over 70 percent, causes serious damage to organic and inorganic materials because they will absorb the water vapor. In fact, most decay of organic objects can be attributed to extremely high humidity. Pests, too, will reproduce and flourish in warm, humid environments and can ruin organic materials. Mold and mildew stain and disfigure paper, and textiles and wooden objects swell. Wool, cotton, and linen absorb moisture and their dimensions change. High humidity can also cause adhesives to break down and leather to expand. For example, high humidity effects a framed painting in a number of ways: the wood stretcher frame absorbs moisture and swells, causing the canvas to stretch, the canvas (made of woven fibers) begins to sag, and the painted surface cracks and eventually loses its paint.

Inorganic materials—ceramics, glass, metals, stone, and concrete—are also negatively effected by high humidity. Glass may weep or sweat, metals will corrode, and stone and concrete may spall. Another problem arises when inorganic materials contain or come in contact with chlorides. High humidity activates chlorides, causing crystals to grow and, eventually, pitting and surface loss of stone, ceramics, and concrete, and causing corrosion of metals.

Extremely dry conditions, below 30 percent relative humidity, which usually occur during the dry winter months or in arid climates, can also be a problem for organic materials. Wood will shrink, crack, or warp and finishes may checker. Paneling and carved wood embellishments may peel or loosen because adhesives have dried out. Textiles may become desiccated, losing their flexibility and, eventually, the fibers will break down completely. Paint will dry up and chip from surfaces. Inorganic materials, however, generally do quite well in dry conditions.

An even more harmful situation than too high or too low humidity are fluctuating temperatures and humidity. Repeated cycles of rising and falling humidity cause the most serious damage. Annual cycles in northern climates can range from nearly 100 percent relative humidity in summer with no dehumidification to as low as 10 percent in winter if heating is provided without humidification.[4]

Fluctuation can also occur if air-conditioning systems are run only during the day to save on operating costs. With the change in temperature when the air-conditioning is turned off, the relative humidity will change, too. Objects will accommodate to the change by shrinking and releasing moisture during the drier part of the day and expanding and absorbing water molecules when the relative humidity rises.

Temperatures may also vary considerably during colder months. The practice of setting the thermostat at, say, 68°F during the day when the museum is open, primarily for the comfort of the visitors and staff and turning it down at night—sometimes as low as 50° or 55°F—might be seen as conscientious budget management. But it should be avoided at all costs. It is much more expensive to repair objects damaged because of fluctuating atmospheric conditions than to pay the increased cost of maintaining an even temperature both day and night.

It is unreasonable, of course, to expect that all historic house museums will be able to attain the ideal levels of humidity and temperatures. However, if the staff works to eliminate the greatest extremes in relative humidity (below 30 percent and above 70 percent), many humidity-related problems can be avoided.

Humidity Levels

CHECKING HUMIDITY LEVELS

There are several accurate and easy devices for measuring relative humidity: psychrometers, hygrometers, thermohygrometers, and hygrothermographs.

The **sling psychrometer** can be purchased for $45 to $75 at scientific instrument or supply companies. This device has two thermometers, one for a dry-bulb reading, and one for a wet-bulb reading. A cotton wick fitted to the wet bulb is saturated with distilled water and the device is whirled around. Readings are taken from both thermometers, and the relative humidity is easily calculated on a psychometric table, included with the instrument.

To obtain accurate readings the procedure must be followed

carefully. Wicks must be clean and fit snugly. New wicks should be soaked in at least three changes of distilled water each overnight. The instrument must be whirled in a steady, even motion for 3 to 4 minutes for an accurate reading. (Care must be taken when "slinging" an instrument in the proximity of collections.)

A more accurate and easy to read instrument is the **aspirated psychrometer.** It operates with a small fan powered by a flashlight battery. The fan draws cool air across wet- and dry-bulb thermometers; readings are calculated on a psychometric chart, often printed directly on the instrument. (The wet bulb is snugly fitted with a clean wick and kept wet in distilled water in the instrument's reservoir for several readings.) The psychrometer can be purchased for around $130 through scientific instrument companies such as Cole-Parmer.

A new product recently offered through instrument companies is the **hand-held relative humidity meter.** These meters are lightweight and compact and can be brought into any area. The readings are digitally displayed and provide measurements from 10 to 100 percent relative humidity. This psychrometer costs around $130 and is preferred over the sling type because it is simple to use (there is no need for making calibrations from a psychometric chart), and it does not need to be whirled around collections.

Other affordable devices for the small museum are the **hygrometers** and the **thermohygrometer** (the latter used to indicate both relative humidity and temperature). These instruments base readings on either hair bundles or cellulose sensors that expand or contract as they absorb or release moisture. Both are accurate and easy to read and are available in several different models and prices. The most common are the dial-face models that can be easily mounted on a wall. These range in cost between $25 and $85. The digital thermohygrometer, which displays simultaneous readings of both relative humidity and temperature, is particularly easy to use. It runs for a year on a AAA battery and costs around $60.

The most inexpensive relative humidity indicator is the **paper hygrometer,** which contains cobalt salts that change color as the relative humidity rises or falls. The device works well in a closed environment, such as an exhibit case, but should be avoided as the only method of testing in larger spaces, where it can be inaccurate. The paper hygrometer can be ordered through conservation supply companies.

The **hygrothermograph,** like some of the hygrometers, bases readings on hair bundles or synthetic fibers. This instrument is most useful for recording; it yields a continuous permanent record of temperature and relative humidity. Inside a clear acrylic case is a drum wrapped in a chart with two fiber-tipped arms that record directly on the chart. The drum rotates once a week. This apparatus is helpful in determining changes in relative humidity over time, and the paper chart provides the museum with a permanent record. The primary drawback is the expense; the hygrothermograph usually costs more than $500. Another limitation is that it must be recalibrated frequently. However, the hygrothermograph can be recalibrated against a battery-operated psychrometer.

MAINTAINING AN ACCEPTABLE LEVEL OF RELATIVE HUMIDITY

As a general rule, the museum should have a number of humidifiers in use in the winter months and dehumidifiers in place in the summer months, even with air-conditioning.

Dry Environments In dry environments water vapor can be added to the air by using portable humidifiers. The number and the size of the humidifying units will depend on the size of the historic house. Experiment with the numbers and types and consult a retailer, such as Sears, where humidifiers are sold.

Two types of humidifiers are available. One is a spray humidifier; the other is an evaporative type. The latter is preferable because spray humidifiers may overcompensate, filling an area with too much water vapor and, if distilled water is not used, coating objects with a fine film of particulate matter. A common problem with portable humidifiers is that they run out of water quickly, resulting in a rapid drop in the relative humidity. Or the controls may be altered by visitors passing through or by staff who are not aware of how the device functions. Too much humidity during the winter months can be disastrous to the house's structure: vapor condenses and freezes within walls, leading to deterioration of brick surfaces.

In the winter months the thermostat should be kept no higher than 70°F. The higher the temperature, the easier it is for objects to lose moisture. Some museums intentionally keep their indoor temperatures just below 65°F because it is believed to be better for the life of the furnishings.

Damp Environments   Use portable dehumidifiers to maintain relative humidity below 60 percent. The number and size of the units used will depend on the house. Dehumidifiers will need daily regulation. The water collected in them must be emptied daily. It may be possible to place them in areas near a sink or drain, where the water can be channeled away with hoses; however, the units will need to be monitored daily for leakage and overflows. Monitoring can become problematic on week-ends or during holidays when the staff rotates, so make accommodations for these changes.

The use of silica gel is another way to help reduce high humidity. It is a porous, granular, noncrystalline form of silica that acts as a drying agent.[5] Stable, noncorrosive, and chemically inert, silica gel is especially useful as a desiccant in small areas such as exhibit cases or small storage areas. Some grades are specially colored to indicate when the gel is dry (blue) or when it has reached a level at which it is no longer useful as a good desiccant (pink). Silica gel can be purchased from chemical and laboratory suppliers, as well as conservation supply companies. (To be effective, silica gel must first be "conditioned" to the desired relative humidity. For instructions on this procedure, refer to the Canadian Conservation Institute publication *Silica Gel.*)

AIR-CONDITIONING

Typically, high humidity and excessive heat go hand in hand. If central air-conditioning is being considered by the museum, it is important to conduct a feasibility study first. Basic questions need to be asked. Can the system be installed without damaging the historic structure or compromising the esthetics of the museum? It is best to consult with an architectural expert before making a commitment to an air-conditioning system.

The use of room air-conditioning units in historic buildings is not recommended. They cause fluctuating temperatures, not only in the areas of use but also in surrounding areas. Further, the units are often used sporadically, making it difficult to maintain a constant temperature.

In historic houses lacking central air-conditioning, there are several ways to cool the interior. First, window coverings can be closed at the hottest and brightest times of the day. Exposure will be different for each room, but it is easy to determine when damaging rays are streaming into a room. If there are no window coverings, then it is essential to install window blinds or to add ultraviolet-inhibiting film to windows to prevent excessive heating.

Cool interior rooms by placing electric fans at intervals, hidden from visitors' eyes. If possible, place fans in windows on upper floors to draw in cooler night air: it will, to some extent, exchange with the warmer air on lower floors, cooling them. (If windows are to be opened during the night, use removable screens on the windows to eliminate the possibility of insects, bats, birds, and other creatures from entering the house.) Some historic houses were built with roof openings to facilitate the release of hot air trapped inside the building during the summer months. These, too, should be opened at night to allow cool air to circulate. (Make sure to fit these openings with screens to avoid pests from entering.)

Controlling Light

Light is a primary adversary of organic historic materials and can be difficult to control in historic house interiors. Too much sunlight, as well as artificial lighting, can cause textiles to dry out and fade, wood-paneled walls to lose color, and fabrics and leather to become brittle. Although some substances—such as wool, linen, and silk—are more sensitive to light than others, inert objects such as ceramics and glass may also be affected.

In general, three "types" of light are used in museums: sunlight, incandescent light, and fluorescent light. Sunlight is harmful to historic objects because it generates heat and transmits ultraviolet rays as well. Incandescent light (tungsten lighting), too, is a concentrated source of heat, but has little or no ultraviolet radiation (although some bulbs, such as tungsten-halogen [quartz-iodine], may produce a significant amount of ultraviolet radiation). Fluorescent bulbs function with virtually no heat buildup, but the ballasts (the device used to start the voltage) do produce heat and can overheat a display case or add heat to a room. The primary problem with using fluorescent lighting is the transmission of ultraviolet radiation.

Controlling the amount of ultraviolet light entering the historic house museum is fundamental. But how do you know how much ultraviolet light is present in the exhibit areas? How is this light measured?

Light levels can be measured by using a light meter. Many types are available; one that is highly recommended is the model that gives a digital reading in both foot-candles and lux (a unit of illumination). This costs about $300 and is available through

Art Preservation Services
253 East 78th Street
New York, New York 10021

If the museum cannot afford a light meter, a public agency such as the state historical society may be willing to lend one for a short time. Light levels can also be estimated using a 35-mm single lens reflex camera with a built-in light meter, and a sheet of white matte board or boxboard. This procedure is outlined in the Canadian Conservation Institute's pamphlet *Using a Camera to Measure Light Levels.*

A general rule is that light levels should not exceed 15 foot-candles or 150 lux. The ideal is no more than 10 foot-candles of light for organic materials. For particularly light-sensitive objects, keep levels between 2.5 and 5 foot-candles, or around 25 to 50 lux. If you find the levels in your museum are too high and cannot be controlled, follow the measures outlined below to safeguard your collection.

The table on page 113 shows the light sensitivity of various materials.

An object's rate of deterioration is directly related to the amount and type of light to which it is exposed, and to the length of exposure.[6] It is important to remember that the effects of light are cumulative. A sensitive object left for an extended period even in a "safely" lit environment will eventually show effects of light degradation. In the historic house, light damage is particularly noticeable in rooms that have been exposed to sunlight for long periods of time.

Keep in mind that historic curtains and draperies will also be strongly affected by sunlight. Historically, housekeepers closed window coverings during the bright, hot times of the day. Although this kept the sun from objects within the room, as well as lowering temperatures, it speeded the deterioration of the window covering itself. In some museums where curtains have hung for decades with no ultraviolet protection, dry rot has advanced so far that they actually fall apart when touched. Printed or colored fabrics will lose their color almost completely, and white areas will become yellowish in color. If possible, replace original curtains with reproductions and carefully store the originals to ensure their longevity.

Light Sensitivity of Materials

Material	Recommended Light Levels
Extremely sensitive	25–50 lux, 2.5–5.0 foot-candles
Textiles	
Paper	
Dyed leather	
Feathers	
Vegetable-dyed materials	
Lacquer	
Multimaterial construction	
Moderately sensitive	150 lux, 15 foot-candles
Bone, ivory, horn	
Cellulose materials, such as wood, tapa, baskets, reeds, grass, leather, parchment, rawhide, skin	
Fur	
Furniture	
Least sensitive	1,000 lux, 100 foot-candles
Metal	
Stone	
Ceramic	
Glass	

Adapted from William Lull and Linda Merk, "Lighting for Storage of Museum Collections: Developing a System for Safekeeping of Light-Sensitive Materials," *Technology and Conservation* 7, no. 1 (1982): 20.

Leather, too, will deteriorate when exposed to sunlight. During the late nineteenth and early twentieth centuries, embossed leather was sometimes used as a wall and ceiling covering in houses, and as upholstery for furniture. Unprotected, leather splits and cracks, especially in areas where pressure is applied, such as seats and armrests. Sitting on a chair that has a cracked leather seat increases the stress and may further damage it. Visitors (and staff) should never be allowed to sit on *any* historic furniture, especially those with leather and fabric coverings.

Historic houses can be protected from light damage in a number of ways.

- Pull blinds, shades, louvers, or draperies as part of the daily routine. If no window coverings exist, consider installing awnings or plantings to diffuse the incoming sunlight (silk plants can be placed near inside windows to diffuse incoming light.)

- Consider applying ultraviolet-inhibiting film to the windows. The film, which is very effective and easily applied, is made by several companies. An effective, long-lasting brand is Scotchtint P–60, available from distributors of sun filtering products.[7] Scotchtint P–60 is a nearly clear, aluminum-based film, composed of two layers of adhesives, one of aluminum, a barrier coat, and a layer of polyester to prevent the aluminum from corroding. It offers total protection from ultraviolet rays and blocks 33 percent of infrared exposure. An asset of the film is that it can be fitted to the inner frame of the window and is virtually invisible. Use of ultraviolet film not only protects historic rugs and furnishings but also allows more flexibility in displaying light-sensitive objects. The film filters ultraviolet radiation for about ten years; then it will need to be replaced.

- Use slipcovers or fabric covers (muslin) to protect fabrics and furnishings that are vulnerable to sunlight. Housekeepers from earlier times used this method to protect furnishings during the summers. Also, cover historic carpets with heavy muslin (available from wholesale fabric supply companies) when rooms are not in use.

- Place sensitive materials, such as oil or watercolor paintings, books, or textiles that are displayed open away from windows and in the darker parts of the room. Careful consideration must be given before using any unstable object in a period room display or exhibit where further damage may be incurred by light exposure.

- If fluorescent lighting is used, warm white fluorescent tubes or low ultraviolet fluorescent lamps are the least harmful. The tubes should always be covered with ultraviolet filters (available through conservation supply companies), and the fixtures should be no closer than 2 feet from museum objects. (The filters must be well fitted to prevent uv leakage.)

- Incandescent lighting is dangerous because of the heat it generates. If it is used in exhibit cases, make certain that the cases are vented to allow heat to escape. If your museum uses incandescent fixtures that replicate historic lighting, keep them at least 3 feet away from curtains, furnishings, and paintings. The heat generated from an incandescent fixture with candle flares can easily scorch or ignite objects within close range.[8]

- Photoflood lights, often used by photographers, also generate heat, often extreme. Use caution when such lights are used; placed too close to an oil painting, they will literally cook it.[9] Also the re-

By placing protective sleeves over fluorescent bulbs, sensitive museum objects can be protected from harmful ultraviolet rays. (Photograph by Bernice Wenzel, courtesy of the American Swedish Institute)

peated flash from photographic equipment will harm sensitive materials, such as textiles and paintings. The museum may wish to establish a rule that visitors cannot take photographs in the museum, a common answer to the problem. (If such a rule is instituted, the museum should have postcards or slides of the historic house available for purchase.)

- When displaying light-sensitive materials in an area without ultraviolet-inhibiting film on windows, use a piece of plexiglass with ultraviolet inhibitor such as UF-3 to cover the vulnerable article.

- Turn off all lights in period rooms or rooms containing historic materials when no visitors are present. This will partially eliminate the stress of ultraviolet emissions (while saving on the utility bills). It may be possible to ask visitors to switch lights on and off as they move from room to room or to station guards on each floor for this task.

Controlling Insects and Rodents

It is not unusual to find insects and rodents in historic houses. These pests can be very destructive, especially to organic materials. However, pests can be controlled if preventive measures are used.

Preventing a pest infestation in the museum can be achieved by good housekeeping and regular monitoring of collection and exhibition areas. By scrupulously observing the following safeguards, you may never be faced with an infestation.

- Keep all food and plants away from collections, and restrict food consumption to an area a safe distance from collections. Food attracts pests and can also be damaging to artifacts.
- Keep storage and work areas uncluttered and free of dust and dirt. Clean frequently.
- Schedule regular checks of collections storage and exhibit areas every few months and keep records of any evidence of pests.
- Set out sticky traps (glue boards) in storage areas to see if anything turns up. Sticky traps, cardboard forms containing a strong glue that holds fast any pests that wander across them, are available at hardware stores or from extermination companies. Pests can then be identified and appropriate measures taken to eliminate them. Change the traps frequently! The bodies of dead bugs can entice other pests to feed on them.

Pests Commonly Found in the Museum

CLOTHES MOTHS

Clothes moths are the insects most commonly found in the historic house. Two frequently found species, the webbing clothes moth and the casemaking clothes moth, infest woolens and animal fibers. Both can be identified by their yellowish or buff-colored wings and soft bodies. The cycle of the clothes moth begins when the adult lays its soft white eggs, which hatch into white larvae. The larvae spins a cocoon and then transforms into an adult moth. At maturity the larvae are the most destructive, feeding on the fabrics in

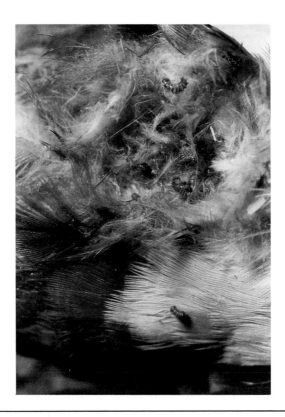

Collections must be protected from insects that can do extensive damage. Here feathers have been attacked by dermestids and moths. Larva of the Odd Beetle can be seen. (Photograph by Tim Ready)

which they live. A thin, silky webbing is always associated with a moth infestation, as well as telltale holes in the fabric. Frass (moth excrement, webbing, and other fuzzy debris) also indicates the presence of moths.

CARPET BEETLES

The yellow to brown, hairy larvae of carpet beetles can be found in stored woolens, carpeting, drawers, cupboards, or any place where lint has accumulated. The adult beetles are small, black to mottled black and white, ovoid-shaped insects and usually do little damage. It is while the beetle is in its larval state that it feeds on wool, fur, feathers, hair, animal fibers, and bristles.

POWDER-POST BEETLES

This common wood-boring insect bores tiny holes in wood and, like clothes moths and carpet beetles, is most harmful in the larval state. Some wood with these telltale holes are free from the insects and only the damage remains. However, a light-colored powder on or around a wooden artifact is a sign of a live beetle infestation.

SILVERFISH AND FIREBRATS

Silverfish and firebrats (much like silverfish, only they prefer warmer climates) can cause great damage. Paper is their main food staple, but they are attracted to starch in some types of fabric, such as silk, cotton, linen, and rayon. In eating the starches, they abrade the surface of textiles. Silverfish and firebrats are more damaging to paper, such as documents, books, and works of art on paper. They thrive on the paste or glue in paper, creating holes as they feed.

Watch carefully for these elliptically shaped insects. They dash about with serpentine movements, running for cover when lights are turned on. Silver or gray in color and covered with scales (hence the name "silverfish"), they are easily recognized. They seem to prefer humid areas, although they can be found throughout a building, wherever they can procure a meal. Silverfish and firebrats are very adroit; they can make their way inside framed watercolor paintings to get at the paper.

The best protection against silverfish and firebrats is to keep paper materials in metal cabinets with gasketed doors. Inspect books, documents, works of art on paper, and textiles frequently for their presence.

COCKROACHES

This persistent insect has been around for millions of years and will probably outlive homo sapiens. Although roaches can be found throughout North America, they are particularly ubiquitous in the South. They can be identified by their broad, flat and oval shape and their tan or brownish color. Because roaches feed at night, it is often difficult to detect their presence. Cockroaches feed on any number of materials, including glue, leather, bookbindings, envelopes. If you have these pests in your museum you will find that they can seriously damage paper, leaving holes much as silverfish do. Unfortunately, damage to books or prints may be the first evidence of an infestation.

Cockroaches can be excluded by using insect-tight metal storage units and controlled by rigorous housekeeping. Check boxes and bags that are brought into the museum, making certain no roaches or their egg capsules are carried in. Egg capsules are dark colored and range in size and shape from a grain of rice to a kidney bean. Store these containers outside the building, or at least away from collections. Keep kitchen and lunchroom areas clean and food stored in sealable bags or containers. Make sure there are no leaks under sinks or from faucets—cockroaches need water to survive. Keep water in the sink's trap and plug or screen rarely used drains to prevent roaches from traveling through plumbing. Use roach traps such as the Roach Motel or a sticky trap to determine where the roaches are coming from and to try to eliminate them at the source. If you choose to use an insecticide, use with caution, it can be harmful to humans and collections. If your museum is persistently plagued with cockroach infestations, it may be necessary to engage professional exterminators.

RODENTS

Rodents are a frequent source of trouble in historic house museums. One of the most common and destructive rodents is the house mouse. Many museum materials have been ruined because mice have found them perfect places for their nests. Textiles have been shredded to create the nests for future generations, leather chewed and eaten, clothing destroyed, wooden household articles gnawed completely through. Mice can set up housekeeping easily in most houses, since they use organic materials for both food and nests.

A good way to prevent mice from destroying objects is to inspect artifact storage areas frequently. Do not allow them time to make a comfortable home. Watch for droppings or other traces of their presence, such as urine or shredded cloth and paper. If you find a nest, remove it and all historic materials from the area immediately.

Use snap traps, sticky traps, and automatic traps such as Ketch-All brand models to catch mice. Once they are caught, destroy them. Avoid anticoagulant rodent bait. Rodents do not die until days after eating it, while they continue to damage collections. They may die in an inaccessible place and attract other pests, such as dermestids (beetles) and moths, to feed on the body. Once trap stations are set, check them regularly. Dispose of mice promptly.

Squirrels have been known to gain entrance to houses through chimneys, open windows, roof openings, and vents. Usually they enter the house accidentally and want to get out as much as you want them out. But they will need to be trapped and removed because they will chew on anything to get out of the house. Once they have been trapped (which may require the help of a local exterminator), close off or repair the places where they entered the building.

Bats can gain access to houses easily through very small openings. They, too, will need to be excluded, by closing off their entrances to the house. Bats are migratory and will leave a residence for other destinations during the year. After they are gone, repair any openings, plug holes, and caulk thoroughly.

Safe Elimination of Insects Through Freezing

In the past the most common way smaller museums rid objects of common insects was to place in close proximity chemicals such as Para-dichlorobenzene (PDB), naphthalene flakes (moth crystals), or Vapona (such as Shell No-Pest strips). These substances were readily available and were largely successful in eliminating the insects. Unfortunately, all these chemicals are extremely toxic to humans, even with limited use. They should never be used in the museum, under any conditions. But how can a museum deal with pest eradication without chemical fumigation?

An alternative to use of chemicals for insect control is to freeze organic materials. Freezing is an easy method of eradicating moths, dermestids, and silverfish in textiles, wood, books, documents, or any material of plant or animal origin. It is preferred treatment today because it is generally safe both for artifacts and humans and has a 100 percent kill rate when done properly. Freezing, however, should not be used on plastic or wax objects. Also, some synthetic materials and objects may react adversely to freezing. Contact a conservator if you have questions about freezing a particular object.

The basic principle behind the procedure is that living cells are

Some organic material can be frozen to eradicate insect infestations. A common household chest or upright freezer can be used. By attaching a thermocouple to the freezer, interior temperatures can easily be read. (Photograph by Tim Ready)

made up of 90 percent water. During freezing, the water crystallizes into ice, rupturing cell walls and killing all stages of insect life, from eggs to adults.[10]

To carry out this process, the museum will need to acquire a freezer, either a chest or vertical type. Install it in an area where objects are prepared for storage and make certain that it can attain a temperature of −20°C (4°F) temperature that is effective for insect eradication. Then proceed with the following steps.

1. Check the object to be frozen for weaknesses. When freezing painted wooden objects, exercise care. Wood will contract at a different rate than the painted surface, damaging the paint. If any object appears unstable, do not freeze it!

2. Prepare infested materials for freezing by placing them in a clear polyethylene bag. Remove excess air and seal the bag with a tie or tape. Keep bagged material at room temperature (18°C) until placed in the freezer.

3. Place the bag in the freezer, making certain that air can flow around it.

4. Use an indoor–outdoor thermometer or a thermocouple (instrument with a probe end and connecting wire for measuring temperature). Place the probe end on top of the bag and the display end (component where temperatures are digitally displayed) on the outside of the freezer door. This device makes it easy to read the temperature of the interior artifacts. The temperature must drop to at least −20°C within eight hours. Maintain this temperature for a minimum of forty hours.

5. Remove the bag from the freezer and slowly thaw it to room temperature. It is helpful to place materials in an insulated container to ensure slow defrosting.

6. After the material has thawed, repeat the freeze-thaw cycle. This will eliminate even dermestids, which can produce protective antifreeze chemicals once, but not twice. By freezing objects twice, you are assured of total eradication.

7. After the objects have completely thawed the second time, the dead insects and frass can be removed by brushing or vacuuming. Before doing this be sure that the artifact is strong enough to withstand the vibration or suction of either of these procedures. Clean the deinfested object at a safe distance from the collections and dispose of all plastic and vacuum bags.

8. Keep records of the procedure, including the date and time of freezing, the length of time the object remained in the freezer, the temperatures that were attained, and the type of insect(s) present.[11]

Keeping the Historic House Clean

In preserving the historic house museum, it is of major importance to keep the furnishings, flooring, and exhibits free from dust and dirt. Dust particles are abrasive and are a primary cause of damage to fabrics, historic rugs, textiles, and works of art (see Chapter 7).

Protection begins at the front door. A large, oversized mat should

At the Lincoln Home in Springfield, Illinois, special runners are used to prevent the abrading of historic carpets caused by visitor traffic. (Photograph courtesy of the Department of the Interior, National Park Service, Lincoln Home National Historic Site)

be placed outside the door to encourage visitors to remove grit, dirt, mud, or snow from their shoes. Another stiff mat should be placed inside the entryway, with a sign asking visitors to clean their shoes thoroughly before entering.

Another practice that is becoming commonplace in European house museums is to ask visitors to use shoe covers to cut down dirt being tracked through the house. Nonskid shoe covers—one-size-fits-all, polypropylene socks with an elastic top that can be stretched over virtually any shoe—can be purchased quite inexpensively through scientific or laboratory supply companies.

Another protective measure is to cut down on abrasion caused by visitor traffic is the museum carpet runner.[12] The runner, which can be placed directly on top of a historic rug, is made of wool edged with a cotton strip but, unlike regular carpet, has no backing. The runner can be special ordered to match the colors of existing carpets and in widths to accommodate wheelchairs and baby strollers. Signs can be placed around the rooms requesting visitors to stay on the runner. Or stanchions can be situated to guide visitors along the runner and away from unprotected carpets.[13]

Another agent that works to destroy historic objects is air polluted with particulates and gases. Air pollution is especially prevalent in urban areas, and museums located in industrial areas are most at risk because of emissions from automobile exhausts and factory smoke. Compounds such as sulfur dioxide (which combines with water to form sulfuric acid), nitrogen dioxide, and ozone can destroy organic and inorganic materials alike, corroding metal, affecting stone and plaster, concrete, paint, metals, cellulose materials, and dyes. These compounds can be even more destructive when mixed with water molecules. In coastal areas—and even inland—air contains highly corrosive chloride salts, which can have devastating effects on historic materials.[14]

The most effective way to protect the historic house from airborne pollutants is by using an air-conditioning system with a filtering unit. If such a system is beyond the budget of the museum, other methods can be implemented. Explore the possibility of using a portable filtration system just for the storage areas. This system, which will control particulate matter as well as contain gaseous media, can be added to rooms targeted as high priority, at a cost of $400 to $1000.[15] If a filter system is used on the furnace, make certain that the filter is changed frequently.

Muslin bags can be used to protect wood, glass and ceramics, leather, clothing, and textiles from particulate pollution while in storage. The bags can be made easily from unbleached, washed muslin with a simple drawstring opening. Silver and other metal artifacts can be wrapped in acid-free paper and placed in polyethylene bags. Be certain not to seal the bag completely, because it is important for the air to circulate. A cloth covering (sometimes called a drugget) placed over displayed historic carpets also offers some protection against air pollution. (Coverings can be made from heavy cotton muslin with the edges hemmed). Druggets or a sheet of clear polyethylene can be placed over carpets when the museum is closed, or kept in place at all times if the carpets are very fragile.

Another method of fighting particulate air pollution is to be sure that the exhibit and storage areas are dusted and vacuumed daily.

Finally, collections should be monitored regularly. If metals change color, leather appears brittle, or textiles are deteriorating, immediate action must be taken. If the objects or materials are on display, remove them and wrap them carefully in muslin or acid-free paper and place them in a safe storage area.

Proper Handling of the Collection

The handling of art objects and antiques requires special knowledge to avoid senseless and irreversible damage. Even workers who are only indirectly involved with the museum's collection can wreak havoc in the historic house. Ladders that are too tall or too large for interior spaces can swing out of control and damage chandeliers or mar wood paneling. Workers may carelessly handle tool boxes, hardware, and other equipment, damaging fragile rugs or furniture. Staff members or volunteers may improperly lift furniture or heavy objects, causing breakage or structural weakening, not to mention serious physical harm to themselves. Careless housekeeping can also create problems. There are several rules that should be stringently followed to avoid mishandling of historic objects in the museum. Take the time to think through the special handling procedures for your museum. Put them into a written format and distribute copies to the staff and volunteers, and keep copies on hand for reference. It is important that your museum staff adhere to these guidelines.

General Handling Procedures

Before moving an object from one place to another, plan the move fully. Know where the object is going and exactly how you will get there. Clear the path from anything that may be in the way. Always discuss the plan with the moving crew and make certain that everyone understands his or her role. Demonstrate proper handling techniques to the crew and have all necessary tools and equipment available before beginning.

- Use ladders of the appropriate size in the historic spaces. If a large ladder is needed, two people should move it around the interior.

Collections in museums must be handled carefully. Here a volunteer wears white cotton gloves to handle properly historic photographs in the archives of the Hennepin History Museum in Minneapolis, Minnesota. (Photograph by Bernice Wenzel)

- Before moving furniture, tie down with cotton cording all loose parts, such as drawers and leaves. Remove marble or glass tops before picking up furniture.
- Never drag furniture or works of art, always lift them.
- When lifting furniture or heavy objects, always have an adequate number of people assisting; it is worse to have too few than too many in the delicate process of moving large historic pieces. Always lift furniture from the bottom, never by the arms or back, and keep the piece in its upright position, not on its side or upside down. Move only one piece at a time and never stack one piece upon another.
- When touching any historic object, wear white cotton gloves. If it is not possible to wear them, wash hands frequently. Latex or grip-type gloves should be worn when handling slick-surfaced artifacts in glass, porcelain, or polished stone because they can easily slide out of one's hands.

- When carrying a large object around the museum, do not walk backward or obstruct your view with the object. If you cannot see around an object, it is too dangerous to move without help.
- When carrying a small artifact around the museum, be sure that it has been carefully padded and placed in a carrying box. It is much easier to move a box than to grapple with an awkward vase or a cumbersome platter. Never let the object protrude over the sides of the box; this makes it vulnerable to breakage. Smaller pieces should not touch one another. It is best to pad each piece with heavy acid-free tissue paper or cotton padding to prevent them from knocking together.
- When moving historic rugs, wall hangings, bed coverlets, and the like from period rooms, roll the pieces on a cardboard tube and be sure that enough people are on hand to assist in moving them. Do not bend textiles and never let them sag in the middle. This will create stress and break the fibers.
- Before moving a painting, print, or antique mirror, check to see that it is in stable condition. Look for a canvas that may have become loose or the back of a mirror that has slipped in its frame.
- When carrying paintings, mirrors, or any framed artwork, keep one hand on the bottom for support and the other hand on the side. This eliminates stress and distributes more evenly the object's weight. Never carry framed objects with one hand or tucked under your arm, no matter how small they are.
- When moving any object, be sure not to lean it against a wall. Framed works that have been innocently rested against a wood-paneled, painted, or papered wall scratch and mar the wall's surface.
- Never smoke, eat, or drink around artwork or historic objects!
- If carts are used in the museum, be sure not to overload them.

NOTES

1. Nathan Stolow, "The Action of Environment on Museum Objects, Part 1: Humidity, Temperature, Atmospheric Pollution, *Curator* 9, no. 3 (1966): 178.

2. A. Bruce MacLeish, *The Care of Antiques and Historical Collections*, 2d ed. (Nashville, Tenn.: American Association for State and Local History, 1985), p. 21.

3. Stolow, "Action of Environment," p. 178.

4. William P. Lull, with assistance of Paul N. Banks, "Conservation Environment Guidelines for Libraries and Archives in New York State" (Draft used in workshop, New York, September 1990), pp. 2–3.

5. Canadian Conservation Institute, *Silica Gel,* Technical Bulletin, no. 10 (Ottawa: Canadian Conservation Institute, 1991), pp. 2–3.

6. Three main categories of light-sensitive materials have been outlined by MacLeish in *Care of Antiques and Historical Collections.* These are cellulose materials, present in paper, wood, and some textiles; organic materials, such as leather, silk, wool, bone, and ivory; and paint pigments and various painting media, such as synthetic resins and oils and water color pigments.

7. The 3M Company in Saint Paul, Minnesota, is the manufacturer of Scotchtint P–60. Contact their customer service department for a list of distributors of this product.

8. Margaret Fikioris, "Textile Conservation for Period Room Settings in Museums and Historic Houses," in *Preservation of Paper and Textiles of Historic and Artistic Value II,* ed. John C. Williams (Washington, D.C.: American Chemical Society, 1981), p. 257.

9. MacLeish, *Care of Antiques and Historical Collections,* p. 21.

10. Sherry Butcher-Younghans and Gretchen E. Anderson, *A Holistic Approach to Museum Pest Management,* Technical Leaflet, no. 171 (Nashville, Tenn.: American Association for State and Local History, 1990), pp. 1–8.

11. The information on freezing was taken from ibid.

12. Margaret Fikioris, conservator, was the first to use these carpet runners at Winterthur Museum.

13. Fikioris, "Textile Conservation," pp. 259–60.

14. Ralph Lewis, *Manual for Museums* (Washington, D.C.: National Park Service, 1976), p. 70; Garry Thompson, *The Museum Environment* (London: Butterworths, 1986), pp. 130–60.

15. William Lull in his work "Conservation Environment Guidelines for Libraries and Archives in New York State (unpublished handout), recommends the company Dust Free, Inc., P.O. Box 454, Royse City, Texas 75089, for small environmental control equipment. Contact Mark K. Mullaney, director of marketing, (214) 635-9564.

7

Historic Housekeeping

There are houses which have soul and spirit, inclined to joy or sorrow; there are places of dignity and grandeur. There are facades of brick and stone that hold images; there are little silent places where, in half-forgotten whispers in dusty corners, the stories of ages find voice.

Margaret Meade-Fetherstonhaugh, *Uppark and Its People*

THERE ARE A wide range of concerns involved in cleaning the historic house, and before a cleaning routine can be established, a great deal of research and analysis is required. The cleaning techniques used in the museum will depend on the object cleaned, what it is made of and how it was made, and its condition. Cleaning painted surfaces will require different techniques than cleaning wood. There are different procedures for cleaning metal fixtures, historic wallpaper, rugs, chandeliers, or decorative elements.

If you do not know how to clean properly the special materials that make up the historic house and its furnishings, it is best to do nothing at all until you have learned the appropriate methods. Much irreparable damage is done at the hands of those who are eager but untrained.

It may be necessary to consult with specialists before cleaning sensitive materials. For example, if there is extensive woodwork in the house, a specialist familiar with the wood species, millwork methods, and historic techniques in staining and finishing should advise on cleaning methods and the products best suited to use on woodwork.

Cleaning the varied furnishings in a historic house is a demanding job. It is essential to know the composition of each object and understand how to clean it properly. "Little Girl's Room," the Vogler House, Old Salem Restoration. (Photograph courtesy of Old Salem Restoration, Winston-Salem, North Carolina)

Establishing a Housekeeping Routine

Before cleaning is started, several questions need to be asked.

- Has adequate research on appropriate cleaning methods been conducted and consultations with specialists been completed?
- Has a written report on housekeeping policies and procedures been completed by the curator? Are there written instructions for daily treatment of the historic structure?

• Who will be doing the housekeeping, a contracted cleaning service or the staff? Is the service or staff knowledgeable and well-informed as to the proper cleaning techniques?

The Housekeeping Staff

The role of the cleaning staff is fundamental to the operation of the historic house museum. Members of the cleaning staff must be highly informed and well trained, applying prudence in all aspects of its care.

The relationship between the curator and the housekeeping staff is one of the most significant in the museum. The curator must communicate with the staff members daily, keeping them abreast of issues ranging from conservation measures to plans for changing exhibits. The staff, in turn, must provide daily information on the general state of the house and the condition of the objects on exhibit. Consequently, all are informed of problems in the museum that need attention.

The number of people on the housekeeping staff will depend both on the physical size of the museum and its resources. If funds are limited (as they often are), volunteers can be recruited and trained as housekeepers. Appoint persons who are dexterous, communicative, and responsible. Remember that they will be continually in contact with important historical materials and need to have a strong sense of the significance of the objects and their fragility.

The Housekeeper's Notebook

In order to perform effectively, members of the cleaning staff must have specific information on procedures, supplies, and schedules. They need to be aware of the consequences of under- and overcleaning and the possible irreparable effects of using the wrong solutions and chemicals or of applying cleaning materials with inappropriate equipment. It is important to compile data about the historic house and to keep this information in a notebook, where it can be referred to easily. This notebook should contain:

It is important for the cleaning staff to have a strong sense of the furnishings historical significance, fragility, and value. Exquisite furnishings in the Port Royal Parlor. (Photograph courtesy of the Henry Francis du Pont Winterthur Museum, Winterthur, Delaware)

- A detailed cleaning schedule.
- A detailed list of cleaning procedures for each area. For example: carved woodwork, slate floors, glass or Plexiglass exhibit cases, wood floors, marble fireplaces.
- Reports from specialists that explain processes of care and preservation of the historic house.

The Housekeeper's Logbook

The housekeeper should keep a complete record of all cleaning activities. Entries should be made daily: a list of tasks completed, materials used and how they were applied and notations of damage or areas of concern, followed by the initials of the housekeeper in charge. A copy of the cleaning schedule and dated photographs of areas or artifacts showing signs of wear or damage should also be included in the logbook. (The logbook can consist of a spiral notebook placed inside a three-ring binder. A copy of the cleaning schedule can be kept in a pocket of the binder, and the photographs can be placed in polyester sheets that fit the rings.) The housekeeper's logbook is an important document, serving as a chronicle of the museum's changing condition.

The Cleaning Schedule

Set the schedule the members of the cleaning staff will follow and determine the supplies and methods they will use in the cleaning process. Establish the hours; will the staff work the same hours as the curator so that there can be an exchange between them?

The cleaning staff and curator each should have a copy of the cleaning schedule. Another copy should be filed in the curator's office as a record of established procedure. The schedule should be divided into sections: daily, weekly, biweekly, monthly, quarterly, semiannual, and annual duties. It should cover the following tasks.[1]

- Dusting (chair legs, window ledges, ornate wood surfaces, picture frames, etc.).
- Vacuuming (historic rugs, hanging textiles, frames, baseboards).
- Spot-cleaning walls and other high-traffic areas.
- Removing garbage.
- Cleaning of bathroom.
- Cleaning of kitchen or lunchroom.
- Cleaning of glass cases, mirrors, picture glass.
- Washing windows.
- Washing blinds and modern draperies.
- Buffing and waxing wood floors.
- Waxing woodwork.
- Cleaning chandeliers and light fixtures.
- Cleaning storage areas.
- Cleaning walkways and entryways.

Preparing a schedule is useless if it is not going to be followed. It is the responsibility of the curator to make certain that *all* of the tasks are being carried out and that they are executed with care. A breakdown in communication between the housekeeper and the curator can result in improper handling (or even the destruction) of historic materials and a generally unkempt museum.

Procedures

As mentioned earlier, a detailed set of procedures should be kept in the housekeeper's notebook and carefully followed. Whenever a new person is installed as housekeeper, the procedures should be carefully reviewed to ensure complete understanding of historic house care. The following are specific procedures.

General Dusting

For dusting woodwork, moldings, mantels, picture frames, louvers, and other horizontal surfaces, a clean, soft cotton cloth should be used. It should be large enough to cover a substantial surface adequately, but small enough to be easily managed in the housekeeper's hands. The cloth can be either dry or slightly damp, allowing for the dirt and dust particles to be more easily picked up. A good source for soft cloths is a diaper service, where clean diapers may be purchased at little cost. They have a large cleaning surface and can be washed and reused. Other suitable cloths are cotton towels, either bath or dish size cut to an appropriate dimension, pieces of flannel, or other soft and absorbent fabrics, such as white T-shirt material.

It is important to remember that dust cloths should be washed frequently in a mild soap solution and rinsed several times in clear water. When a cloth's surface is soiled, fold the cloth to a clean side and continue dusting until all sides are soiled. Then replace the cloth with a clean one. The grit on a soiled cloth can cause damage by abrading surfaces with the grit from the soil.

Dust cloths, as well as dust mops, should not be treated with oils or sprays. Although a treated cloth tends to pick up dust more easily, it leaves an emulsion on the surfaces that will attract dust. Instead, it is far better to dampen a cloth with a small amount of water.

Cleaning delicate carved historic woodwork with a cotton swab. *(Photograph by Bernice Wenzel, courtesy of the American Swedish Institute)*

Dusting with a Vacuum Cleaner

A vacuum cleaner is an efficient tool for dusting because it removes dust from a surface instead of merely pushing it around. A canister-type vacuum with a soft bristle attachment can be used effectively on horizontal surfaces, baseboards, and door frames. It should not be used, however, on historic wallpapers, built-in wood carvings, or wood paneling, which need special care.

Hand Dusting with a Soft-Bristled Brush

Certain objects will require special care in their cleaning. Picture frames, decorative plasterwork, carved wood friezes, pillars, ceilings, wood paneling and accessories, such as paintings, porcelain objects, books and inlaid furniture, should be hand dusted regularly with a soft-bristled brush of an appropriate size. Be sure that the brush is clean before use. Paintings should be dusted with hor-

izontal strokes beginning at the top of the painting working down-
ward (after it is certain that the painting is in stable condition).
Dusting porcelain can be precarious. Take precautions to stabilize
the piece or hold it with one hand, brushing the dust off with the
other. When dusting books take care not to touch the leather cover
with an ungloved hand; the hand's oils can discolor book covers.
Dust inlaid furniture carefully, checking the floor after dusting for
any fragments that may have come loose. Loose inlays should be
reported immediately to the curator and recorded in the housekeeper's logbook. Loosening is part of the aging process; the glue
used in attaching inlay pieces will eventually desiccate and the inlay
will loosen. A conservator or wood specialist should be called to
attend to this kind of deterioration.

Cleaning Glass and Plexiglass

Glass and Plexiglass surfaces—windows, mirrors, exhibit cases—can
be cleaned with an ammonia solution or commercial cleaners and
wiped either with paper towels or lint-free cloths. Prepare an ammonia solution by mixing warm water in a large plastic bucket with
a small amount of ammonia (work with the solution to find the
desired proportions). This solution will remove fingerprints and
dust and soot that has built up over time. Plexiglass should be cleaned
biweekly with an antistatic solution available from museum conservation catalogs or locally through plastic specialists.

Washing Windows

Washing windows is a job that is best done with two people. One
can clean the higher windows while the other works on the lower
panes. This buddy system can ensure safety if a ladder is used, with
one person steadying the ladder and assisting the other when step-
ping up and down.

Before washing is started, all coverings should be removed
and any furniture close to the windows should be moved aside.
Take care that the cleaner does not drip on wooden sills and
ledges.

Vacuuming

Vacuuming must be performed with special care. Select a vacuum that is easy to manipulate, one that will not damage historic furniture if it is bumped against wooden legs, corners, or walls. Extra padding might be added to the vacuum's base to prevent accidents. The museum may need two vacuums: a large commercial machine for cleaning synthetic carpet in public areas and a small, more manageable type for carpeted steps, hanging textiles,and historic rugs. Synthetic rugs in heavy traffic areas must be vacuumed daily to remove the dirt and grit that visitors bring into the museum. Also, hardwood floors can be vacuumed with special brush attachments.

Vacuuming Historic Rugs

Periodic cleaning will remove dust and grit that abrades fibers and may seriously damage rugs. If rugs are walked on as part of a house tour, they will need to be cleaned more frequently than those blocked off from visitor traffic. (Runners are highly recommended on historic rugs). A delicate balance must be achieved in vacuuming rugs often enough to keep them clean but not so often that they are damaged by overcleaning.

Special care must be taken vacuuming historic rugs. Always be certain that the historic rug is in stable condition before attempting to clean it. A small, slow-action vacuum used with a monofilament screen is best for removing dirt (at no time should a large, powerful machine be used on old rugs). The screening, which will prevent threads from being pulled from the rug into the vacuum, can be purchased at any hardware store and in any size. To prepare the screen, simply cut it into the desired size for the area to be cleaned and sew cotton strips around the screen's edges to give it support. Several different screen sizes might be kept on hand. For smaller rugs, a 2×2-foot size is suggested; adjust the size of the screen depending on the size of the rug. For very large rugs, you may wish to make a more rigid frame for the screen, using wood strips coated with polyurethane to prevent acids in wood from reaching rug. Attach the screen to the frame with rustproof staples and always work with the screen staple-side up. Monofilament screening should also be used for vacuuming historic upholstery, draperies, and window coverings. A soft bristle upholstery brush used with the screen is a safe cleaning technique for most fabrics.

Spot Cleaning Painted Walls and Other Painted Surfaces

Some painted surfaces in the historic house will not respond to cleaning with water alone. For the stubborn fingerprints and stains that blemish such surfaces, a good cleaning agent is a combination of a soap, such as Orvus, and water. (This product can be purchased through conservation supply companies.) To mix the solution, add about 1 percent Orvus in a small container of water and gently rub the surface to be cleaned. Rinse the area with a different cloth and dry it with a third one. Do not use detergents on historic wallpapers or painted plasterwork.

Caring for Historic Wallpaper

Paper has been used as a decorative wall covering since about the late seventeenth century in America, but it was especially popular in eighteenth- and nineteenth-century homes, where it was not uncommon to find multiple patterns of wallpaper used in one room. Although vulnerable to light degradation and dampness, historic wallpapers have survived, in some instances layered one upon another.

A general rule is not to dust or try to clean historic wallpapers because of their fragile nature. Keep window coverings drawn in papered rooms to prevent fading, and try to lower humidity levels to prevent mold growth. Do not allow staff or visitors to touch wallpapers or to brush against them with shoulders or bags. If wallpapers are heavily soiled or torn, contact a conservator to administer treatment.

Cleaning Plasterwork on Ceilings and Walls

Cleaning plasterwork in the historic house is an arduous task but should be carried out at least once a year. Ornamental plasterwork

In house museums where historic wallpapers have survived, the best care given them is preventive maintenance. This same care should be applied to rooms with repro-duction wall coverings to ensure their longevity. (Photograph courtesy of the Department of the Interior, National Park Service, Lincoln Home National Historic Site)

easily accumulates dust and dirt particles, which settle on depressions and protrusions of moldings and cornices.

Cleaning can be done (carefully) with a hand brush and a small vacuum cleaner. Use the brush for cleaning the plasterwork and the vacuum for removing the loosened dust. A good, small, but powerful vacuum cleaner is the Data Vac. It is lightweight, and can be held by a shoulder strap. The Data Vac comes with several feet of hose and different nozzle attachments. It is available at computer stores or office-supply companies. Cover the areas beneath the plasterwork where dust is likely to fall, with polyethylene sheets. While cleaning, watch for signs of cracking or any other damage.

Note all findings in the housekeeper's logbook and report findings to the curator.

Cleaning Blinds and Window Shades

Blinds, louvered shutters, and shades should be cleaned regularly, since a large amount of dust and dirt enters the house through windows, particularly in urban areas where factory smoke and automobile exhausts add to airborne pollution.

For cleaning venetian blinds and louvered shutters, use a soft, slightly damp cloth. Turn the blinds (louvers) to the closed position, and wipe them from the top slat down. If plain water does not remove the soil on the blinds, try a solution of soap (such as Orvus) and water.

Historic window shades should be dusted with a soft brush or wiped with a dry cloth. If dusting with a dry cloth does not clean shades, a slightly damp cloth might be more effective. Be sure to test a spot before proceeding with damp cleaning; the dust or grime may smear instead of being lifted off.

Cleaning and Waxing Wooden Floors

As a rule, wooden floors should be dry mopped daily. For a more thorough cleaning use a damp mop with a cloth or string-mop head. Dip the mop into a bucket of clean water, and wring it until it is only damp. Use a back and forth motion to clean the floor, making sure that the mop does not strike the wood baseboards. Areas that are difficult to reach, such as the corners and areas close to walls, should be cleaned by hand with a damp cloth.

Waxing floors is acceptable if done only occasionaly, but before waxing, make sure polished floors are historically accurate for the house. Always use a nonskid paste wax (paste waxes can be removed with denatured alcohol or a commercial floor-wax remover, while other commercial waxes must be stripped).[2] Apply the wax with a soft cloth, using a circular motion, and polish with a similar motion. If the room is large, it may be necessary to rent or buy a floor-polishing machine.

The polishing machine can do a number of tasks associated with polishing, or buffing, a floor. It can be used to scrub stubborn areas (often polishing machines are outfitted with scrubbing brushes and buffing pads or brushes) and to spread the wax. It is the buffing of the wood floors that gives them a luster. Floors can be buffed anytime a luster is required. Often, through daily use, floors will begin to dull from the dirt and soil that is tracked into the area and ground into the floor. To renew the shine, first dry mop the floor, and then buff it with a soft cloth or the polishing machine. Again, be sure that it is historically accurate to shine the floors in your historic house. Undoubtedly some floors were never intended to have a luster. A word of caution about using a polishing machine. Remember to remove all furniture in the path of your work. Also, avoid running the machine to the edge of the baseboards. These areas should be polished by hand. (Use the appropriate size polisher for the room; an over-size machine may be difficult to handle and can result in damage.[3])

Cleaning Tile, Stone, and Marble Floors

The best way to clean stone and tile floors is wet mopping. This technique is similar to damp mopping, but less pressure is used when wringing out the mop. If the floor is particularly soiled, use a non-ionic soap, such as Orvus, in the water and wash with more pressure. Ideally, three buckets should be used. A bucket with hot water with soap, an empty bucket with a wringer, and a bucket of clean warm water. First, dip the clean mop into the soapy water and gently squeeze out excess water. Mop a small area of the floor, and then place the mop in the wringer and squeeze out the dirty water. Go over the area again. Then rinse the mop in the clean water, squeeze out the excess, and rinse the area. Continue until all the soap has been removed. While the floor is drying, place caution signs to inform staff and visitors of the slippery floor.[4]

Cleaning Chandeliers

Accumulations of dust and grime on historic house chandeliers will cause them to lose their sparkle and diminish their beauty. Chandeliers should be cleaned about once a year, depending on the conditions inside the museum. The task should be done with the greatest of care—chandeliers are often extremely fragile. The housekeeper is usually responsible for cleaning the chandeliers; however, this task can be hired out to experts, such as exhibit technicians, who are familiar with the special handling necessary in cleaning fixtures. It is also possible to hire a cleaning service, but be sure that such workers are thoroughly trained and experienced.

Cleaning chandeliers is a laborious task that usually requires working on a ladder. It may be necessary to remove any furniture directly below the fixture, but if it hangs over a dining room table made of hardwood and in stable condition, you may want to make use of it. Place a couple of layers of pads on the table (table pads, or moving pads) and a thick piece of plywood that is smaller in size than the padding. Then place a step ladder of suitable size on top of the plywood in order to reach the chandelier. The plywood will help to distribute the weight of the ladder, and the padding will protect the table from both the board and the possibility of making impressions from the weight of the ladder. For light fixtures not easily reached by a ladder, it may be necessary to rent scaffolding from a local scaffolding and platforms company. (The company will often set scaffolding up, as well as deliver and pick up.) Scaffolding is usually rented by the day; therefore, if the system is to be cost effective, the housekeeper should see that all chandeliers in difficult-to-reach spots are cleaned on the same day.

CRYSTAL CHANDELIERS

To clean crystal chandeliers, use a solution of one-quarter isopropanol alcohol (available in hardware or drug stores) to three-quarters distilled water. This solution can be placed in a plastic spray bottle. Spray just enough solution onto cotton diapers or lint-free cotton flannel to dampen slightly. Care must be taken not to saturate the cloth.

Holding the wires or chain ropes of the crystal drops with one hand (a dry cotton glove should be worn on this hand to protect the wires from the solution), gently wipe crystal from top to the bottom. It is advisable to spread moving pads or other soft padding in a wide area beneath the fixture. If the crystal drops do happen to fall off, they will land on a soft place. No drying should be necessary, if the correct proportion is used. The alcohol will evaporate.[5] Often crystal ornaments are attached to the fixture with fine wire, which can rust and begin to deteriorate. If this happens, the wire eventually will not be capable of holding the glass crystal.

METAL CHANDELIERS AND CANDLE HOLDERS

Cleaning metal chandeliers and candle holders made from materials such as silver, brass, copper, or pewter require special care. When working with metals, always wear cotton gloves. Brush any dust or grit from the fixture with a soft brush or cloth, being careful not to rub grit across the surface. Dirt is abrasive and can easily scratch metal. This light dusting should be done regularly to prevent buildup. For a more thorough cleaning, use a solvent such as denatured or ethyl alcohol (available at hardware stores), applying it directly to the fixture with cotton swabs. The solvent will remove oils and surface dirt and grime. Never touch metals directly with hands because of the oils on them.

Polishing Metal Fixtures

If metal fixtures are very dirty or heavily tarnished, they can be polished. It is recommended, however, that a conservator be contacted to discuss the appropriate method for applying and removing polish or that sources such as the AASLH technical leaflet *The Care of Antique Silver* and the Canadian Conservation Institute pamphlet *The Cleaning, Polishing and Protective Waxing of Brass and Copper Objects* might be consulted.

All polishes are made of abrasive materials and the purpose of the polish is to remove enough of the surface so that the underlying metal, which is brighter and cleaner looking, will show through. Therefore, while polishing does remove the dull patina on an object's surface, it also removes a small amount of the metal.

Commercial polishes should never be used on historic metal; they are far too abrasive. The safest polish is a homemade one: mix into a paste two parts denatured alcohol, two parts distilled water, and a small amount of precipitated chalk (available at jewelry or dental supply stores). If chalk is not available, other, less abrasive materials, such as rottenstone or talc (available at conservation supply companies), can be substituted.

After cleaning the fixture with the polishing paste, treat it with microcrystalline wax (available through conservation supply houses). The application of a thin layer of wax will protect the metal from fingerprints and atmospheric pollutants or high humidity.

Glass globes, chimneys, or other glass accessories belonging to the light fixture should also be cleaned. Dip the glass into a solution of ammonia and water in a plastic bucket, rinse in a different bucket and dry with a clean cloth.

Cleaning Storage Areas

Collections in historic house museums often are stored in closets, attic space, unused rooms, and even such areas as boiler rooms and former coal bins. Too often, these areas are neglected, with serious consequences. It is essential to keep them clean and to check regularly for pests of all types.

Cleaning Entryways, Walkways, and Porches of the Historic House

The visitor's first view of the historic house is of the grounds and the entrance. An entry area strewn with leaves and cigarette stubs will often leave a visitor with a negative impression, even though the interior may be immaculate. Brooms, hoses, sprinklers, or shovels, when found on the historic houses's grounds or porch, not only give a cluttered appearance but also can pose hazards to the visitor. Always store these tools in an appropriate place. Sweep the walkways, porches, and entryways regularly. Repair broken or pitted paths, and in areas where winter weather brings snow and ice, be certain that the walkways and steps are not slippery. If steps are in poor repair, call in a specialist to mend them or have them replaced—visitors can be seriously injured from tripping or falling on crumbling steps. Rope off any unsafe areas from visitor traffic, both inside and outside the house. The use of caution signs to inform visitors of places they should not explore is also recommended. Sometimes even signs and ropes will not discourage the determined visitor from investigating every nook and cranny of the house. For this reason, it is a good idea to lock doors to rooms that visitors are not authorized to enter.

NOTES

1. For a thorough guide to housekeeping and scheduling of cleaning duties, refer to Ralph H. Lewis, *Manual for Museums* (Washington, D.C.: National Park Service, 1976), chap. 11. Another excellent book that offers advice on cleaning and preserving historic buildings is J. Henry Cham-

bers, *Cyclical Maintenance for Historic Buildings* (Washington, D.C.: National Park Service, 1976). Hermione Sandwith and Sheila Stainton, *The National Trust Manual of Housekeeping* (London: National Trust, 1984), is an invaluable resource in "keeping" the house.

2. American Association for State and Local History, *Housekeeping Techniques for the Historic House,* Conservation Techniques for Historic Houses Series, no. 8 (Nashville, Tenn.: American Association for State and Local History, 1978).

3. Lewis, *Manual for Museums,* pp. 225–31.

4. Ibid., pp. 224–25.

5. This method of cleaning chandeliers was developed by Susan Wood, exhibit technician, the Minneapolis Institute of Arts.

Architectural Preservation: Maintaining the Historic House Exterior

Preservation means stabilizing a structure in its existing form by preventing further change or deterioration.

Orrin Bullock, *The Restoration Manual*

THIS CHAPTER CONCERNS the preservation of existing historic structures. The term *preservation,* as used here, describes the process of continual maintenance of a property in a historically concerned and sensitive manner to ensure its survival.

Preservation is different than *restoration,* which refers to the "recreating of the original architectural elements in a building so that it closely resembles the appearance it had at some previous point in time."[1] Issues of restoration will not be covered here, since this book presupposes the historic house has been restored. However, general references on the subject can be found at the end of the book.

In discussing principles of preservation, it is necessary to know that there are established recommendations and guidelines. Most historic house museums are listed on the National Register of Historic Places, which ethically commits them to follow standards and guidelines set by the Secretary of the Interior for preserving and retaining the historic character of a property while allowing for efficient contemporary use.[2] These standards and guidelines should be used as the framework for establishing the historic house's maintenance and repair plan. Copies of the *Secretary of the Interior's*

Shadows-on-the-Teche in New Iberia, Louisiana, is listed on the National Register of Historic Places. *(Photograph courtesy of the National Trust for Historic Preservation)*

Standards for Historic Preservation Projects with Guidelines for Applying the Standards are available through the Government Printing Office in Washington, D.C.

"Maintenance Is Preservation"

Maintaining a historic building requires applying both logical principles and practical approaches. Daily—as well as weekly, monthly, and yearly tasks, including inspection and repair—are involved. The work can be tedious, time consuming, and seemingly endless; when

Hamilton House in South Berwick, Maine, has been refurbished to reflect its early-twentieth-century appearance. *(Photograph by J. David Bohl, courtesy of the Society for the Preservation of New England Antiquities)*

one cycle of maintenance is completed, a new one begins. Yet maintenance of historic properties is vital.

Deterioration of historic houses is a continual and, unfortunately, an inevitable process. Damage caused by natural elements is unending. Improper treatment by well-meaning, but uniformed caretakers or neglect of basic repair is often a factor in a building's deterioration. The loss of even the smallest embellishment may diminish a building's historical integrity. The destructive forces of our environment can be held at bay only through painting and repainting surfaces, removing abrasive dirt, making repairs routinely, and vigilantly inspecting the structure. The goal of these efforts is to preserve the structure in its original form or as close to its original form as possible and to extend the building's life.

Exterior Maintenance

The perceptions and skills of the person who actually conducts the exterior maintenance of a house will vary from museum to museum. At one historic house a resident caretaker may be expected to maintain the property; at another, a custodial team will be in charge; at a small historic house, a regularly scheduled volunteer. However, it is the curator, site manager (primary on-site supervisor), or director who is responsible for seeing that the work is done properly. The supervisor's duty is to train the caretaker or staff, schedule the work, and follow-up to ensure that it has been well done. He or she must be explicit in communicating what is expected from the museum's maintenance force. The supervisor is not always an expert and should consult with professionals if problems arise. A written description of each task should be documented in a **maintenance manual.**

Maintenance Plan

Maintenance requires a plan, one that must be rigorously carried out. The National Park Service (NPS) lists four components of a good plan: **inspections, work schedules, building records,** and **reference support materials.** NPS also recommends including a means of evaluating maintenance activities to determine strengths and weaknesses within a system.[3]

1. Inspection. Draft an inspection schedule. Full-scale inspections should be made twice yearly, in the spring and the fall. Special inspections should be conducted at unscheduled times as well—for example, when it rains or after a severe storm, to determine how gutters are functioning or if there are signs of leaks in the roof.[4]

A thorough inspection requires a complete examination of the house—do not neglect areas because they are difficult to reach, cramped, dirty, or unpleasant. Maintenance, in the words of one state historic preservation officer, "is all a matter of astute observation." One needs to know what to look for and, when a problem is identified, to determine the proper approach to remedy the situation.[5]

2. Work schedules. Work schedules list tasks, both routine and occasional, and specify the frequency with which they must be carried out. Priorities should be set and followed. After a schedule has been established, it should be assessed periodically to ensure that it remains pertinent to the needs of the building. The schedule will also need modification according to the season. Record the schedule in the maintenance manual.

3. Building records. Knowledge of the structure is essential for proper preventive maintenance. Information about architectural style, building date, architect(s), and general contractor or builder will provide insight into the operation of the house. Learn how it was constructed, the materials used, and where the materials were procured. Become familiar with how the elements of nature affect the building. Identify areas of weakness in the structure and monitor them carefully. Watch for patterns of wear and determine their sources.[6]

All maintenance inspections and repair work should be documented and kept in a **maintenance notebook.** This notebook should contain the dates of inspections and a detailed account of the findings—locations of problem areas, plans for repair, and, after repairs are complete, a description of techniques used to make them. Assessments of past repairs can also be recorded, as well as comments on past companies' performances. Keep a photographic record in the notebook showing changes or the evolution of a repair, from the initial problem to the completed repair. Avoid using Polaroid prints or instant photos; they will fade quickly, and there is the possibility they will contaminate files because of leakage from the chemicals they contain.

4. Reference support materials. These materials include the **performance standards** and **treatment specifications** for performing work on a property and can be compiled by the site manager, director, or curator. Performance standards describe when maintenance work should be undertaken; for example, when repainting is necessary. Treatment specifications are descriptions of appropriate cleaning and repair methods: in other words, how to go about doing a maintenance job.[7]

Maintenance Manual

All reference information about the house should be kept in a maintenance manual. For assistance, see *Cyclical Maintenance for Historic Buildings* by J. Henry Chambers. This handbook, used with guidelines from the National Park Service, will aid the maintenance staff in hammering out a practical maintenance manual. The following categories, adapted from Chambers's handbook, should be included in the manual:

- History of the building. A concise history of the building to familiarize staff with the building's past.
- Catalog of documents. Copies of known documents relating to the building: historical, architectural, construction, and legal records should be included. Be sure that the documents are copies; all originals should be kept safely in a vault off the premises.
- Evaluation of the resource. A description of the current physical condition of the building and its components.
- Survey forms. Forms describing the exterior of the building and including information on roofs, gutters, porches, windows, cellars, and outbuildings.
- Treatment forms. Forms describing standards and methods for specific treatments, such as the proper method of cleaning gutters and downspouts. Treatment forms indicate the frequency with which maintenance should be completed on specific parts of the building. Treatment leaflets such as those in the series Preservation Briefs, Tech Notes, and others are available from the state historic preservation office or the National Park Service.

Roseland Cottage (The Bowen House) in Woodstock, Connecticut, was built by Henry Chandler Bowen, businessman and well-known abolitionist. Roseland Cottage is an important surviving example of a Gothic Revival summer estate. Gardens and grounds reflect the landscaping principles of Andrew Jackson Downing, the famous nineteenth-century landscape architect whose concepts exerted a major influence on residential design. (Photograph by J. David Bohl, courtesy of the Society for the Preservation of New England Antiquities)

- Resource personnel. Names, addresses, and telephone numbers of consultants and contractors who have worked on the building.

- Sources of special equipment. Listings of local sources, with current addresses and phone numbers, such as platform and scaffolding companies.

- Sources of materials. Suppliers of special materials as well as craftsmen or other specialists, such as marble and stone suppliers and roofing specialists.

- Safety considerations. Information on allowable floor loads and special procedures designed to protect the building, such as the proper technique for walking on a slate roof. Include a current copy of building codes and other regulatory measures affecting the museum and its operation.
- Emergency numbers. Current numbers and names to notify in emergencies, such as fire and police departments, utilities companies, and special maintenance contractors.

A Commitment to Maintenance

A strong maintenance plan must be supported by the board of trustees. To be carried out properly, it must be well funded. Proper tools and adequate equipment and materials are crucial to good maintenance standards. Make the acquisition of necessary supplies part of annual budget. After all, preserving the historic building is as important as preserving the collections within its walls.

Preventive Maintenance

Weather—wind, rain, snow, sleet, and sun—continually works to deteriorate the structure of the historic house. Consequently, it is paramount that the property be made as weatherproof as possible to withstand the constant attack of the elements.

It is generally agreed that the element most destructive to a house is water (or ice). Left standing, water will

- Create an environment for rot to thrive.
- Weaken roofs and penetrate the building's interior.
- Cause masonry and brick to spall, fracture, and deteriorate.
- Rust metals.
- Cause paint to peel.

To protect a structure, the first rule is to keep it dry and as watertight as possible. Conduct periodic and comprehensive checks for signs of water damage, such as staining, growth of moss and lichens, and softening of wood. Identify vulnerable areas and places that have been damaged by water in the past.

Constant vigilance, perpetual weatherproofing, religious gutter cleaning, and continual caulking and painting will help to keep water

Built in the 1880s, this three-story Victorian frame and brick mansion was designed to suit the life-style of Theodore Roosevelt. It includes a large porch, gun room, library, and the North Room, a showcase for Roosevelt's personal relics. (National Park Service, Sagamore Hill National Historic Site, Oyster Bay, New York)

problems under control. Never become complacent about the extent of waterproofing done on a structure. Water will penetrate the smallest crack.

What to Look for in Determining Water Problems

Certain areas of the historic house, such as the roof, are particularly susceptible to water damage, and they must be monitored regularly. Locate the source of water or persistent moisture that is plaguing the health of the house, and quickly eliminate it.

When searching for vulnerable places, look for open joints or seams that are not protected by caulking or paint. Water will easily penetrate the end grain of wood on siding, doors, window frames, shutters, and decorative elements. One expert explains why end grain absorbs water by characterizing a board as a "series of drinking straws running parallel to the length of the board."[8] The straws draw water into the wood's structure, and there it remains until the cycle of decay begins.[9] Wood ends should be treated with a water repellant and painted to ensure a longer life.

Search the roof surface for signs of deterioration, such as cracks, cupping, curling, or waviness. Also look for loose or missing sections. Make regular checks in attic and top floors for discoloration and stains that may have been caused by water leaking from the roof.

Clogged gutters cause water to back up under the roof, forming ice dams in cold weather. Clean gutters annually and carefully inspect their joints and seams. Solder all cracks on metal gutters and caulk joints to keep them watertight. Always use proper sized downspouts to direct water away from the house foundation.

Monitor the chimney area and make sure the flashing is in good condition and caulking is solid. Seal open joints with caulking or roofing cement—caulking should be a high grade of polysulfide, butyl, or silicone rubber.[10] Look for cracks and missing bricks or mortar in the masonry. If the brickwork is deteriorating, it may be time to replace bricks and repoint. Look inside the chimney top for stains, which indicate leaks.

Flashing, the metal used to seal joints and prevent leaks, must be in place where the roof meets chimney, walls, dormers, and adjacent roofs. If flashing is damaged or loose, caulk, cement, or solder any gaps or holes that appear. Also, use proper eave flashing to direct water away from the house.

Monitor shrub growth and vegetation growing close to or directly on the house. It is recommended that ivy and vines not be allowed to grow on historic building; the padded "foot" that attaches the vine to the stone and mortar will eventually cause it to weaken and break apart. Vines also hold moisture—gathered on the leaves—close to the brickwork, eventually causing deterioration. Moss and lichens also retain moisture, leading to rot, and bushes growing around a house may also hold water that has been bounced off the siding or has run off the roof.

Sunnyside is a restored nineteenth-century home of Washington Irving, author of such classic stories "The Legend of Sleepy Hollow," and "Rip Van Winkle." Irving purchased the original cottage and, with the assistance of architect and painter George Harvey, remodeled it, adding Dutch-stepped gables, ancient weathervanes, and Gothic and Romanesque features. Although the roof forms a beautiful skyline, complex designs such as these can be difficult to maintain. (Sunnyside, Historic Hudson Valley, Tarrytown, New York)

Monitor wood located near the ground, such as steps, porches, and low windows, which may stay wet for long periods of time, inviting decay. If this remains a persistent problem, it may be necessary to change the grade around the house, creating a slope where water runs off.

Check windows and doors for gaps and cracks that may allow water to enter, damaging interior walls. Unchecked, moisture in window frames and doors can initiate rot. Waterproof by painting window sashes and sills with a high-quality oil-based paint.

Look for peeling paint under eaves or soffits, a sure sign of moisture problems. Always check wood siding and trim for loose or damaged clapboards and inspect decorative trim for cracks and loose fit. Caulk edges to prevent water from entering.

Roof Maintenance

Roofs, continually exposed to weather, take the brunt from natural forces. A weak roof or one in poor repair can lead to deterioration of the entire structure. The materials used in roofing vary widely, and each type requires different procedures for proper care.

Wood shingles have been and in many areas continue to be the most common roofing material used in this country because of the ubiquity of wood and the visually pleasant designs they form.

The basic rule for preserving wood shingles is to keep them free of all debris from surrounding trees and from such live organisms as moss, mold, and other fungi. These can be removed by scrubbing the roof with a solution of water and bleach. (The proportions of bleach and water will depend on the growth, if moss is heavy try a more potent bleach solution.) Moss left to grow unchecked can even cause mini-dams to form on roofs.[11]

Wood shingles are highly flammable. They should be treated with a fire retardant (this is required by some local codes), even though this process can make the wood shingles brittle.[12] The most effective and lasting treatment is pressure-impregnating the wood with treated salts after it has been cut.[13]

The life expectancy of wood shingles is fifteen to sixty years, depending on local climate and environment. They naturally erode from rain, snow, and sun, and should be replaced when they have lost about half of their original thickness.[14]

Slate roofs, although they are costly to install, are the longest lasting and in many ways the easiest to maintain. Slate is durable, fire resistant, and is prized for its aesthetic qualities.[15] Preservatives or other treatments are not required, and rot is not a problem as it is on wood. The suspectible areas on a slate roof are around nail holes and flashing where water can seep inside, freeze, and cause breakage; deteriorated flashing should be replaced and gutters checked periodically.[16] Slate eventually can delaminate and erode, and become brittle with age. It can even break from prolonged exposure to pollution and rain. Avoid walking on slate roofs, instead use a chicken ladder or ladder and planks to distribute weight on the slates. Another method of inspecting roofs too difficult to reach is to use binoculars.

The longevity of a slate roof will depend upon the quality of the materials and installation. Poor quality slates installed with inferior nails will need to be replaced much sooner. Properly installed, a slate roof should last between 100 and 150 years or even longer, depending on the type of slate used.

Clay tile was used as roofing material as early as the seventeenth century in the United States. Although heavy, clay tiles require little maintenance and they withstand a high degree of weathering. Cracked or broken tiles can also be replaced easily. The maintenance of clay-tile roofs should consist of regular monitoring for broken or missing tiles, which may cause leaks, and for moss or lichen growth, the presence of which often indicates a water problem.

Metals have been quite popular as roofing materials because they were inexpensive, fire-resistant, easy to install, lightweight, and generally required little maintenance. By the nineteenth century, the most common metal roofing materials used were tinplate (tin-plated iron), terneplate (leaded tin), tin shingles, and galvanized sheet metal. During colonial times, the metals most often used on buildings, such as church roofs, were lead and copper.[17]

Tinplate and terneplate were most often applied in sheets measuring 10 by 14 inches.[18] To retard corrosion, tinplate was painted, usually brown or red but sometimes green to simulate the patina or copper.[19] Tin shingles, designed to simulate tile or wood, were also used, as were galvanized sheet-metal shingles (galvanized with zinc to prevent rust) designed to look like pantiles.[20] The life expectancy of a metal roof depends on the metal from which it is made and the local environment. Galvinized roofs survive for 20 to 30 years; lead-coated copper, for 70 to 100 years; and terneplate, depending on abrasion, for about 50 years.

All metals are susceptible to pollution damage, chemical action, and metal fatigue. Tinplate and terneplate will deteriorate when in contact with copper or asphaltic or bituminous materials, such as roofing compounds and building papers, as well as paints containing bitumen, asphalt, and aluminum.[21] Avoid allowing these materials to come in contact with metal roofing. Most metal roofs must be primed (with linseed oil and iron oxide primer) and painted (brown—iron oxide—or, red—calcium carbonate, ferric oxide or ferrous sulfate).[22]

Although maintaining a metal roof is fairly simple, inspections must be made regularly. If a very small area of corrosion or a puncture is located, repair it by placing a drop of solder in the hole. Larger areas will require a patch of the roofing metal.

Each season monitor the condition of the paint on the roof. Make plans to touch up areas and eventually repaint the entire roof. When painting a metal roof always be certain paint is made specifically for use on metal.

Asphalt shingles have been used since the late 1890s and are the most common roofing material on American houses. One reason for this popularity is their low cost and relative fire resistance. However, they deteriorate more quickly than wood, metal, or slate roofing; asphalt shingles are expected to last from fifteen to a maximum of twenty-five years.

Asphalt shingles are made of felt saturated with asphalt and covered with mineral or ceramic granules. When inspecting an asphalt-shingled roof, look for wear of the granular surface. If it is worn smooth, it is time to replace the shingles. Nail heads appearing underneath the shingle and "lumpiness" may indicate multiple roofs underneath the present one. If this is suspected, it may be necessary to remove old shingles when it is time to reroof.

Roof Inspections

Roofs should be examined twice yearly for proper preventative maintenance. First, check the flashing. It is a particularly important protection. If there are signs of disintegration, replace or repair it immediately.

Look for changes and for variations and inconsistencies, such as waviness, lumpiness, sags, or concave surfaces. If possible, get up close to inspect the roof, giving special attention to areas susceptible to damage from nearby trees or power lines. Look for gaps and missing or damaged portions. Study the roof from the interior of the house, checking roof boards and rafters for leaks and testing for dry rot and the soundness of wood with a pick (an ice pick or pen knife works well). Inspect top-floor ceilings and the attic for stains and discoloration.

When conducting an inspection, use a checklist to ensure that nothing is overlooked. Record findings in the museum's maintenance notebook.

When roof replacement is necessary, preserve the house's integrity by using historically appropriate materials. Before repair work

Sagamore, the Adirondack mountain retreat at Raquette Lake, New York, was built on the notion of self-sufficiency. Artisans working at the site created the buildings and their furnishings from local materials. From this and other similar retreats the "Great Camp" tradition endured. The main lodge, a mix of Swiss Chalet and rustic log construction, was built in 1897 by railroad magnate William West Durant, and later was owned by Alfred G. Vanderbilt. It is currently used as a conference center. (Photograph by Barbara R. Lewis)

is started, record exactly what was in place before the replacement—the size, shape, color, and the pattern and design of materials to be removed. Carefully photograph the roof to document its original appearance.

Wall Maintenance

The exterior walls of a house serve as the bastions of the house, holding the great weight of the structure. In these walls are wood or masonry or a combination of the two. Whatever their composition, preventive maintenance plays an important role in their survival. Like the roof, walls should be prudently inspected twice yearly. Examine them for cracks, gaps, signs of warping, and settling. Look for open joints around door frames, window frames, and trim.

Search for areas on walls where water may enter. Since cracks are likely to be found in areas where dissimilar materials meet, check around such places for evidence of water damage, such as stains and discoloration. Carefully search wood walls for signs of mildew or mold growth—indicators of prolonged moisture. Look for peeling or blistering on painted surfaces; either can indicate water damage. Use a small pick or pen knife to test areas for rot. Monitor places where caulking was previously used; it may be time to seal these areas again.

Another potential problem is differential settling of the building, indicating weakness in the foundation. This is often indicated by undulating siding and large cracks. Do the walls bulge? Are they plumb? Examine exteriors carefully for such signs; if they are detected, consult an expert such as an architectural historian because structural damage may have occurred.

WOOD SIDING

There are several kinds of wood siding: among them horizontal clapboards, vertical board-and-batten, and shingles in a variety of patterns and textures. Prudence in inspecting for the enemies that destroy wood and immediate action taken when a problem is found will help to preserve wood and prolong its life.

Decay or rot is the primary foe of wood. Three types of fungus feed on wood houses: mold fungi, stain fungi, and decay fungi.

Mold and stain fungi are more nuisances than destroyers, although they will cause discoloration of wood. Decay fungi are the most destructive. The two most common types of decay fungi, brown and white rot, feed on the cellulose of wood cells. Rot can extend as much as 4 feet into the wood beyond the visible infected area and eventually will destroy the structure of the wood.[23] White rot causes wood to lose its color and become "whitish." It consumes lignin (an organic substance that, along with cellulose, forms the "woody" component in wood), leaving the wood fibrous and stringy.[24] Brown rot may be identified by the brown stain it leaves on wood, by cracks and, eventually depressions. The fungi weakens wood by consuming the cellulose; the wood eventually cracks and begins to collapse.[25]

The primary preventive treatment for brown and white rot is simple: keep the structure dry, because these fungi need water to live.[26] Earlier in this chapter some of the ways were outlined on keeping houses watertight, thus preventing conditions in which fungi thrive. A few of these methods bear repeating, and others need to be stated.

- If possible, keep exterior woodwork at least 8 inches above the ground. Wood that comes in direct contact with the ground may absorb moisture from the soil.
- Keep wood painted or stained; exposed wood will allow water to penetrate, especially at the end grain. Always keep joints tightly fitted, firmly caulked, and well painted.
- Allow air to circulate, do not pile objects against or near walls.
- Watch for peeling or cracked paint on wood surfaces, which can indicate a water problem. Find the source of the water, eliminate it, and caulk and repaint the wood surface.
- Use gutters and downspouts to direct the roof runoff away from vulnerable wood siding.
- Repair roof leaks immediately to prevent water from running inside walls and destroying plaster and woodwork. Always keep gutters clean.

After efforts are made to eliminate sources of water that are feeding rot fungi, it is necessary to destroy the fungus. A fungicide can be used on the wood, both that which is being directly attacked and adjacent susceptible areas. However, fungicides are hazardous and should be applied by professional workers from a local exterminating company.[27] If wood is too rotted to treat with a fungicide, it will need to be replaced with lumber treated with a preservative.

Other enemies of wood are wood-inhabiting insects, such as termites and beetles, which will also damage the structural timbers of a historic building. It is necessary to monitor for termites in wood structures, most commonly, subterranean and dry wood termites, which feed on cellulose or starch in wood.[28] Subterranean termites, found in northern climates, can be identified by the shelter tubes they construct on the interior of buildings. These tubes, made from mud and dirt, are usually visible on walls of damp crawl spaces and basements.

Dry wood termites, found primarily in the warmer and moister climates typical of the southeastern states, do not build shelter tubes. However, they can be identified by their fecal pellets, which often appear spilling from cracks in wood. Another telltale sign is the wings that fall from the insects during a period in their life cycle.[29]

Powder-post beetles are wood borers, and at the active larval stage will tunnel inside wood, causing great damage. Watch for exit holes made by the adults and for fine powdery dust beneath the holes.[30]

Other common problems are gaps, cracks, and splits. The larger cracks can be repaired with wood filler and caulking. For smaller cracks and splits, caulking alone will work. After repairing the surfaces seal them with paint.

MASONRY WALLS

The use of masonry walls—those made of brick, stone, stucco, and concrete—is a time-honored building tradition, and many historic houses employ these durable materials. Even though masonry is reputed for needing little maintenance, things can go wrong without preventive care.

The primary problem in a masonry building is a breakdown in the mortar joints that hold the brick, stone, or concrete together. Where there is joint failure, water will very likely find its way inside the house. The rule of thumb is that "the mortar must be softer than the material it bonds."[31]

Masonry walls can also bend as a result of ground settlement or because they are structurally inadequate. They can crack where different materials come into contact, such as a stone window sill surrounded by brickwork. Masonry can also fail above windows and door openings because of the stress of the weight above.

Water left to sit in a joint or allowed to flow constantly across mortar joints will cause premature erosion. A visible sign of water damage is efflorescence, a white discoloration on the face of the brick or stone caused by crystallization of salts on the surface.

Cycles of freezing and thawing also wreak havoc with joints and play a role in the deterioration of masonry. Water frozen inside saturated brick or stone will expand and cause chips to break off; a process called "spalling."

Badly deteriorated masonry will need special repair—called **pointing, repointing,** or **tuck-pointing.** Pointing, a process by which the old mortar is carefully chipped out and replaced with new mortar to reestablish a firm bond, will restore the visual character of masonry and help to preserve historic brick or stone. The work must be done with care by a good tuck-pointer (a specialist from the masonry trade) using hand tools, such as a hammer and chisel, to remove old mortar. Improper cutting can widen joints and damage the brick "crust." The mortar, too, must be chosen carefully to approximate the color, thickness, and proportions of the original. If mortar is too rigid, there is risk of serious damage to stone and brick during the expansion and contraction that takes place in climates with severe temperature changes. Cement mortars, such as portland cement, are more likely to remain inflexible; consequently, cracks will develop in the wall and spalling will occur. Lime mortars are softer and more likely to expand and contract with freeze and thaw cycles.[32]

A good repointing job can last from 50 to 100 years. When considering repointing a historic house, the curator or site manager should plan the work carefully. The planning and execution of a tuck-pointing job takes time.

Finding Architectural Replacements

Regular maintenance will reduce the need for replacing features on the house, and regular repair will help maintain the original materials; eventually, however, the museum will need to address the issue of replacing historic fixtures and decorative materials with reproductions. For example, cornice molding on the exterior of the house may have deteriorated and it may be necessary to replace it. It is generally agreed that replacements should be identical, or replacements-in-kind. By using similar materials, sizes, finishes, and designs, the integrity of the house can be preserved.

Before restoring any element of the house, carefully research the original materials and their source. Merchants should be sought who will provide accurately produced replacements of high quality. If members of the maintenance force are uncertain of the extent of a replacement project or where to find appropriate materials, they should do nothing until a restoration specialist has been consulted to make recommendations on how to proceed.

But where can one find quality historic reproductions that are acceptable for museum use? In the past decade, there has been a resurgence of companies that supply reproductions of architectural elements and decorative materials. Unfortunately, many "modern reproductions" are not historically accurate in terms of color, texture, and detail. Consequently, reproductions must be selected with great care and with the advice of specialists.

Excellent resource books, cited in full in the References section of this book, are available that discuss correct replacements for originals include works such as *Floor Coverings for Historic Buildings* by Helene Von Rosenstiel and Gail Caskey Winkler, *Lighting for Historic Buildings* by Roger W. Moss, and *Wallpapers for Historic Buildings* by Richard Nylander. An informative general discussion of reproductions can be found in William Seale's *Recreating the Historic House Interior.*

Another indispensable resource is the *Old-House Catalogue,* where one can find suppliers of everything from metal ceilings and roofing materials to interior and exterior light fixtures, furniture, fabrics, wallcoverings, and reproduction hardware. The catalog also lists services that may be needed by owners or managers of historic houses. This informative book is published annually and can be found in most area libraries or can be purchased in bookstores.

Organizations can also assist in making correct choices about reproductions in the historic house. The Society for the Preservation of New England Antiquities and the National Trust for Historic Preservation can be consulted for products and services. Also, consult with staff of state and local historical societies and the state historic preservation office. Making visits to similar historic house museums may serve as a source for comparison.

NOTES

1. Patricia Poore and Clem Labine, eds., *The Old-House Journal New Compendium* (Garden City, N.Y.: Doubleday, 1983), p. 50.

2. If your museum is not yet listed, consider applying for registration. Inclusion on the National Register recognizes the significance of the listed property and that measures be taken to ensure its protection. House museums that are nonprofit organizations are also eligible for certain federal preservation grants if they are listed on the National Register.

For more information on applying for National Register status and assistance in evaluating a property contact the office of the state historic preservation officer.

3. Kaye Ellen Simonson, *Maintaining Historic Buildings: An Annotated Bibliography* (Washington, D.C.: National Park Service, 1990), p. 1.

4. Ibid., p. 1.

5. A commonly stated phrase used by Minnesota's state historic preservation officer, Charles Nelson.

6. Simonson, *Maintaining Historic Buildings,* p. 1.

7. Ibid.

8. Clem Labine, former editor of the *Old-House Journal,* has made the analogy of a board's end-grain to drinking straws.

9. Clem Labine, "Old-House Maintenance: Dull, But Essential," *Historic Preservation* 39, no. 1 (1987): 23.

10. Gordon Bock, "Inspecting Chimneys," *Old-House Journal* 17 (1989): 35.

11. "Preventing Rot in Old Houses," *Old-House Journal* 2, no. 11 (1974): 1.

12. Charles Nelson, Minnesota's state historic preservation officer, personal communication February 1991.

13. Sharon C. Park, *The Repair and Replacement of Historic Wooden Shingle Roofs,* Preservation Briefs, no. 19 (Washington, D.C.: National Park Service, 1989), p. 9.

14. "Preventing Rot in Old Houses," p. 5.

15. Sarah M. Sweetser, *Roofing for Historic Buildings,* Preservation Briefs, no. 4 (Washington, D.C.: National Park Service, 1978), p. 4.

16. Ibid.

17. Ibid., p. 2.

18. John G. Waite, "Tinplate and Terneplate Roofing," in *Old-House Journal New Compendium,* ed. Poore and Labine, p. 128.

19. Sweetser, *Roofing for Historic Buildings,* p. 3.

20. Ibid., pp. 2–3.

21. Waite, "Tinplate and Terneplate Roofing," p. 128.

22. Ibid., p. 129.

23. Charles Nelson, personal communication, January 1991.

24. Clem Labine, "Defeating Decay," in *Old-House Journal New Compendium,* ed. Poore and Labine, p. 308.

25. "Detecting and Defeating Rot in Old Houses," *Old-House Journal* 2, no. 10 (1974): 6.

26. Labine, "Defeating Decay," p. 308–9.

27. A word of warning! Fungicides and insecticides are very dangerous and should not be used by nonprofessionals (Charles Nelson, personal communication, October 1991).

28. Ralph H. Lewis, *Manual for Museums* (Washington, D.C.: National Park Service, 1976), p. 271.

29. Wendy Jessup, Wendy Jessup and Associates, specialists in the care of cultural property, personal communication, October 1991. Jessup recently wrote "Biological Infestations," a chapter to be included in the National Park Service's *Museum Handbook,* pt. 1: *Museum Collections.* For more information, contact Curatorial Services, National Park Service, P.O. Box 37127, Washington, D.C. 20013-7127. For more information on pest con-

trol, contact Wendy Jessup, 1814 N. Stafford Street, Arlington, Virginia 22207, or call (703) 528-4339.

30. Sherry Butcher-Younghans and Gretchen E. Anderson, *A Holistic Approach to Museum Pest Management*, Technical Leaflet, no. 171 (Nashville, Tenn.: American Association for State and Local History, 1990), pp. 6–7.

31. Charles Nelson, personal communication, January 1991.

32. Jonathan T. Schechtman, "Wet Basements," in *Old-House Journal New Compendium*, ed. Poore and Labine, p. 110.

9

///

Museum Security:
Protecting the Historic House

Museums, by their very nature, must be security conscious.
G. Ellis Burcaw, *Introduction to Museum Work*

PROTECTING COLLECTIONS AND a house from light, pests, extreme temperatures, and fluctuating humidity were discussed in Chapter 6. Equally important is protecting the museum against vandalism, theft, fire, and natural disasters. Regardless of the size or location of the historic house, provisions must be made to ensure the safety of the museum, the visitors, and the staff. Security rules and regulations pertain to everyone. Special treatment that may infringe upon security must not be given to individuals because of their status or rank.

Vandalism and Theft

Aside from normal wear and tear, house museums are often susceptible to abuse by visitors. In the homey atmosphere and informal ambience of the setting, some visitors feel comfortable enough to reach out and touch furnishings and objects on display, even though they may have been asked not to do so. Some visitors are simply careless or inconsiderate, dropping gum on historic carpets, littering, or defacing artwork on display. Others will actually steal objects—either as a souvenir of the site or to sell for profit. Theft in the house museum is a topic that requires much scrutiny by the staff, and plans must be in place to deal with theft when it occurs. By far the easiest way to control theft is to take steps to prevent it.

A primary method of securing the house museum is to employ security guards, either paid or volunteer (many house museums must rely on volunteer security staff because of the expense of hiring guards). Guards positioned around the house will not only watch for acts of theft and vandalism, but also serve as troubleshooters when emergencies arise, such as a medical accident or a fire. The very presence of a security guard will deter individuals who may have entertained thoughts of pilfering. It is suggested that guards continually observe visitors, but in such a way that the visitor is unaware of it.[1] (Guards can observe visitors from upper floors or go about room checks or invent tasks to do while surreptitiously watching them.) The staff, too, should assist the guards in observing visitors: interpreters, tour guides, demonstrators, and receptionists as they go about their work must remain alert to the possibility dangers of vandalism and theft.

Museum Guards

Because of their importance to the museum, guards need special training and regularly scheduled, continuing instruction. Professional security officers from police departments, larger museums, and security companies can be brought in to share ideas and offer suggestions to the museum's security force and to instill in them a sense of their importance.

Museum guards should be uniformed and readily identifiable to visitors. The dress standard might be a light-colored shirt, navy pants or skirt, and navy blazer. A museum crest or badge will further aid in making the guard easily distinguishable when assistance is needed.

Guards must also be well informed about the museum. As front-line staff, they are continually asked for directions and questioned about the history of the house, current exhibits, and the museum's policies—such as use of strollers or whether photography is permitted. Visitors often draw conclusions about the museum from its staff. An agreeable impression is made when guards are knowledgable, friendly, and helpful.

While guards are on duty, they will need to patrol the museum and remain mobile. After closing, they must make thorough checks of exhibit rooms, rest rooms, closets, and any other areas that may serve as hiding places for potential thieves. If all-night guards are employed, an outside patrol should be made at least once every hour.[2]

The museum should draft a protection policies handbook, clearly spelling out rules and procedures for dealing with security and safety: What is to be done if a visitor is injured in a fall on narrow steps or hits his or her head on a low doorway or has a heart attack? What action should be taken if someone is caught vandalizing the building or stealing? Who fills out accident or theft reports?

The protection policies handbook should be compiled by the site manager, director, and security personnel. It should either be small enough to be kept with the guards at all times, or be kept readily at hand.

One staff member—the site manager, curator, director, or care-taker—should serve as the chief of security. It is recommended that this person "hold and issue all keys, keep a check-in and check-out ledger for week-ends and after-closing hours, supervise the guard-ing of exhibit galleries, be on good terms with the police and the fire department, and receive extra training in security matters."[3]

All staff members must be aware of messengers and delivery-men who enter the museum ostensibly to repair equipment, take meter readings, or make inspections of the boiler or air-conditioning, or the security system itself. It is a common ruse for thieves to gain access to a building dressed as repair personnel. Once inside, they can go about discreetly stealing objects and concealing them in closed-lid tool boxes. It is advisable to ask repairmen for identification. In some house museums, the security chief lives on the site. A guard on site may deter potential thieves and can deal with emergencies that occur after closing.

The extent of security measures a house museum employs will depend on the rules at that particular site. Some museums will not allow visitors to wander around on their own. Instead, they provide tours for groups that are limited in size. The tours are led by an experienced guide, quite often two, who position themselves in the front and at the rear of the group. With two guides working to keep a group together and allowing no one to stray, it is easier to avoid theft. In house museums where visitors, alone or with a group, are allowed to guide themselves, measures must be taken to further protect the historic settings and the house itself:

• Station guards in areas that are particularly vulnerable.
• Keep doors locked leading to areas where objects are stored and

in sections where the public should not have access.

• Block vulnerable areas with barriers. Barriers act as both physical and emotional deterrents, keeping visitors from pocketing objects and also from damaging furnishings by touching or bumping into them.

A wide variety of barriers can be used, anything from a simple rope tied across the entryway of a room to a full-sized sheet of Plexiglass placed within the door frame, to an electric eye or an alarm device placed under the carpet at the entrance of the rooms.[4] Of course, the effectiveness of the different types of barriers varies. Anyone can quite simply lift a rope and enter a room, while a full-door barrier is much more difficult and time-consuming to penetrate.

Unfortunately, selecting room barriers is complicated by the effect that they have on the visitor. For example, it is more difficult for a museum-goer to appreciate a period room when it must be viewed through a Plexiglass door. The possibility of creating a "less real" effect is one that should be carefully considered when deciding how best to secure the house museum.

Security measures should also be taken when displaying objects in exhibit cases. Use standard display cases and attach the Plexiglass top to the base with tamper-proof screws. These screws have specially machined heads that must be tightened and loosened with a custom tool, a deterrent to thieves armed with only an ordinary screwdriver. To find companies in your area that sell these special screws, check the Thomas Register of American Manufacturers, published annually, or look for it at your public library.[5] Or call or write for a catalog from Tamper-Pruf Screws, a company that deals specifically with security screws and fasteners.[6]

When possible, tie objects to their supports with monofilament, a very fine plastic line that usually cannot be seen and will not detract from the "feel" of the room. Be aware, however, that monofilament can be cut easily with any sharp-edged object. To tie an object down, wrap the monofilament line around the base of a sculpture, for example, and tie it to a leg of a table on which the sculpture sits.

Paintings can also be affixed to walls with security screws. It is also recommended that objects placed on walls be hung by double wrapping wires or monofilament around the hooks that hold them. This helps prevent their easy removal.[7]

Electronic Devices

Many security measures can be used. The devices chosen will depend on cost and necessity. No matter where the museum is located or how sophisticated the security seems, no museum is impenetrable. All efforts must be made to thwart would-be vandals and thieves, because as stewards of important historical and cultural collections, no museum can afford to go without protection. Consult with professional security companies to decide on the best approach to take in securing the house museum.

Electronic sentries can be used to supplement the security force and to protect the museum when guards are not present. A wide range of devices is available. Motion and sonic detectors (available from security-equipment companies) installed in special areas of the museum, such as exhibit rooms, will alert staff to movement and sound in areas when none should exist. Burglar alarms can be placed on doors, windows, and other vulnerable openings of the museum. These alarms, which emit highly audible sounds when activated, may be connected to the central station of a security company whose staff will notify the police if a theft or break-in occurs at night or when the museum is closed.

In exhibit areas, simple battery-operated devices that sound an alarm if an object is moved may be used and, in a restricted area such as a period room, a pressure sensitive pad placed just inside the room (hidden discreetly under a rug) will activate an alarm if someone steps on it.[8] Closed-circuit television, which allows security personnel to survey several areas of the house at once, is another device often used in museums. Exterior lights that provide overlapping cones of illumination should be installed in parking lots, driveways, and entryways. Lighted areas tend to deter burglars and vandals, whereas dark zones encourage them.

Before installing any electronic equipment, careful thought must be given to how it will appear in the setting. All equipment should be placed in the least conspicuous spots so that the historical ambience of the site will remain as undisturbed as possible.

Common Deadbolt Lock

High-quality deadbolt locks on exterior doors and doors to collections areas and high security locks on windows and roof openings will help to reduce the possibility of a break-in. Choose deadbolt locks that are made of brass with a hardened steel bolt. The bolts should be 1 inch in diameter with a solid, free-spinning collar (locks with a fixed collar can be pried off by using a wrench or pliers; once the collar is removed, a burglar can use a screwdriver to turn back the bolt, unlocking the door). High-security locks for windows (such as the double-hung windows commonly used in older homes) are the pin tumbler sash type that lock on the inside with a key. They can be purchased from and installed by a locksmith.

Keys for all locks must be carefully controlled and given only to staff who regularly use locked areas. A current log of individuals holding keys must be kept by the museum's security officer, and extra keys must be kept in a secured box or safe.

Visitor Protection and Safety

Visitors come to house museums expecting to enjoy their experience and rarely give a thought to dangers that may be present in the historic setting. In fact, museum-goers often become so engrossed in the atmosphere of the house that they ignore even the most common hazards.

To ensure a safe environment, museum staff should assess all areas of the house and grounds for potential hazards and have a plan of action to follow when accidents occur. All staff should know emergency numbers and the location of first-aid kits. It is imperative that the museum's front-line staff be trained to handle emergencies. First-aid training is often provided through the local Red Cross office, which will also provide follow-up refresher training.

A few general rules will help ensure visitor safety

- Lock all areas that visitors should not enter. A persistent visitor with a strong curiosity will not be deterred by a mere closed door.
- Install handrails to steady visitors on stairways and in rest-room stalls.
- Keep the house and grounds scrupulously clean and repaired. Steps and sidewalks should be kept in a solid state; cracks must be filled and evened off. All debris must be cleared away. Never leave rakes, hoes, shovels, or machinery around the grounds. This gives an impression of disorder.
- Regularly inspect outdoor sculptures, reflecting pools, or other decorative objects for potential dangers they may pose to the public.

Decorative outside objects may create an **attractive nuisance**—a situation in which children are attracted to physical objects on the museum's grounds and subsequently suffer injury from coming in contact with them. The museum may be liable in such cases. (For example, a child drawn to a sculpture on the lawn of the museum, falls when trying to climb onto the sculpture and suffers an injury.[9])

- Remove snow from walkways, and use a deicer when freezing rain or snow coats sidewalks and entries.
- Block off or cover slippery floors or walkways to prevent accidents. A sign stating that a floor is slippery or wet is not enough. People often miss or do not read signs, especially in museums.
- Beware of uneven floors or floor coverings that fit improperly. They can cause visitors to trip and loose their balance, resulting in injury.
- Steep or irregularly worn stairs are hazardous. Direct all museum traffic in these areas and make certain that each visitor is aware of the danger.
- Install additional lighting in dimly lighted areas where visitors might miss a step.
- Make certain all equipment, tools, and chemicals are safely stored and kept locked. Rat poisons and other toxic substances must be kept out of reach of children.

Disaster Preparedness Planning

The year 1989 was disastrous for museums around the world. In May, a tornado ripped through a restored Moravian community, Old Salem, in North Carolina, downing aged trees and damaging buildings and fences. On September 22, Hurricane Hugo hit Charleston, South Carolina. Museums and historic houses in the area were whipped by 135-mile-per hour winds, and a 17-foot wall of water pounded the shore.[10] The Loma Prieta earthquake struck the San Francisco Bay area on October 17, damaging historic buildings and museums collections. In December, Romania's National Museum was severely damaged during a civil revolution. It was reported that paintings were pierced by bullets and damaged by fire. Galleries in the museum were said to have been gutted by fire and archival materials destroyed.[11]

These events were well publicized, but many more go unnoticed. Museums are constantly faced with such hazards as high winds, floods, tsunamis, chemical spills, fire, bomb threats, and even breaks in plumbing or leaks in roofs.

During the past decade, disaster planning has been the topic of discussions, workshops, and countless journal articles. This attention has spurred museums to write their own plans for facing disasters and to conduct drills to familiarize their staffs with procedures in the event of disaster. The planning has paid off: many museums located in Charleston were prepared for Hurricane Hugo. Members of Charleston Archives, Libraries, and Museums (CALM), a consortium of twenty-two cultural institutions that had spent years focusing on disaster preparedness and recovery planning, were left with relatively minor damage.[12]

All museums are well advised to write a disaster-preparedness plan and to see that each staff member has a copy. Consider some of the steps to take in formulating a plan:

- Identify the potential dangers to the museum (for instance, tornadoes are a definite threat in the Midwest or Plains states, while hurricanes are more prevalent in coastal areas). It is recommended that museums review *Protecting Historic Architecture and Museum Collections from Natural Disasters,* edited by Barclay G. Jones. This valuable book can help staff to assess potential hazards in the museum's geographic area.[13]

- Create a list of objects in the collections that should receive top priority for protection during a disaster.

- Obtain blueprints of the building and make sure they are easily accessible to staff. They can be helpful because they show where heating and air-conditioning, ventilation, alarm systems, and other pertinent utilities are located.

- Plan preventive measures. For example, sprinklers reduce damage from fire or install window shutters to protect the panes from high winds.[14]

- Have supplies and equipment on hand to help secure the building and collections, such as plywood sheets to nail over outside windows to prevent glass from shattering and tarps or sheets of polyethylene to cover windows and to protect furnishings and room interiors. Make certain that all staff knows where the supplies are stored.

- Decide who will be first and second in charge in the event of an emergency. Make certain that staff members understand their responsibilities when disaster strikes. Procedures, even the most obvious ones, need to be carefully spelled out in the plan. Panic born from unexpected disasters can cause humans to think and act irrationally. However, having a step-by-step set of procedures will help.

- Test the plan by conducting drills for various types of emergencies. Drills will help staff to understand the emergency program. Rehearsals can include training in the use of fire extinguishers, first-aid and lifesaving techniques, locating and closing down building utilities, evacuation of personnel and visitors, and removal of collections to safe locations.
- Work with other museums in the area to create a network of help and resources in case of emergency. There is greater strength in fighting the aftermath of a disaster if museums agree to combine their expertise and to work together.
- Know what to do after the disaster. Have a network of people and services to contact to assist in cleanup and post-disaster conservation and restoration for both collections and buildings.
- List emergency phone numbers.

Fire Prevention, Detection, and Suppression

Fire poses a major threat in the historic house museum. It can destroy the entire collection and furnishings, as well as the museum's very structure. As with other methods of protection, prevention is the best possible defense against fire.

Staff and volunteers must know what to do to prevent fires, and they must understand proper safety procedures. Time and effort should be spent instructing staff on visitor evacuation, use of a fire extinguisher, and collections salvage methods. Invite the local fire department to inspect the building and make recommendations on updating fire protection and safety. Personnel from the district fire station should be familiar with the museum; this will help immensely in case of fire.

Fire drills are a serious matter, and all museum personnel must know their responsibilities and how to carry them through. It is recommended that staff work with the local fire department in determining the most expedient evacuation procedures. Fire drills should be held twice a year and assessed for efficiency after each one.

There are strategies that are very effective for fire prevention.

- Keep the museum scrupulously clean, uncluttered, and free from debris. Keep all combustible materials away from heat sources, and place flammable liquids and materials in proper metal storage cabinets (those that meet the fire code). Consult your state Occupational Safety and Health Administration (OSHA) office for information on safety standards and procedures for public spaces.
- Enforce no-smoking rules in areas that are sensitive and present the threat of fire. Never allow smoking in collections areas, exhibit spaces, shops, or areas where machinery is stored or utilities are located.
- Keep exits, stairways, and corridors free from obstructions. Be sure that fire exit signs are well lit to aid in emergency evacuations.
- Contact your local fire department to assess your building and make recommendations on the number and types of fire extinguishers best suited to your building. There are three classes of fire: those involving (1) ordinary combustible material or (2) flammable liquids, and (3) electrical fires. Each must be doused with the proper extinguishing agent. (Extinguishers can be purchased from suppliers of fire-protection-equipment.)
- Use an appropriate number of smoke detectors in the building. Contact your local fire department for its recommendations about the number to use and the best placement for them. (For more information about smoke detectors, refer to the following section.)
- Conduct periodic checks of fire extinguishers and smoke and heat detectors.
- Have electrical wiring checked regularly by a qualified electrician. Old, outdated wiring should never be used to carry more electricity than it was designed for. Discuss the electrical needs of the staff, and define the realistic capabilities that can be placed on the existing system.[15]
- Check heating systems and hot-water equipment regularly to ensure that they are functioning properly.
- Make certain that key staff are familiar with the museum's structure: building materials, construction techniques, and location of all utilities. Keep an extra set of blueprints on hand.
- Be sure that all workers who enter the museum observe the fire-safety procedures and regulations used by the museum staff.

- Always keep a duplicate set of the museum's catalog off the site in the event of fire. At the museum, store collections records in a fireproof steel cabinet or vault.

Fire Detection

As public buildings, museums are required to have an early warning system that complies with the National Fire Protection Association (NFPA) standards and local fire codes, and they must be inspected regularly. Also, as institutions that preserve our cultural and historical heritage, the buildings should be well equipped with fire-protection equipment. The sophistication of the detection and extinguishing systems will depend upon the museum's needs and their cost. Automatic detectors trigger an alarm when smoke or abnormally high temperatures are detected. Detectors should also be wired to alert a monitoring station—the local police or fire station or commercially operated centers.[16]

There are two basic types of smoke detectors: photoelectric and ionization. Each works on a different principle. Photoelectric detectors have a lamp that shines a light beam just out of direct view of a light-sensitive photoelectric cell. With the introduction of smoke particles, the beam of light scatters and some of the reflected light is detected by the photocell unit. As more particles enter, more electricity is generated, and when the particles become dense enough the alarm is activated. Photoelectric detectors work well in the presence of smoke and smoldering fires. These devices must be "hard wired" to a permanent electrical supply and usually have a battery backup to keep them operating in the event the power goes out.[17]

The ionization detector uses a small amount of radioactive substance to create ionized air. When smoke particles enter the detector they disrupt the flow of electric current to the point that the alarm sounds. Ionization detectors require little power and can run easily on batteries; they will work even during a power failure.[18]

Another automatic detector is the thermal, or heat detector, which operates by detecting rising temperatures in a room. When a preset temperature is reached, an alarm is triggered. Heat detectors are useful as a backup to smoke detectors, but they should not be used alone; they do not detect smoldering fires that emit smoke and little heat but may release poisonous gases. Heat detectors work well in areas such as furnace or boiler rooms and attics.

Because they are activated by different conditions, smoke and heat detectors should be used together in varying combinations. Be certain that the photoelectric detector has a built-in battery backup in case of power outage. Batteries in all types of detectors should be checked and replaced routinely.

Fire Suppression

House museums, because of their nature, also require protection from fire: a fire-suppression system. Museum staff may feel secure after installing the proper number of smoke and heat detectors throughout the historic structure. But if a fire-alarm sounds, someone must be present to hear it, report the fire, and attempt to extinguish it. If the alarm is tied to a monitoring station, time is lost as the fire team is being dispatched. Meanwhile, the collections and building burn. With a fire-suppression system in place, immediate action may be taken to extinguish the fire.

The two most commonly used automatic fire-suppression systems are gas-suppression and water-sprinkling systems. Gas suppression has been used successfully in collection areas for many years. An advantage to the system is that no water is introduced into the area, thus avoiding damage to historic rooms, collections, or furnishings.

Unfortunately, the Halon gases used in suppression systems and in hand-held extinguishers contain flourohalocarbons, substances linked with depletion of the ozone layer of the earth's atmosphere. For this reason Halon does not have a future as a fire suppressant; in fact, production of the gas is now restricted. Therefore, museums are left with only one viable option for fire suppression: water-sprinkling systems. Automatic sprinklers can work well in a variety of areas since there are several types from which to choose.

WET-PIPE SPRINKLERS

Recommended for areas where people work and gather, the wet-pipe sprinkler, activated by heat, is the most common and least expensive system in use. The pipes, which are mounted on the ceiling, are constantly filled and automatically release water if a fire breaks out. The system should not be used in areas where there is danger of the pipes freezing or of mechanical damage to the pipes.

A drawback of the wet sprinkler is accidental discharge and the water damage that follows. But this happens only rarely.

DRY-PIPE SPRINKLERS

The pre-acting, or dry-pipe, sprinkler system is more expensive than the wet-pipe, but eliminates the possibility of water damage from broken or frozen pipes or from accidental release of the sprinkler heads. Water is not discharged into the pipe until heat and smoke activate the system.

FLOW-CONTROLLED OR ON—OFF SPRINKLERS

The flow-controlled system is well suited to gallery and collection spaces. Like the other systems, it is activated by heat, dispensing the minimum amount of water needed to extinguish the fire; then the sprinkler heads shut off automatically. If the fire reignites, water is again discharged. This system avoids the problems caused by a spray of water that may continue until fire fighters have shut off the system manually, which may not happen until long after the fire is out.

While protection of human life is paramount in making a historic building fire safe, consideration should also be given to installing fire and security devices in such a way that they have a minimal impact on the historic structure. The publication *Fire Safety Retrofitting in Historic Buildings* by the Advisory Council on Historic Preservation offers suggestions for treatments of specific areas within historic buildings as well as examples of the successes of the union between safety and preservation.

NOTES

1. Ralph H. Lewis, *Manual for Museums* (Washington, D.C.: National Park Service, 1976), p. 282.

2. William A. Bostick, "What Is the State of Museum Security," *Museum News* 46, no. 5 (1968): 17.

3. G. Ellis Burcaw, *Introduction to Museum Work*, 2d ed. (Nashville, Tenn.: American Association for State and Local History, 1983), p. 105.

4. Bostick, "State of Museum Security," p. 15.

5. The Thomas Register can be purchased through the Thomas Publishing Company, One Penn Plaza, New York, New York 10001, (212) 695–0500.

6. Tamper-Pruf Screws, 8800 T E. Somerset Boulevard, Paramount, CA 90723, (213) 531–9340. There is also a New York–based company that manufactures only security screws: Tamperproof Screw Company, Inc., 30 Laurel Street, Hicksville, New York 11801, or call (516) 931–1616, extension 400.

7. Jack Leo, "How to Secure Your Museum: A Basic Checklist," *History News* 35, no. 3 (1980): 10.

8. Ibid., p. 10.

9. Marilyn Phelan, *Museums and the Law* (Nashville, Tenn.: American Association for State and Local History, 1982), p. 60.

10. Phillip Babcock, "Ready for the Worst," *Museum News* 69, no. 3 (1990): 50–54.

11. Evan Roth, "Romania's Revolution Rocks Museums, Too—For Good and Ill," *Museum News* 69, no. 3 (1990): 25.

12. Joy B. Dunn, "The CALM before the Storm," *History News* 45, no. 1 (1990): 22–24.

13. Babcock, "Ready for the Worst," pp. 50–54.

14. Ibid., p. 50.

15. Joseph Chapman, "Fire," *Museum News* 50, no. 5 (1972): 33.

16. The ASIS Standing Committee on Museum, Library and Archive Security, *Suggested Guidelines in Museum Security* (Arlington, Va.: American Society for Industrial Security), p. 6.

17. "Smoke Detectors," *Consumer Reports* 41, no. 10 (1976): 555.

18. Ibid.

Telling the Story:
Interpreting
the Historic House

Tho' the pipes that supply the bathroom burst
And the lavat'ry makes you fear the worst
It was used by Charles the First
Quite informally
And later by George the Fourth
On a journey North.

         Noël Coward, "The Stately Homes of England"

AFTER THE HISTORIC house has been saved and restored, its financial future secured, the collections organized and documented, it is time to concentrate on interpreting the house. But what is "interpretation," and how can it be accomplished in a way that presents historical information accurately, holds the visitor's interest, and meets a sound educational objective?

Interpretation, the structure in which information about the historic house is presented, is an attempt to stimulate the senses and arouse the imagination. It can be an interchange with a costumed interpreter portraying a pioneer woman churning butter. It is the realization that the butter that she is making looks, smells, and tastes like the unsalted butter one buys in grocery stores today. From the experience the visitor understands a number of historical realities—that the methods of food preparation in the past may be strikingly different from those used today, that butter making, a labor-intensive task that was usually performed by women, that pi-

Good interpretation is a way of educating visitors in a stimulating and thought-provoking manner. At Old Salem Restoration, costumed interpreters demonstrate domestic skills as they hang out freshly scoured wool behind the Vierling House. (Photograph courtesy of Old Salem Restoration, Winston-Salem, North Carolina)

oneer women depended on their own labor for self-sufficiency, and that butter was a significant part of the diet then, just as it is today.

Such a demonstration helps visitors to connect with the past and to learn what life was like for a particular family or in a particular era. Enjoyment of the ambience of the historic house is augmented by sensing past traditions, folkways, and customs that were a part of America's history.

The interpretive approach should aim to be multifaceted and broad in scope but not unfocused or confusing. It should capture the true characters of those who lived at the historic site. If possible, try to incorporate the personalities and views of servants, slaves, gardeners, handymen, chauffeurs, neighbors, and even the minister who dined with the family every third Sunday.

In interpreting an event that took place at the site, try to enlarge the focus and expand the associations. Explain the dramatic events that led up to it and discuss the people involved. Then, explain what life was like following the event, describing how it affected not only the "famous" people but those whose views are seldom heard. Try to shed light on how the event might have changed future views, products, language, behavior, politics, economics, law, and geographic delineations.[1]

Types of Historic House Museums

Thousands of historic house museums are open to the public and each one attempts to educate visitors in one of three primary ways. They fall into a few categories. as follows:[2]

The Documentary Historic House Museum

By far the most common type of historic house museum in the United States is that which commemorates a rich or famous individual or family—a town's founding father, a celebrated writer, a former U.S. president, or an industrial magnate. The primary interpretive aim is to chronicle the life of an individual or relate an important historical event. Some of these museums, such as the grand estates of Thomas Jefferson and Henry Flagler (Florida's real-estate tycoon and railroad builder) give a view of elitist society. Others are more modest, such as Noah Webster's simple four-room saltbox farmhouse in West Hartford, Connecticut, or Betsy Ross's urban, artisan-class brick home in Philadelphia. Each of these houses not only provides a glimpse into a famous person's life but also shows how various social classes might have lived at the time.

Some of the most famous documentary sites are Colonial Williamsburg and George Washington's Mount Vernon in Virginia, the Abraham Lincoln Home in Springfield, Illinois; Edgar Allan Poe's home in Baltimore; Helen Keller's childhood home in Tuscumbia, Alabama; and Clara Barton's home in Glen Echo, Maryland.

The Representative Historic House Museum

Some historic houses have been restored to interpret a particular style of architecture from a particular period. They are exemplified by the southern antebellum plantation (often used to portray the life-styles of wealthy landholders), by wayside inns, or by pioneer log cabins. The focus is on a way of life rather than on a particular individual or family. Good examples of representative house museums are the Botsford Tavern near Detroit, Michigan, which depicts a mid-nineteenth century home and inn, and the houses built during different times in such well-known historic villages as Old Sturbridge Village in Sturbridge and Plimouth Plantation in Plymouth, both in Massachusetts; the Henry Ford Museum and Greenfield Village in Dearborn, Michigan; and Old World Wisconsin in Eagle, Wisconsin.

The Aesthetic Historic House Museum

The historic house that serves as the setting for special collections, where decorative and fine arts, furniture, and antiques from various periods are displayed—may be classified as "aesthetic." The house serves as a backdrop for the objects, with no particular attention paid to former residents or the events that took place there. Houses of distinctive architectural design also fit into this category. The Taft Museum, located in a Federal-period house in Cincinnati, places emphasis on its collections of fine art and furniture, not on the period rooms themselves. The most famous museum of this type is The Henry Francis du Pont Winterthur Museum in Wilmington, Delaware. In the multitude of rooms collections of furniture and decorative arts are displayed—objects all appreciated for their own merit.

Combinations of the Three Types

Not all museum houses neatly fit these categories—often they combine two or even three purposes. Take, for example, the home of the famous scout Kit Carson. His adobe house, at first glance, may be classified as a documentary site because three rooms of the dwelling are furnished as they were when Carson lived there with his family during the mid-nineteenth century. The remaining rooms, however, are set up as a museum that displays artifacts from Native American and Spanish and American settlers of the region. These displays portray the ways in which people lived in New Mexico's past. This museum also would be considered a representative site.

Another hybrid is the C. M. Russell Museum in Great Falls, Montana, dedicated to the painter of the American West. The museum consists of three buildings: Russell's studio, a documentary site; the house where he lived after he married—which, because it contains few of the original furnishings might be classified as a representative site; and a modern museum building that houses many of Russell's works—a clear example of an aesthetic site.[3]

Many historic house museums also serve as the headquarters for historical societies or as local and ethnic museums. They, too, combine one or more of the types of sites in their interpretive programming. Consider the American Swedish Institute, located in the Swan J. Turnblad mansion in Minneapolis, Minnesota. This historic house museum seeks to interpret the traditions of Swedish immigrants. Interpretation at the institute endeavors to tell the story of the original owner and founder of the museum (documentary), to show elegant interiors with works of art created by Swedish immigrant artists (aesthetic), and to explain the Swedish immigration period with displays of artifacts (representative).

Preparing an Interpretive Program

To begin planning an interpretive program, it is suggested that the curator and staff return to the mission statement. A rereading of this document allows them to focus on the true function of the museum. In addition, the curator will need to decide how to com-

The American Swedish Institute is a Swedish ethnic museum and cultural center housed in the Swan J. Turnblad mansion. Turnblad, a Swedish immigrant, built this miniature castle in 1904 to display his newly achieved wealth and status. (Photograph courtesy of the American Swedish Institute)

municate the museum's mission. To accomplish this, the museum must define its goals and objectives. The goals will be defined in general terms; the objectives should be the specific course of action. The end product will be a document that states what the interpretive program will teach the visitor and how these goals will be carried out.[4]

After the objectives have been established, write the interpretive program, basing it on historical facts about the house gleaned from documents, photographs, diaries, journals, local records, oral histories, and the like. Collect the facts carefully, always focusing on the topic, and plan techniques for communicating ideas to visitors. Avoid presenting a romanticized view of the house and the events surrounding it, or elevating the former residents to the stature of "great men or women." Try not to cover too many ideas and, for the most part, avoid those that are not solidly linked to the main thesis of the museum. Too much information can cause visitors to feel confused and disoriented, and they may leave without understanding why the house was significant enough to be saved or restored.

A thorough understanding of the commonly held thoughts and views of the time period being interpreted will enable the museum staff to create the most accurate interpretation. Many questions must be asked to fill out the story of the house.

• What were the roles of the residents (family) of the house in the community? How did they relate to neighbors, servants, or workers?

• What was their economic status? Did it change over time? If so, what forces enabled wealth to be accumulated quickly or lost rapidly?

• What were their social values and political views and the extent of their involvement?

• How were they connected to the local church or synagogue, and how did their religious beliefs connect them to other people in the community?

• What were their kinship patterns? Did they live in a nuclear unit, or did several generations reside in the house? What were the reasons for this pattern?

• How did they entertain? What clubs did they belong to? Were they listed in the social register?

• What do the living spaces in the house reveal about the residents? Are there public spaces and private spaces? Did their religious views affect the arrangement of furnishings?

• Were children's rooms or areas adjacent or close to adult spaces? Was the arrangement different from or similar to today's patterns? What did it indicate about the culture?

• What levels of technology were at work during different stages of the house's history and what effect did the changes have?

• What event(s) took place at the site? What effect did they have on local, state, or national history? What mark's did they leave on the house and its surroundings?

- What is the architectural style of the house? Why was it chosen? How did it come to be used in this region?
- How did the style of the house fit into the surrounding community? How was the house furnished? What does this information tell about the values of the time?
- What were the common decorative styles during the period(s) represented? What do they indicate about the people who furnished the home?
- What was the style of the gardens and plantings of the grounds? What influenced the designs?
- How did the craftsmanship and artistry of the period compare to that of today? What changes in technology have caused transformations in the way furnishings were made?
- What is the aesthetic focus of the museum? What does this style reflect of the times, attitudes, culture, social views?

The Importance of Historical Accuracy

An accurate account of the history of a house or its residents is necessary for sound interpretation. Whether it be a resident's political life, a historic event that took place at the site, or the history of the house itself being unraveled, the story must be grounded in and related to solid fact. Unfortunately, the fiction that surrounds historic houses is sometimes passed on as fact in interpretive programs. Such fiction may be entertaining to the visitor, but only serves to undermine the integrity of the historic house.

But where does one find out information about a house, its builders and its residents? How does one learn more about the history of a community? How do you separate fiction from fact, local legend from reality? Where do you start?

Conducting Historical Research

Begin historical research by heading to government offices, public libraries, and historical societies. All information collected, including photocopies of documents, should be kept in a notebook that can later be used by the museum staff. Maintain a bibliography of all sources used in research. This is valuable information that will be used again and again.

PUBLIC RECORDS

Public records are an excellent resource. They are most often located at the county courthouse and can contain a wealth of pertinent information.

- Vital statistics, such as records of marriage and divorce, births and deaths, and adoptions.
- Probate records, including such documents as wills, deeds, estate proceedings, and possibly inventories of household articles from disposition proceedings.
- Legal descriptions of property, abstracts of title, mortgages, plat maps, and information related to real estate, including early property tax records. (Tax records contain changes in ownership and reveal the value of property over time because of improvements made to the property.)
- Records of lawsuits.

In larger communities, building permits and building index cards, which list all the permits issued for a structure, can be found at the inspections department in city offices. These cards often include details such as the architect, builder, owner(s), dimensions, and original costs and may contain information on the original construction of a building and later additions and modifications.

LIBRARIES AND ARCHIVES

County libraries and archives offer such resources as city directories, newspapers, written histories, obituary files, biographies of prominent individuals, address files, and photographs.

City directories list alphabetically (although not always completely) inhabitants of a city. In larger communities, listings are updated annually. Individual listings may include race, occupation, number and names of family members, and home addresses.

Newspapers offer valuable clues on the activities of prominent people, the tastes prevalent at the time, and how people were furnishing their homes. Turn-of-the-century newspapers, for example, held descriptive advertisements of real estate, and society pages often described new residential construction.

Photographs are a good resource for those conducting historical research. Besides showing how homes appeared on the outside and in association to neighboring buildings, they provide insight into how people furnished their homes and how they utilized space. Photographs also offer a look at the clothing of the period—everyday apparel, ceremonial costumes, military ensembles, and club regalia—visual documents that can help to associate individuals with organizations, clubs, fraternities, professions, and different levels of military involvement. Even relationships between individuals might be gleaned from photographs.

Photos can be found in the collections of family and individuals who have been connected to the house, in state and local historical society archives, and in special collections in public libraries.

COUNTY, LOCAL, AND STATE HISTORICAL SOCIETIES

County and state historical societies often hold family histories and written histories of the region, personal records on individuals, and newspaper clippings pertaining to residents and events of the time. Company records, documents and artifacts from regional clubs, naturalization records, early state and federal census reports, and, occasionally, architectural drawings may also be found in the collections of historical societies.

For a study of period house plans and interior design, refer to such magazines as *House Beautiful, House and Garden,* and *Better Homes and Gardens,* as well as mail-order catalogs, which can be found in historical society archives and libraries. Some publishers, such as Dover, reprint house plans and pattern books from earlier eras.

ORAL HISTORIES

Interviews can also shed light on questions pertaining to a historic house, its former occupants, and events that took place there. Such encounters can tap memories of the old-timers of the neighborhood, descendants of a family, or an individual's co-worker. An inquiry around the neighborhood may turn up some interesting information. Members of the same social groups or church may offer insight into an individual's life, and former domestic employees, even the surviving family of former business partners, can provide a glimpse into a personality.

When seeking an interview, prepare questions carefully and in advance. Cross check the information collected with facts already known to gauge the respondent's accuracy. Individuals remember incidents differently, so be cautious when collecting oral histories and be critical in assessing them.

Studying the House and Its Contents

The house itself may contain documents packed away in an attic or in empty rooms. Search for personal records like diaries, journals, daily record books, household account books, travel accounts, scrapbooks, photograph albums, newspaper clippings, delivery receipts, postcards, correspondence, and receipts of furnishings and household objects purchased for the home. Question the most recent residents about old records; perhaps they have uncovered something or know where to look. Try to locate any remaining descendants of the original residents; they may have documents, photographs, or letters pertaining to the family.

William Seale, in *Recreating the Historic House Interior,* suggests looking at archival collections from other properties of the same period and in the same area. Local household inventories, he notes, reflect the tastes of an era and can contribute to the understanding of similar houses and their contents.

In creating an interior intended to represent a specific time, culture, or geographic region, it is important to investigate the kind of furnishings that would be appropriate. Illustrations in books, old magazines, catalogs, and advertisements in period newspapers and magazines depict house interiors as they appeared through time and may reveal distinctive regional or ethnic design elements.

The museum may want to hire an experienced researcher to conduct the investigation, such as a local historian, a history professor from a nearby university or college, or a graduate student trained in history or historic architecture. The state historical society will probably be able to supply names of professionals familiar with records in your area. Or contact the state historical preservation office (SPHO) for a referral to a skilled house historian.

When searching for clues about the physical structure of a building, study both the interior and the exterior carefully. Open closets, peer behind fireplace mantles, and inspect window ledges for traces of original colors or wallpapers. Chip paint fragments from walls and ceilings, and have them analyzed to learn what colors were stylish during various stages of the home's occupancy. Study

Period room settings take many forms, from modest to elaborate. This ornate dining room at Lyndhurst in Tarrytown, New York, was designed by A. J. Davis (1864–1867). (Photograph courtesy of Lyndhurst, a property of the National Trust for Historic Preservation)

wear patterns on floors, doors, and walls to help determine how life was lived in a house. For example, look for holes in floors where wall-to-wall carpets were laid or where a rug may have been tacked down.

Record in a notebook all information that is uncovered in the house; draw diagrams and mark anything found that may be useful in reconstructing the original interior. Everything—from holes in walls to placement of moldings—should be recorded. Once such information is on paper, patterns will often appear.

Scrutinize the building for modifications in its original structure, and look at architectural drawings and photographs for evidence of alterations. Or consult a restoration architect to determine the character and date of the house. This specialist will be able to determine if—and usually when—walls were torn down, windows walled up, porches removed, or features added. The techniques employed include X-ray technology to analyze the basic structure, hardware chronology (studying the composition and form of nails, screws, and so forth to ascertain dates), and dendrochronology (tree-ring dating; matching a wooden beam, for example, against a series of tree-ring dates to determine its age when cut). The restoration architect also uses blueprints, documents, and historical records to assist in understanding an historic structure and how it has changed over time.

Archaeological excavations at the Brush-Everard House, Colonial Williamsburg, Williamsburg, Virginia. (Photograph courtesy of the Colonial Williamsburg Foundation)

Refuse left by past peoples, excavated from around a dwelling, can shed light on their life-style, level of technology, habits of leisure and work, and building styles. Here specialists analyze archeological materials found at Colonial Williamsburg. (Photograph courtesy of the Colonial Williamsburg Foundation)

Archaeology

The grounds of historic houses may have included outlying buildings. It is expensive, but prudent, to hire historical archaeologists to excavate in order to uncover locations of previous structures and their floor plans. Archaeologists usually unearth household artifacts. Dishes, bottles of all sorts, pipe fragments, shells, nails, and other everyday objects that were lost or cast aside can be dated by their style and composition. These were days when refuse was dumped into pits dug not too far from the back entrance or kitchen door of a dwelling. Materials uncovered from excavating can fill many gaps in the historical record.

Deciding on an Interpretive Approach

After research is completed, the staff will need to decide how to use most effectively the information collected. How will they go about explaining a celebrated individual or the dramatic historical event that took place at the site? What will be interpreted? Which rooms should be restored or re-created as period rooms, and which might hold exhibits? Will the staff include an overview of the family and highlights of different people who have lived and worked at the house? Or will exhibits portray trends of a particular time in history?

Restoring Period Interiors

Many visitors go to historic houses to savor the feeling of historical surroundings and to admire the furnishings of the interiors. They enjoy the sense of being cast back in time—of strolling through rooms essentially frozen in the past.

Restoring or re-creating historic period rooms is an exacting task that, unless all the original furnishings are still in place, requires considerable research, planning, and financial resources.

Historic interiors are usually represented in two ways. The first involves the use of objects that actually belonged to a specific individual or were being used at the time that person was memorialized. This approach is most often taken at documentary sites. It is the most difficult type of interior to create because personal furnishings are often dispersed after an individual dies.

An outstanding example is the Alexander Ramsey House in St. Paul, Minnesota. Ramsey, the first territorial governor of Minnesota (1849–1858), expressly willed his Second Empire Victorian home to the state. His granddaughters lived in the house until their deaths in 1964, when it was turned over to the Minnesota Historical Society. Because the family knew that the house would one day be open to the public, they preserved everything that belonged to their for-bears—original furnishings, correspondence, even Governor Ramsey's diary, in which he recorded all the purchases for his home. These documents provide insight into the family's daily life in the days before Minnesota became a state.

The house itself is remarkably preserved. Most of the furnishings, from the largest pieces of furniture to the smallest accessories belonging to the Ramseys, are in place and are a solid representation of the late Victorian period.

Another example is the home of James J. Hill, founder of the

Re-creating historic rooms is an exacting task that requires considerable research, planning, and financial resources. Pictured here are the living quarters of the inn-keeper and his wife at the Salem Tavern, built in 1784. (Photograph courtesy of Old Salem Restoration, Winston-Salem, North Carolina)

The Alexander Ramsey House in St. Paul, Minnesota, is typical of the Second Empire Victorian Period. *(Photograph courtesy of the Minnesota Historical Society)*

Great Northern Railroad. Few furnishings, however, remain from the days when Mary and Jim Hill and their children lived in the forty-five-room, Richardsonian Romanesque mansion. The Minnesota Historical Society, which owns and operates this massive sandstone mansion, elected to leave rooms unfurnished where no original pieces exist. At the Hill House, the interpretive focus is explaining the social and technological systems of the household. Guides, as they lead visitors through the house, discuss the family's life, its relation to the community, servants' roles, and the ingenious mechanical, electrical, and security systems, which were the best of their day. The interpretation is scrupulous, with every detail thoroughly researched before being incorporated into the tour. The tours, in fact, are so successful, so compelling, that the visitors often leave believing they have seen much more than is actually

Costumed interpreters at the Alexander Ramsey House in St. Paul, Minnesota, demonstrate the complexities of Victorian dressing to schoolchildren. (Photograph courtesy of the Minnesota Historical Society)

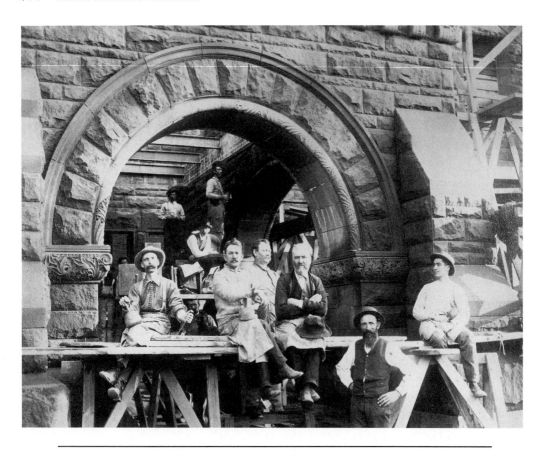

The stories of the "common person" who worked and lived at a house are also important to its history. Pictured here are the stonemasons who built the James J. Hill House, in St. Paul, Minnesota. Swan Pearson, standing with his arms akimbo, received $4.50 a day for his work as general foreman. (Photograph courtesy of the Minnesota Historical Society)

present. The past has come to life, even though the rooms are sparsely furnished or empty.

The second approach to historic interiors is one in which the furnishings are representative of the originals or those that may have been used. These can be reproductions or actual furnishings typical of a particular time period or geographic region, but not necessarily linked to a particular family. Such rooms are easier to create because the furnishings can be collected from a wider range of sources. Or rooms can be furnished with objects that represent the most beautiful and finest, brought together with an emphasis on high quality. Period rooms such as these are common to representative and aesthetic type of historic houses.

Take for example, Strawbery Banke in Portsmouth, New Hampshire, a historic site with forty-two houses that range from the seventeenth to the twentieth century. To furnish them, curators search the New England region for objects they have found listed in deeds and other documents associated with the houses. In

At the James J. Hill House, in St. Paul, Minnesota, the lives of many former servants have been researched and included in a thorough interpretation. Pictured here are Lena Olson (left), the Hills' head cook, and Celia Tauer Forstner (right), the cook's helper (1910–1911). (Photograph courtesy of the Minnesota Historical Society)

At Strawbery Banke in Portsmouth, New Hampshire, the Walsh House (built in 1796) is one of forty-two historic houses at this "representative" site, showing life-styles from the seventeenth to the twentieth centuries. (Photograph courtesy of Strawbery Banke, Inc.)

addition, archaeologists' finds help to fill in blanks. At one house, archaeologists uncovered fragments of tableware used by its former inhabitants. Curators at Strawbery Banke were surprised that they had tableware of the same design in their own collections. The tableware was moved to the house and is displayed there.

The two types of historic interiors described above are general classifications. Overlap does exist. For example, if few original furnishings remain at a documentary site, it is not uncommon for curators to choose to fill in the museum's period rooms with reproductions or furnishings similar to those originally used. If this method is used, it is important to inform visitors that the furnishings displayed were not actually used by the family, but represent the kinds of objects they *might* have had.

This approach is taken at the Will Rogers Birthplace, near Oologah, Oklahoma. This ranch was the birthplace of the famous humorist, performer, and newspaper columnist. Until he was nineteen Rogers, born in 1879, lived in the two-story clapboard home his father built and, although he traveled widely, remained connected to the property and purchased it after his parents' death. Rogers was killed in a plane crash in 1935, leaving the ranch to his wife and three children, who deeded the home to the state of Oklahoma in 1959. In 1932 most of the pieces belonging to Rogers were destroyed in a fire.

It was the curator who decided that, instead of leaving the period rooms empty, the house would be more effective if it was filled with furniture similar to the originals. Consequently, furnishings

An interior of an early-nineteenth-century home owned by Stephen Chase, a well-to-do merchant from Portsmouth, New Hampshire. The room provides a glimpse into the era, region, and social standing of the Chase family by revealing facts about foodways, decorative preferences, level of technology, and personal interests. (Photograph courtesy of Strawbery Banke, Inc.)

The desk of Washington Irving—a gift from his publisher G. P. Putnam—is signifi-cant because of its association with the famous man. (Sunnyside, Historic Hudson Val-ley, Tarrytown, New York)

from the late nineteenth and early twentieth centuries have been collected. Friends and relatives were also generous in contributing objects Rogers had given to them.

This house museum, although a documentary site, relies on ob-jects representing the period—and not those originally used—in order to create an atmosphere similar to that of Will Rogers' time.

In the restoration of an interior belonging to a specific individ-ual or one created as the essence of an era, it is essential to inter-pret truthfully. If the owner of a house was a scholarly man who owned a large library, it is important to reflect this aspect of his personality as part of the visitor's experience. If diaries and oral histories reveal that the books were often piled in stacks on table-tops, shelves, or the floor next to a favorite chair, then they should be displayed in stacks or strewn about. It would be inaccurate to interpret the library as uncluttered.

Curatorial staff should put aside their modern views and ideas about space, arrangement of furniture, color, design, and style when they re-create period rooms. The house should be viewed as its

The North Room of Theodore Roosevelt's mansion reflects his interests and person-ality through his books, hunting trophies, political gifts, artwork, and furniture. This room was added to the home in 1905 to accommodate the many distinguished visitors and heads of state while Roosevelt was president. (National Park Service, Sagamore Hill National Historic Site, Oyster Bay, New York)

Toys carefully arranged to look strewn about, giving the impression of a room played in by children. The John Vogler House "Boys' Room," where Vogler's sons—Timothy, George, and Nathanael—slept. (Photograph courtesy of Old Salem Restoration, Winston-Salem, North Carolina)

occupants would have used it. If there were children, it is important to show their toys strewn about as if they had been playing. If the children slept with their parents which they often did in the eighteenth and nineteenth century, show this by placing the children's belongings in the bedchamber and explain to visitors why this was the custom then and why it is different today.

Be truthful about the arrangements of objects in a room. Let dust pile up in corners if it is deemed appropriate for the time period and cultural views of the family. Today's sterilized interiors are a fairly modern phenomenon. Stack pots, pans, and utensils on the stove or tabletops if they were kept in this way. Hang coats and hats on chair backs, or place them on tables. Burn candles down, toss a newspaper in a favorite chair, or leave boots lying about on the floor for authenticity.

Alternative to Period Rooms: Using Exhibits in the Historic House

Some historic house staff will be frustrated in their attempts to establish an interpretive program because of the lack of historic records, photographs, and original furnishings in the house. Part of the problem can be solved by installing theme exhibits in rooms where no original furnishings exist or in areas of the house that are not original. Exhibits can also be combined with existing period rooms to create a multidimensional interpretation of the house.

An example is the Summit County Historical Society, housed in the Perkins Stone Mansion in Akron, Ohio. This historic house is used as the setting of an exhibit called "Rites of Passage," which focuses on the major events in people's lives in the late nineteenth and early twentieth centuries.[5] The interpretive approach portrays the social transformation of Akron from a predominantly rural to an urban society through the perspective of rites of passage such as weddings and marriages, childbirth and death, and mourning customs.[6] Nine fully furnished period rooms of the house are displayed as they would have been when the Perkins family celebrated one of these rituals.

In the parlor, the wedding celebration of a wealthy family is reflected by costumes, accessories, and an overabundance of greenery and garlands. Wedding gifts typical of the turn of the century are displayed in the dining room. In a front hall and another parlor, both draped in black crepe, mourning costumes and paraphernalia are displayed, as well as funeral furniture such as kneelers, votive lamps, guest register stand, and embalming tables. Details are treated with ingenuity—an enlarged photograph of a period photo depicts a turn-of-the-century wedding cake, and funeral flowers are reproduced based on photos from the period. In these heavily adorned rooms, interpreters discuss trends of the times, such as consumerism, class consciousness, and changing social views and attitudes.[7] Visitors are able to enjoy the historic house setting while learning about the social history of Akron at the turn of the century.

Interpretive Techniques

There are many interpretive techniques available for historic house museums, and many combinations of them can be used. The techniques selected will depend on the resources available such as money, staff, and time. Some of the more common techniques and tools are listed here.

Brochures and Pamphlets

The most basic interpretive tool is a written description of the historic site. Whether the museum is organized as self-guided, with descriptive labels in each room, or is fully staffed by interpreters, a general brochure that serves as introduction and souvenir is essential.

Site Orientation

Museums will often have guides stationed at the main entrance to orient visitors before they are greeted by a tour guide or go off on a self-guided tour. The overview can be a verbal recitation of the house's history or an informative videotape or slide show.

Self-Guided Tours

Self-guided tours are usually assisted by a brochure that includes a brief history of the house and its residents and a room-by-room description. Visitors set their own pace, spending time in areas that interest them and passing over those that do not.

Stationed Interpreters

In many museums, guides are stationed at strategic locations in the house and grounds to inform visitors about that particular area. They may, through vignettes, provide insights into the life of the family and events that occurred at the place. For example, an interpreter stationed in an outbuilding, one that served as slave quarters, might describe some of the realities of slave life or the slaves' religious beliefs and kinship network—helping visitors to make the connection between the setting, the objects, and the people who used them.

Guided Tours

Trained docents accompany visitors through the house, describing its residents, period rooms, and exhibits. The tours, which usually last between forty-five minutes and one hour, are prepared from scripts and attempt to involve the visitor emotionally.

Demonstrations

Demonstrators portray generic characters and usually wear costumes typical of the period. They perform real tasks—weaving cloth, baking pies, blacksmithing, spinning wool, or weeding a garden plot. Some involve the public by asking them to participate in the activity. Demonstrators often speak in the first person, an approach that can captivate the visitors and help them to sense the past. However, there is always the danger that this approach will see rather artificial. Some historic house interpreters are more comfortable using third-person speech, finding themselves better able to answer questions and relay information to visitors. A solution to the first- or third-person dilemma is to combine the techniques, choosing the proper one according to the situation.

It has been discovered at Colonial Williamsburg, for example, that the first-person approach works best for craft demonstrations and for "local color on the street" but works less well in communicating basic information about the site.[8] The interpretive staff will need to experiment in order to create a well-balanced program, one that is both enlightening and lively.

Role Playing or Character Presentation

In role playing, the interpreter presents a real person (or a composite) who was associated with the site, while demonstrators focus on performing an activity or task.

Role playing, for example, may involve a chambermaid who describes her experience while living with a family in 1885. Her per-

A demonstrator at Old Salem Restoration interprets an age-old task, splitting wood.
(Photograph courtesy of Old Salem Restoration, Winston-Salem, North Carolina)

sonality (as the maid) may be a composite of several people who actually worked at the house, with the information that helped to create her character extracted from letters, oral histories, and documents. She may be stationed in the wing of the house where she "once worked," drawing from her surroundings as she relays incidents from the past to the visitors. Role-playing interpreters are not so closely bound to their location as are demonstrators; they may wander throughout the museum, while maintaining character. Such interpreters should wear authentic reproductions of period costumes and use the dialect of the time, and their speech should be in the first person.

When role playing involves portraying a particular person, it is essential that his or her character be well researched, and thoroughly rehearsed before it is presented to the public. It may also be beneficial to try out the character on family members or friends to ensure that the "true" personality has been captured.

In some instances, the role of demonstrator and role player are merged. Take the servant who worked for a prominent family in the late nineteenth century. The costumed interpreter discusses "her" life at the house and how she acquired her job as a domestic, her social standing in the community, how she is compensated for her work, her religious views, the extent of her education, and what she might expect to do with her future. She relates this while she preserves food, washes the family's clothing, or cleans a bedroom.

Living-History Performances

Dramatic skits performed by actors (hired through area colleges or theater groups) are often held anywhere there is room—exhibit areas, on the grounds, in the ballroom or auditorium or lounge area. These presentations are intended to expand the visitors' understanding of the site and may range from a reenactment of an event (a battle scene or robbery held on the grounds), a special ritual, or a ceremony that was part of a family holiday (such as a Hanukkah celebration held in the dining room) to an exchange between family members about their views on social institutions such as slavery or working conditions in factories. Costumes are authentic reproductions, and sets can be as simple as a backdrop of a period room or as elaborate as a stage with props set up in the museum's auditorium or classroom. After the performance, interpreters—and actors—are available to answer questions and to discuss the historical events portrayed.

Lectures, Workshops, and Conferences

Some visitors will be interested in academic interpretation. In offering lectures, workshops, and conferences on topics that deal with the historic house, its collections, and associated exhibits, the museum enables individuals to explore and study more intensively a particular area of interest.

Classes for Students

The house museum can also be used as a classroom setting for students of all ages. There are many ways in which to do this. An example would be to hold a day-long session for elementary-school class during which the pupils wear clothing of the time period and spend the time learning what life was like in another era—even in another social context. They might write their lessons on slates with chalk and prepare their lunches from foods typical of the time and region. For college students, a historic house can be an environment where questions about the family as an economic, social, and psychological unit can be studied. Or classes on architecture, decorative arts, folklife, social history, social and cultural geography, American studies, archaeology, and museum studies might be taught by local teachers and professors. For a good source of curriculum ideas refer to Thomas Schlereth, *Historic Houses as Learning Laboratories: Seven Teaching Strategies.*

Combining Interpretive Techniques

A combination of several of the interpretive techniques usually works best for historic house museums. One model for a house museum might be to implement a variety of interpretive methods during various times of the year.

Visitors receive a color brochure describing the museum's history while they wait in a gathering area and view a short informative video. Exhibits, which further enhance the understanding of the visitors, are located in this area or in areas where tours terminate. Next an interpreter dressed in regular clothes leads the group through the period rooms of the house and the grounds. (In the past, this museum offered self-guided tours and had interpreters positioned at various locations around the house.)

On certain days, in this hypothetical museum, however, there is something more. Costumed demonstrators dressed in reproduced fashions of the time perform tasks of the early householders, describing their tasks as they work. Role-playing interpreters are also present. They speak in the first person, and either perform duties on the spot, like the demonstrators, or wander around the grounds, speaking with visitors. They never drop their characters! The group not only is given a firsthand look at what life was like in another time, but has the convenience of a regular guide who offers a wide range of perspectives about the house and events that made it significant.

At certain times of the year, the museum offers living-history performances, in which scenes of life and events that made the house and family significant are recounted for visitors.

The Interpreters

Training

Interpreters involved in tours, demonstrations, or role playing should be specially trained by the curator or an interpretation specialist. They must learn all that they can about their subject so that they can present a thorough tour and be prepared for the varied questions that will be asked. Visitors will respond to a guide's imaginative explanations during a room-to-room tour of a house, or a lively exchange with a costumed interpreter demonstrating the day-to-day tasks of the household.

The museum should keep all the necessary resources on hand and offer a quiet place for study. Information packets that the interpreter can take home should also be provided. Lectures, workshops, and classes presented by the historians, curators, and museum educators must be considered a staple of the training program.

Guides should be given a written description of the information the museum wishes to convey to the public. While each interpreter will have his or her own manner of delivering a tour, it is useful for everyone to have the same starting point. Guides must also be kept up to date on new developments at the site. For example, a newly installed exhibit or a rearranged period room should not be discovered in the midst of a tour. Such surprises can cause a guide embarrassment, perhaps creating skepticism in the mind of the visitor. Does the guide really know what is going on?

Demonstrators and role players should be well trained in the tasks they will be performing or the roles they will be playing—in housekeeping, beekeeping, gardening, sewing and quilting, and food preserving. All tasks and roles should be practiced and rehearsed (with performances evaluated) before the interpreter goes it alone. It has been suggested that when interpreters are playing a role in the first person, they should receive thorough training in period speech patterns as well as theatrical techniques in order to portray historical characters properly.[9] As noted earlier, first-person interpretations, if not carefully prepared, risk losing their effectiveness, actually coming across as hokey. The preparation for this type of program requires considerable research, training, and administrative support. If time and funds cannot be committed, it is best not to do it at all.

Interpreters should present their tours (or roles) to other interpreters for constructive evaluations. Occasional visitor question-

Girls, dressed in period costumes, are learning to sew, based on a sewing class taught in early Salem. *(Photograph courtesy of Old Salem Restoration, Winston-Salem, North Carolina)*

naires at the end of tours can shed light on how well the presentation was received. Self-evaluation—using a tape recorder or a videotape—is also an effective means of assessment. Interpreters must modify the tour for the age groups involved. Youngsters, of course, will need a different presentation than that given to a group of adults. Be prepared for a variety of ages and try different techniques for each group.

Presentation

It is tedious for visitors to endure a haphazard, fragmented presentation or an expressionless recitation of historical facts. Ill-prepared, dull presentations will cause visitors to wander away from the tour, either physically or mentally. Children, especially, will protest with poor behavior or vocal criticism. On the other hand, good interpretation will stimulate visitors to ask questions and perhaps draw comparison to their own lives.

Interpreters should speak clearly, establishing eye contact with visitors. They should convey information with enthusiasm, never in a condescending or superior tone. When questions arise, they should be addressed clearly and concisely. If the answer to a question is not at hand, the interpreter should admit uncertainty, and seek to have it answered by a curator or site manager at the end of the tour.[10] Unfortunately, some historic houses are so steeped in myth that it has been difficult to correct misconceptions, and many questions have been left unanswered. Faced with such situations, the interpreter should state that few historic records are available but that research continues and, as facts are uncovered, they will be passed on the visitors.

Costumed interpreters demonstrate pie making in the kitchen of the Alexander Ramsey House, St. Paul, Minnesota. (Photograph courtesy of the Minnesota Historical Society)

The gardens and grounds of house museums can provide lovely settings for picnics, wedding ceremonies, and special events. (Lyndhurst, Tarrytown, New York, a property of the National Trust for Historic Preservation)

Guides should be able to inform visitors about the locations of necessary facilities, where they can rest, how long the tour will be, and how far they will have to walk. They must also explain why artifacts, wallpapers, historic fabrics, silver light fixtures, and other objects cannot be handled—educating visitors of the importance of protection and preservation.

When conducting tours, interpreters should explain the lives of the residents in the way they were actually lived. It is important to present a balanced view and not to shy away from controversy. On the other hand, dwelling on sensational aspects should be avoided— a suicide in the dining room, a murder in the parlor, or a spouse's illicit affairs.

In order to achieve a more comprehensive interpretation of the house, try to include other historic features at the site, such as the gardens and grounds, outbuildings, family gravesites, slave quarters, and other architectural components—all of which are part of the house's history.

All interpreters—volunteer or paid staff—must maintain a high degree of professionalism when explaining a house museum to the public. Often the guide is the only contact that visitors have with the museum, and their views about the site are formed on the basis of this association. Therefore, competency, sincerity, friendliness, and enthusiasm are of utmost importance in selecting individuals as interpreters.

Museum Accessibility

It is a museum's responsibility to provide all people with an opportunity to share in the experience it has to offer. In fact, on July 26, 1991, the Americans with Disabilities Act (ADA), which prohibits discrimination against persons with disabilities and mandates the removal of barriers faced by the disabled, was signed by George Bush. Because of this law, museums are determining their level of accessibility and implementing changes to provide further access to the disabled.

Accessibility is a complicated issue. Making a museum house accessible to the disabled may be as simple as installing a wood ramp at one of the entrances to allow access to the first floor. But it may also involve changing the physical appearance of the historic house, as well as potentially costly modifications—installing curb cuts, enlarging sidewalks and walkways, and adding larger doors and even elevators.

One question arises because of a law under the Historic Preservation Act of 1966, which directs that if a museum is on the National Register of Historic Places the building must be protected and kept from being altered in any way that might compromise its historical integrity. How, then, can the staff of a historic house museum, with an eye to preserving the building's physical structure, modify it to allow access to the disabled mandated by the Americans with Disabilities Act? The ADA is designed to work *with* the Historic Preservation Act. Physical access to public buildings is paramount to ADA; however, it is meant to be implemented without placing "undue burden" or "undue hardship" on public or private museums. Consequently, the ADA suggests alternative methods of access when alteration will threaten or destroy the historic significance of a building or if an institution cannot afford to make the alterations. For example, if it is not feasible to install an elevator, the museum might instead show videotapes of its upper floors to visitors who are unable to climb stairs. Contact your State Historic Preservation officer to determine if ADA guidelines would threaten or destroy the historic significance of your facility.

An important feature of the ADA is that each museum is examined case by case. An accessibility consultant will evaluate your building according to ADA guidelines, and can suggest how to make changes without too much difficulty or expense. Examples are installing access ramps; making curb cuts; repositioning shelves, tables, chairs, vending machines, or telephones; adding raised markings on elevator control buttons; widening doors; installing accessible door hardware; installing grab bars in toilet stalls; and removing high-pile, low density carpeting.

It is important to begin planning for the modifications needed in making your museum accessible. Become familiar with the ADA. Build accessibility improvements into your five-year plan; goals are more easily met if they are spread out over a period of time. Improvements may require fund raising. Contact your State Historic Preservation Office for availability of funds. (At present there are no federal funds to assist historic house museums in improving physical access; however, this may change in the future.)

Request a copy of the Americans with Disabilities Act rules and regulations from

> Department of Justice
> Civil Rights Division
> P.O. Box 66118
> Washington, D.C.
> (202) 514–0301

Modifying for Access

Staff and volunteers should have formal training in the requirements of different disabled groups, techniques for communicating and providing assistance, and information on the location of accessible facilities.[11]

The museum must offer places to rest in the lobby or waiting area, and along the tour route for those who might experience fatigue. Visitors should also be informed at the onset of how far they will be walking on the tour. If the full tour is too long for some visitors, consider offering an abbreviated tour as well. Public rest rooms and drinking fountains should be modified to accommodate wheelchair users. It is also useful for the museum to designate a staff person to assist disabled visitors in getting in and out of their vehicles, and going up and down ramps.

Some changes to increase access to the visually impaired can be made quite simply. Enlarging the type size on exhibit labels, making a second set of labels in braille, or offering hand-held magnifiers will assist visitors in reading standard labels. (Contact the nearest agency for the visually impaired and its staff will be able to refer you to braille sign-makers in the area.) Audio guides are a useful aid. The equipment needed to prepare them is inexpensive and readily available: a cassette tape recorder, headphones, blank tapes, and an interpreter to record the tour through the house.

Tactile accessibility should also be explored. Can some objects from collections be made available for disabled visitors to experience by touching? Obviously, a program of this sort should not be implemented without supervision, but it is an option to consider. A visually impaired visitor can greatly benefit from being able to touch a heavy pewter stein or a crudely carved wooden bowl.[12]

For the hearing impaired, the museum should provide closed captioning on video productions, and sign-language interpreters should be available when needed. It is helpful to get to know several interpreters and to teach them about the museum and its collections. Their expanded knowledge and understanding will enhance the tours for deaf visitors. Most states have an interpreter referral service or center where interpreters can be located. For the number in your state, call the National Registry of Interpreters for the Deaf in Silver Springs, Maryland, (301) 608–0050. This organization will provide the number to the nearest referral center.

Specially designed tours should also be made available for the learning impaired. Teachers and advisors with specialties in learning disabilities can make suggestions in creating meaningful tours.

Disabled visitors need to feel welcome in the museum environment. Genuine friendliness and helpfulness are elements that all historic house museums can incorporate into their programs.

Facilities, Gift Shops, and Conveniences

It is important for visitors to be made comfortable during their stay, so it is necessary to provide adequate facilities inside, and outside, if outdoor use is permitted. Make sure to have adequate accommodations, such as benches and chairs for people to pause and absorb what they have learned as they rest. Remember, museum fatigue affects both the feet and the psyche of those who join the historic house tours. Also provide an adequate number of rest rooms, drinking fountains, and trash receptacles for visitor convenience.

Maintenance staff should make regular checks to keep rest rooms clean and well supplied. If the museum provides eating facilities, such as lunchrooms or picnic areas, they must be kept clean and free from food and debris. Trash receptacles must be monitored, emptied, and cleaned frequently.

If vending machines are provided for visitors, make certain that they operate properly and are well maintained, and that there is change available for using the machines. Some museums sell snacks such as cookies, rolls, coffee, fruit, and sandwiches. These must be kept fresh—to prevent food poisoning—and food handlers must adhere to state health codes for preparing, handling, and selling food to the public.

Outdoor Facilities

House museums offer a range of outdoor facilities, from elaborate formal gardens restored to their historic appearance to simple grounds. Many museums provide facilities such as picnic grounds, rest areas, walkways through wooded areas, and even outdoor arenas where programs are held.

In most museums, visitors are left to enjoy the grounds at their leisure, and tours are self guided. However, some do have staff who specialize in horticulture or landscape architecture to guide tours and answer questions. Other museums provide only prearranged tours or special tours during certain times of the year.

Whatever the arrangements, visitors should be informed in advance about what they can expect once outside the museum building. It is essential for visitors to know the museum's rules for using the grounds; these should be listed on signs or relayed by a tour guide. Do not expect visitors to read rules printed only in a brochure. If grounds are extensive, provide a map showing locations of picnic areas, rest rooms, accessible walkways, and trash receptacles.

Consider assigning a guard—either paid or volunteer—to patrol the grounds in order to answer questions, assist visitors, alert the maintenance staff when supplies are low in rest rooms, and reinforce the museum's rules.

It is imperative to keep grounds well maintained to lend to the beauty of the surroundings, as well as to provide a safe environment for visitors. Grass should be kept well manicured, and bushes and trees well trimmed. Low-hanging branches or overgrown walkways not only look bad, but pose a hazard. Always put away lawn equipment and chemicals after use, and keep garden hoses, sprinklers, trowels, and rakes away from areas where visitors may walk.

Renting Facilities

Some museums open their outdoor facilities to the public for rental. Weddings, receptions, conferences, business events, and parties are popular events held on museum grounds. It is important to have a written policy that outlines procedures, rules of use, responsibilities and liabilities of renters, and a fee schedule. In addition, a contract must be drawn up between the renter and the museum.

The museum may want to obtain a special insurance rider when the grounds are being rented to cover damages that may be incurred. (The expense for this extra coverage should be paid by the renters.) The museum's insurance company can provide specific information.

Gift Shops

Operating a museum is an expensive endeavor, and it is generally agreed that starting a gift shop is a good way to earn capital to help defray expenses. In fact, a well-managed gift shop is a means of providing funds to add exhibits, make repairs to the structure, and create programs. Frequently, small museums use profits earned from gift shops, coupled with membership and entrance fees, to keep the doors open and the museum running.

Most often, the museum will set up the store, establishing a location within the building or on the grounds, purchasing the stock, and hiring or recruiting a manager to run it. However, gift shops in museums occasionally are operated by independent nonprofit organizations that raise money to support the museum. Because they are independent, they have their own board of directors and are largely self-governed. Sometimes the museum may rent space to an independent shop if some of the profits are returned to the museum.

Most museum gift shops operate as nonprofit entities and benefit from the museum's tax-exempt status. But before opening a store, be sure to seek legal council on the proper procedures; the process is complicated, and laws change pertaining to such businesses. It is also helpful to contact the Museum Store Association for advice about where and how to begin. This nonprofit membership organization was formed to provide its members with skills for effective store management, resources for locating relevant products for the store, and information on government actions that affect the museum store industry.[13]

WHAT TO SELL

The type of merchandise sold in the shop should relate to the identity and personality of the museum house and its former inhabitants. Artifacts in the house can offer clues about what to stock. Reproductions of teapots, glass and wooden bowls, quilts, and coffee grinders are products that are often available. Books relating to architecture, life during the period, or activities in which the family was involved, and even history books of the region or state are related items that could be sold.

If children were an important component of the museum's story, sell old-fashioned, handmade games, toys, and dolls, and childrens' books, paper dolls, and patterns for doll clothes.

If gardening was an emphasis of the historic family or even of the time period, sell seeds, books on gardening, and simple gardening tools. Offer objects that are associated with articles made and discussed at programs or demonstrations at the site—handmade baskets, silver jewelry, silk flowers, or wooden household utensils.

For ethnic museums, it is important to purchase merchandise that reflects the heritage. A trip to the country being represented may be necessary in order to stock authentic objects.

Ask visitors what they would be interested in buying. Offer a range of prices and quality to make objects affordable to the diverse people who will shop.

THE WORK FORCE

Volunteers make up the staff at gift shops in many museum houses, although it is not unusual for store managers to have paid positions because of the demanding nature of the job. Store managers often recruit the volunteers and organize and direct them, as well as conduct the business of buying and selling the store's merchandise. This is a time-consuming and important task that requires a responsible and dedicated person. (Generally the more income earned by the store, the more paid positions there are.)

Museum shop volunteers should be recruited and managed in much the same way as volunteers working in other areas. The rules of thumb are make sure that the job description is clear and that each person knows what is expected of him or her and how the shop is operated; correctly match the right person with the right job; offer job changes to prevent burnout; praise and encourage the staff's efforts; consider carefully who will work, and make sure there is always a leader (a knowledgeable and capable volunteer or employee) scheduled to solve efficiently the inevitable problems that arise with customers.

Those working in museum shops have a dual role; they must understand the merchandise they sell, and they must know the museum. Visitors will expect shop staff to be knowledgeable about exhibits, programs, and even the collections. They will ask questions pertaining to the museum—the times it is open, where facilities are located, and when the presentations begin. Regularly scheduled meetings, even a gift shop newsletter, will help the staff keep up to date. It is also helpful to have on hand "Information Sheets" that answer stock questions and provide an update.

NOTES

1. Fred E. H. Schroeder, *Interpreting and Reinterpreting Associative Historic Sites and Artifacts,* Technical Report, no. 6 (Nashville, Tenn.: American Association for State and Local History, 1986), p. 7.

2. William Alderson and Shirley Payne Low, *Interpretation of Historic Sites,* 2d ed. (Nashville: American Association for State and Local History, 1985), pp. 12–21.

3. William T. Alderson, personal communication, January 5, 1991.

4. For a detailed discussion of goals and objectives in planning interpretive programs, turn to Carolyn P. Blackmon, Teresa K. LaMaster, Lisa C. Roberts, and Beverly Serrell, *Open Conversations: Strategies for Professional Development in Museums* (Chicago: Department of Education, Field Museum of Natural History, 1990).

5. Jeffery Smith, "Rites of Passage," *History News* 44, no. 1 (1989): 29.

6. Ibid., pp. 29–31.

7. Ibid., p. 30.

8. Alderson, personal communication, January 5, 1991.

9. Warren Leon and Roy Rosenzweig, *History Museums in the United States* (Champaign: University of Illinois Press, 1989), p. 89.

10. Alderson and Low, *Interpretation of Historic Sites,* p. 60.

11. Larry Molloy, "Museum Accessibility: The Continuing Dialogue," *Museum News* 60, no. 2 (1981): 56.

12. Ibid., pp. 53–54.

13. The Museum Store Association, Inc., is located at 501 South Cherry Street, Suite 460, Denver, Colorado, 80222. The phone number is (303) 329–6968. The Museum Store Association provides a quarterly magazine, a membership directory, and other special interest publications. It organizes an annual meeting dealing with current topics in various locations around the United States.

11

Volunteers in the
Historic House Museum

I have often admired the extreme skill they show in proposing
a common object for the exertions of very many and in induc-
ing them voluntarily to pursue it.

Alexis de Tocqueville, *Democracy in America*

WHEN FRENCH STATESMAN and writer Alexis de Tocqueville traveled in the United States in 1831 and 1832, he was amazed by the
generosity of Americans in lending their time and expertise voluntarily. Today that same spirit persists for the benefit of individuals, institutions, and communities. In this tradition, volunteers
continue to fill vital roles in American museums, with some 70,000
serving throughout the country.[1] Without volunteers the majority
of smaller museums, especially historic houses, would not be able
to open their doors.

A recent National Trust survey indicates that more than 65 percent of historic property museums are run solely by volunteers.
Frequently, they are residents of the town where the museum is
located or are members of local groups that strive to preserve and
administer the historic structure. Volunteers often undertake the
major tasks of establishing a board of trustees, appointing a director or curator, recruiting guides, and even finding local assistance
for the museum's cleaning and maintenance needs.

Volunteers come to the house museum because they are interested in the history of their community or region and they want to
offer their time and their knowledge. Because they often bring

special skills and professional experience to the museum position, they have greater expectations of what museums can offer them.

Curators of historic house museums must know how to recruit, organize, manage, and train volunteers. Where does the museum find volunteers and how are they recruited? And once recruited, how are they retained?

Recruiting Volunteers

An understanding of what motivates people to volunteer will aid in both recruiting and retaining volunteers. One or more of the following motives often prompts people to seek volunteer positions in historic house museums.

- Self-fulfillment and personal esteem through ties with organizations they value.
- A personal commitment to better the community.
- A desire to work for social change and reform by aiding in the preservation of historic sites and properties.
- A need to increase or sharpen marketable skills and to gain references for employment.
- A desire to continue the use of special skills after retirement (as computer programmer, draftsperson, writer, researcher, electrician).
- A desire to meet people and make new friends.
- A means to earn academic credit (as a student intern).

Regardless of the reasons volunteers choose to work at museums, once they are there, their roles and responsibilities must be clearly defined. A systematic approach to structuring the individual's positions and roles will help to create order and will give volunteers a sense of direction and purpose within the organization.

How and Where to Find Volunteers

A good method of establishing a volunteer program is by advertising openings in local newspapers, the museum's newsletter or a flyer in a regular museum mailing, and press releases sent to schools and professional groups. Radio spots (public-service announcements) can also stimulate interest in potential volunteers.

A successful volunteer program is often the best way to recruit volunteers. Word-of-mouth recruiting is frequently used by smaller museums and fills their volunteer needs. And holding an open house in which the existing volunteer staff members perform their jobs and discuss their responsibilities is also a good way to entice potential volunteers. Other methods of finding volunteers include slide-show presentations before targeted audiences, such as retired teachers or soon-to-retire employees from large companies in the community.

An example of an ad in a newsletter might be:

MUSEUM TOUR GUIDES NEEDED

Outgoing individuals with a love of history will find volunteering as a tour guide enjoyable and rewarding. Share your knowledge of our historic building and your enthusiasm for our cultural heritage. Training in guiding tours will be provided.

Use a wide variety of outside special-interest publications to announce positions. Keep local organizations in mind—weavers' guilds, lace-makers' associations, and woodworking and blacksmith guilds are excellent sources. Not only can their members provide skills needed by the museum, but they also have great enthusiasm for their crafts. Reaching out into the community by contacting such organizations can increase the visibility of the museum.

An example of an ad for the newsletter of a local weavers' guild might be:

The historic house museum is looking for volunteers to help preserve its textile and costume collections. Due to a major reorganization of the storage areas, volunteer help is needed for rolling large textiles on tubes, lining storage areas with muslin, padding costumes with acid-free paper, and stabilizing textiles for exhibition. A three-session training course will be provided for all volunteers. Contact the curator for details.

Government Agencies

There are agencies whose sole purpose is recruiting and referring volunteers, and they can also be valuable resources. For example,

Voluntary Action Centers (VAC), also known as Volunteer Bureaus, operates 387 volunteer clearinghouses throughout the United States. VAC, an excellent source for locating potential volunteers, offers its services to all museums. (Refer to your state office on volunteer services for Voluntary Action Centers in your community or contact The National Volunteer Center [VOLUNTEER] in Arlington, Virginia.)

The Management Assistant Project (MAP), is run through the United Way. MAP fills requests for professional assistance for museum management problems, ranging from establishing personnel policies to recruiting trustees. Although MAP charges a fee for its service, it can be negotiated or waived altogether, depending on the finances of the organization. To learn more about MAP, contact your local United Way office.

The Retired Seniors Volunteer Program (RSVP) matches qualified volunteers with positions in community organizations. RSVP is found throughout the country listed under the state ACTION office (the umbrella agency for federal government volunteer programs).

Many state governments have an office on volunteerism, check the state office listings in your telephone directory.

Corporate Retiree Programs

Many corporations offer volunteer services through their corporate retirees' program, matching former employees with appropriate volunteer positions in the community.

Honeywell, Inc., a large corporation based in Minnesota, offers one such program. This service, staffed by former Honeywell employees, taps a wide range of expertise, providing historic house museums with retirees skilled in areas from photography and lighting to office work and management consulting. Requests for volunteers are recorded on a computer database that matches qualified retirees to position openings.

Internships in the Museum: Help from Colleges and Universities

Museum internship programs offer students a challenging environment in which to work and an opportunity to earn academic credit while gaining experience. Internships can vary from a one-month "career exploration" course to programs that last a full school year.

Museums use interns to research collections or to assist in registering, storing, inventorying, and cataloging them. Interns can also help to plan and prepare exhibits by researching and writing labels and copy for pamphlets and catalogs. Students with the requisite skills can be assigned basic carpentry or photography. The curator may limit applicants to those with a background in American history, American studies, museology, or other fields.

All internships should include a written agreement or "learning contract" between the curator (or director, or site manager), the student, and the faculty adviser from the academic institution. This agreement should describe in detail the nature of the job, the number of hours the job will entail, and how many academic credits the job will carry. The intern, curator, and adviser should establish a method for evaluating the intern's service. Will it be a written record or journal of days spent at the museum? Will it be an oral presentation given in class or seminar? The adviser may ask the museum staff to assess in writing the intern's competence, attitude, initiative, and other traits observed during the internship.

Basics of a Volunteer Program

Applications and Interviews

Interested potential volunteers should complete a detailed application, including work experience and references. Carefully review the applications and call references, determining whether the applicants would work well in the museum. Then meet with each volunteer in person, and make clear the expectations of the museum: a commitment to the goals of the museum and its mission, mandatory training sessions, and a contribution of a minimum number of hours.

Placement

Consider the interests, former training, talents, and motivation of individuals before placing them. Be sensitive to both the needs and the expectations of the volunteer and the museum. Ask questions. Do not assume that because those with experience, for example, as a computer operator or an electrician, will wish to do similar work in the museum. Volunteers may be looking for a challenge—for new and very different work from their everyday occupation.

Job Descriptions

Working together, supervisor and volunteer should write a description of the volunteer's job. The description should include the volunteer's qualification, occupation, and employer or former employer and specify special skills that are needed. If the supervisor is also a volunteer, he or she should work with the director or board to define the job.

Job descriptions can be helpful in documenting volunteer assistance when applying for grants. Generally, a strong volunteer program indicates excellence in museum standards and a dedication to the museum from individuals and benefactors.

Training

Training volunteers not only provides the museum with a skilled resource, but enriches the work experience and education of the volunteers. Further, it adds to the confidence of the volunteers in carrying out their jobs—they know that the museum is investing in them.

Skilled staff members should provide the training: the interpreters should train the docents, and the curator should train those who will be working with collections. Training should be continual and adapted to the museum's changing exhibits and programs. Videotape training sessions for future use and for use by volunteers who are unable to attend at scheduled times. "Experts" from outside the museum can also be recruited for training. For example, bring in a head guard from a larger museum to discuss new techniques and procedures for securing the museum.

Basic training should include familiarizing all volunteers with the museum's bylaws, mission statement, collections policy, and code of ethics. All volunteers should have a copy of the *Museum Code of Ethics* (see Chapters 2 and 4). Volunteers serving as curators, directors, or members of the board of trustees must be aware of the specific codes that pertain to their roles and responsibilities in the museum. Managers of historic house museums, whether volunteer or paid staff, are responsible for the care of the objects and buildings held in public trust.

Performance Evaluations

The museum should plan to evaluate the work of its volunteers periodically. By taking the time to evaluate their views and attitudes, as well as their work, the relationship between unpaid and paid staff can be strengthened. Include in the evaluation basic questions on performance: Do the volunteers understand the museum's goals? Is their work commitment being fulfilled? Are they satisfied with the kind of work in which they are involved? In the process, consider if adequate training has been provided the volunteers and if they are serving in appropriate roles.

Volunteers should also be given the opportunity to reevaluate their own positions and goals; this can help to promote their continued interest in the organization. Some museums use peer evaluation to assess the performance and function of volunteers. This system works best where volunteers have received similar training, allowing for balanced comparison of one another's performance and exchange of constructive suggestions.

Regular Informational Meetings

Staff members must meet regularly with volunteers to acquaint them with new procedures, current projects, new positions, and forthcoming exhibitions. These meetings can also serve as a forum for volunteers to present problems and developments in the museum about which the staff might be unaware. Informational meetings should also promote cohesiveness among the volunteer staff and reinforce the connection between the volunteer and the museum.

Scheduling and Documenting Volunteer Time

A schedule of the volunteer's work hours and vacations should be prepared and made available for easy reference. It often works well to have volunteers sign up for a month at a time, with a certain number of hours committed to ensure that the volunteer is recognized as a staff member. (Twelve hours a month is an average commitment.)

A separate chart with the volunteer's name, position, and number of hours contributed is a useful record for the museum. For example, the grant application for the Institute of Museum Service's general operating support program asks about volunteer involvement, which such a chart can document.

Volunteer Recognition: The Key to Success

Formal recognition is essential when acknowledging the service of volunteers. Traditionally, museums have acknowledged their volunteers' efforts with an annual celebration, in addition to plaques, pins, and awards. These serve to strengthen volunteer camaraderie. But the informal appreciation that is shown day to day can be the most satisfying kind of recognition. For example, provide volunteers with a positive work environment; parking, desk space, coffee, refreshments—small measures such as these go a long way in expressing appreciation. Include volunteers in staff meetings and decision making: being personally recognized and greeted by the museum's paid staff or board of trustees is important—recognition that will stimulate a positive work environment.

Recognition for volunteer service can take many forms.

- Profiles in the museum's newsletter.
- Discounts in the museum store.
- Free membership in the museum.
- Complimentary tickets to exhibition openings, receptions, lectures, movies, and special events.
- Presentation of service awards, such as plaques and certificates. Often the governor's office will have signed certificates that can be given to special volunteers.
- Sabbaticals to volunteers who feel burned out.
- Letters of commendation.
- Free enrollment in the American Association of Museum Volunteers, a representative organization of all volunteers in American museums.

National, State, and Federal Volunteer Organizations

National Organizations

The American Association of Museum Volunteers (AAMV, affiliated with the American Association of Museums) is a membership organization specifically designed for museum volunteers. It is open to individual, salaried staff, and group participation and represents more than 22,000 museum volunteers. AAMV's mission is to promote professional standards in volunteering in museums, to serve as a center for information about volunteer activities, and to provide continuing education for volunteers and volunteer managers.

Each state has an AAMV-appointed representative responsible for fielding calls concerning museum volunteering, giving presentations to museums in the state concerning AAMV, and informing museum professionals about the organization. (To locate this representative, contact your state museum association or call the AAMV office; see listing in the Appendix).

There are other national associations that support volunteer leaders, promote the study of voluntarism, and provide information and support. These associations often are affiliated with the national organization Association for Volunteer Administration (AVA).

- Association for Volunteer Administration (AVA). AVA is a professional association for those working in the field of volunteer management who want to develop their professional skills and shape the future of voluntarism. Services include certification, a quarterly journal, and regional and national conferences.[2]
- Association of Voluntary Action Scholars (AVAS). AVAS is an association of scholars and professionals seeking to stimulate and distribute research and inquiry in the field of voluntary activity.
- The National Volunteer Center (VOLUNTEER). VOLUNTEER serves as a national advocate for volunteering and citizen involvement, encouraging the more effective use of volunteers in community problem solving. This organization helps to improve volunteer management skills by providing information-sharing, training, and technical assistance services.
- Nonprofit Management Association (NMA). The purpose of this organization is to stimulate ideas and develop professional skills among those who provide management and technical assistance to nonprofit organizations.

State Government Offices

Many state governments have offices that provide services to the volunteer community. Their mission is to encourage and sustain volunteer programs, citizen participation, and public and private partnerships that contribute to the quality of life for the state's citizens. (Check the telephone directory for the state office listing.)

State-run volunteer services fulfill their mission by

- Lobbying on volunteer issues.
- Conducting research on various aspects of volunteering and disseminating on volunteer programs and resources.
- Communicating with volunteers and community leaders and responding to requests for technical assistance.
- Increasing the visibility and status of volunteers.
- Providing training in volunteer-related issues, trends, and techniques.
- Maintaining a library of resource material.

Federal Agency

ACTION is the umbrella federal agency for volunteer programs. Its purpose is to stimulate voluntarism and to demonstrate the effectiveness of volunteers in problem solving. Its programs concerning museum volunteers are Retired Senior Volunteers (RSVP) and Volunteers in Service to America (VISTA). (Addresses of these organizations are listed in the Appendix.)

Assessing the museum's volunteer needs, planning a workable volunteer program, recruiting volunteers, and acknowledging their work are all essential elements in a well-managed museum. A volunteer program is a symbiotic relationship, meeting the needs of both the participants and the institution. A strong volunteer staff is an invaluable resource in accomplishing a museum's goals.

NOTES

This chapter has been published in part as Sherry Butcher-Younghans, "Using Volunteers in History," *History News* 43, no. 4 (1988): 11–14.

1. According to the American Association for Museum Volunteers there are over 70,000 volunteers who serve in museums in the United States.

2. Descriptions of volunteer organizations are excerpted from a listing of national volunteer resource organizations compiled by the Minnesota Office on Volunteer Services.

APPENDIX

Organizations

Advisory Council on Historic
Preservation
1100 Pennsylvania Avenue, Suite
809
Washington, D.C. 20004
(202) 786-0503

American Arts Alliance
424 C Street NE
Washington, D.C. 20002

American Association for State
and Local History
530 Church Street,
Suite 600
Nashville, Tennessee 37219
(615) 255-2971

American Association of
Botanical Gardens and
Arboreta
Department of Horticulture
Box 3530
Las Cruces, New Mexico 88003

American Association of
Museums
1225 Eye Street NW,
Suite 200
Washington, D.C. 20005
(202) 289-1818

American Association of Museum
Volunteers
Wadsworth Atheneum
600 Main Street
Hartford, Connecticut 06103

American Historical Association
400 A Street SE
Washington, D.C. 20003
(202) 544-2422

American Institute for
Conservation of Historic and
Artistic Work
1400 16th Street NW,
Suite 340
Washington, D.C. 20036
(202) 232-6636

American Institute of Architects
1735 New York Avenue NW
Washington, D.C. 20004
(202) 626-7300

American Library Association
50 E. Huron
Chicago, Illinois 60611
(312) 944-6780

American Society of Landscape
Architects
Committee on Historic
Preservation
1733 Connecticut Avenue NW
Washington, D.C. 20009
(202) 686-2752

American Studies Association
University of Maryland
South Campus
Surge Building, Room 2101
College Park, Maryland 20742
(301) 405-1354

Association for Living History
  Farms and Agricultural
  Museums
National Museum of American
  History
Smithsonian Institution,
  Room 2235
Washington, D.C. 20560
(202) 357-2095

Association for Preservation
  Technology
P.O. Box 8178
Fredericksburg, Virginia 22404
(703) 373-1621

Canadian Conservation Institute
1030 Innes Road
Ottawa, Ontario KIA OC8
Canada
(613) 998-3721

Canadian Museums Association
280 Metcalfe Street,
  Suite 202
Ottawa, Ontario K2P 1R7
Canada

Center on History-Making
  in America
Indiana University
1503 E. Third Street,
  Suite 201–202
Bloomington, Indiana 47405
(812) 855-8639

Institute for the Conservation of
  Cultural Material (ICCM)
P.O. Box 1638
Canberra City
Canberra, A.C.T. 2601
Australia

International Centre for the
  Study of the Preservation and
  the Restoration of Cultural
  Property
Via San Michele 13
00153 Rome
Italy

International Council of
  Museums
Maison de l'Unesco
1 rue Miollis
Paris XVe
France

International Institute for
  Conservation of Historic and
  Artistic Works
6 Buckingham Street
London WC2N 6BA
England

Museum Store Association
501 South Cherry,
  Suite 460
Denver, Colorado 80222
(303) 329-6968

National Council on Public
  History
301 Cavanaugh Hall
425 University
Indiana University
Indianapolis, Indiana 46202
(317) 274-2716

National Institute for the
  Conservation of Cultural
  Property
3299 K Street NW, Suite 403
Washington, D.C. 20007
(202) 357-2295

National Park Service (NPS)
U.S. Department of the Interior
P.O. Box 37127
Washington, D.C. 20013-7127
(202) 208-4747

National Register of Historic
  Places
1100 L Street, Suite 6209
Washington, D.C. 20005
(202) 343-9536

National Trust for Historic
  Preservation
1785 Massachusetts Avenue NW
Washington, D.C. 20036
(202) 673-4000

New York State Conservation
  Consultancy
2199 Saw Mill River Road
Elmsford, New York 10523
(914) 592-4901

Organization of American
  Historians
112 N. Bryan Street
Bloomington, Indiana 47408
(812) 855-7311

Smithsonian Institution
Traveling Exhibition Services
  (SITES)
1100 Jefferson Drive, SW, Room
  3146
Washington, D.C. 20560
(202) 357-3168

Society for American
  Archaeology
808 Seventeenth Street NW,
  Suite 200
Washington, D.C. 20006
(202) 223-9774

Society for the Preservation of
  New England Antiquities
  (SPNEA)
Harrison Gray Otis House
141 Cambridge Street
Boston, Massachusetts
  02114-2799
(617) 227-3956

Society of American Archivists
600 South Federal, Suite 504
Chicago, Illinois 60605
(312) 922-0140

Society of Architectural
  Historians
1232 Pine Street
Philadelphia, Pennsylvania
  19107-5944
(215) 735-0224

Textile Conservation Workshop,
  Inc.
Main Street
South Salem, New York 10590
(914) 763-5805

Urban History Association
Department of History
Lake Forest College
555 N. Sheridan Road
Lake Forest, Illinois 60045
(708) 234-3100

Victorian Society in America
The Anthenaeum
East Washington Square
Philadelphia, Pennsylvania 19106
(215) 627-4252

Funding Agencies that Help
the Historic House Museum

Institute of Museum Services
  (IMS)
1100 Pennsylvania Avenue NW,
  Suite 510
Washington, D.C. 20506
(202) 786-0536

J. Paul Getty Trust
Grant Program
1875 Century Park East,
  Suite 2300
Los Angeles, California 90067
(213) 277-9188

National Endowment for the Arts
    (NEA)
1100 Pennsylvania Avenue NW,
    Suite 803
Washington, D.C. 20506
(202) 682-2000

National Endowment for the
    Humanities (NEH)
1100 Pennsylvania Avenue NW,
    Suite 803
Washington, D.C. 20506
(202) 786-0438

National Science Foundation
1800 G Street NW, Suite 520
Washington, D.C. 20550
(202) 357-9498

Smithsonian Institution
Office of Fellowships and Grants
955 L'Enfant Plaza, Suite 7300
Washington, D.C. 20560
(202) 287-3271

Regional Conservation Centers and Associations

Most of the following are listed in American Association of Museums *Caring for Collections: Strategies for Conservation, Maintenance and Documentation* (Washington, D.C.: American Association of Museums, 1984).

These twelve regional centers function as nonprofit conservation laboratories for use by museums, historical societies libraries and universities.

Balboa Art Conservation Center
P.O. Box 3755
San Diego, California 92103
(619) 236-9702

Center for Conservation and
    Technical Studies
Fogg Art Museum
Harvard University
Cambridge, Massachusetts 02138
(617) 495-2392

Conservation Center for Art and
    Historic Artifacts
264 S. 23rd Street
Philadelphia, Pennsylvania 19103
(215) 545-0613

Intermuseum Conservation
    Association
Allen Art Building
Oberlin, Ohio 44074
(216) 775-7331

New York State Office of Parks
    and Recreation
Bureau of Historic Sites
Collections Care Center
Peebles Island
Waterford, New York 12188
(518) 237-8643

Northeast Document
    Conservation Center
Abbott Hall
24 School Street
Andover, Massachusetts 01810
(617) 470-1010

Pacific Regional Conservation
    Center
Bishop Museum
P.O. Box 19000-A
Honolulu, Hawaii 96817
(808) 847-3511

Rocky Mountain Regional
   Conservation Center
University of Denver
2420 S. University Boulevard
Denver, Colorado 80208
(303) 733-2712

Texas Conservation Center
Panhandle-Plains Historical
   Museum
Box 967, W.T. Station
Canyon, Texas 79016
(806) 656-2238

Textile Conservation Center
800 Massachusetts Avenue
North Andover, Massachusetts
   01845
(617) 686-0191

Upper Midwest Conservation
   Association
2400 3rd Avenue South
Minneapolis, Minnesota 55404
(612) 870-3120

Williamstown Regional Art
   Conservation Laboratory, Inc.
Clark Art Institute
225 South Street
Williamstown, Massachusetts
   01267

Organizations For and About Volunteers

ACTION
1100 Vermont Avenue NW
Washington, D.C. 20525
(202) 634-9108

American Association for
   Museum Volunteers
1225 Eye Street NW,
   Suite 200
Washington, D.C. 20005
(202) 289-6575

Association for Volunteer
   Administration (AVA)
P.O. Box 4584
Boulder, Colorado 80306
(303) 541-0238

Association of Voluntary Action
   Scholars (AVAS)
Lincoln-Filene Center
Tufts University
Medford, Massachusetts 02155
(617) 381-3449

National Volunteer Center
   (VOLUNTEER)
1111 North 19th Street,
   Suite 500
Arlington, Virginia 22209
(703) 276-0542

Nonprofit Management
   Association (NMA)
c/o United Way of Minneapolis
P.O. Box 2350
Minneapolis, Minnesota 55402
(612) 340-7591

REFERENCES

Chapter 2

American Association of Museums. *Museum Ethics.* 2d ed. Washington, D.C.: American Association of Museums, 1991.

———. *Museums for a New Century.* Washington, D.C.: American Association of Museums, 1984.

Burcaw, G. Ellis. *Introduction to Museum Work.* 2d ed. Nashville, Tenn.: American Association for State and Local History, 1983.

Conway, Mary Ellen. "A Made-for-Television Historic House Series: From Opera to Sitcom." *History News* 43, no. 3 (1988): 18–25.

Diamond, Susan Z. *Preparing Administrative Manuals.* New York: AMACOM, 1981.

George, Gerald, and Cindy Sherrell-Leo. *Starting Right: A Basic Guide to Museum Planning.* Nashville, Tenn.: American Association for State and Local History, 1986.

McHugh, Alice. "Strategic Planning for Museums." *Museum News* 58, no. 6 (1980): 23–29.

Malaro, Marie C. *A Legal Primer on Managing Museum Collections.* Washington, D.C.: Smithsonian Institution Press, 1985.

Miller, Ronald L. *Personnel Policies for Museums: A Handbook for Management.* Washington, D.C.: American Association of Museums, 1977.

Phelan, Marilyn. *Museums and the Law.* Nashville, Tenn.: American Association of State and Local History, 1982.

Ullberg, Alan, and Patricia Ullberg. *Museum Trusteeship.* Washington, D.C.: American Association of Museums, 1981.

Weil, Stephen E. *Beauty and the Beasts: On Museums, Art, the Law, and the Market.* Washington, D.C.: Smithsonian Institution Press, 1983.

Yang, Meipu. "Manuals for Museum Policy and Procedures." *Curator* 32, no. 4 (1989): 269–74.

Chapter 3

American Association of Museums. *Museums for a New Century.* Washington, D.C.: American Association of Museums, 1984.

Glickberg, Randi R. "Historic Sites Accreditation." *Museum News* 60, no. 2 (1981): 42–49.

Chapter 4

American Association of Museums. *Caring for Collections: Strategies for Conservation, Maintenance and Documentation*. Washington, D.C.: American Association of Museums, 1984.

———. *Museum Ethics*. 2d ed. Washington, D.C.: American Association of Museums, 1991.

———. *Museums for a New Century*. Washington, D.C.: American Association of Museums, 1984.

Babcock, Phillip. "Ready for the Worst." *Museum News* 69, no. 3 (1990): 50–54.

Bandes, Susan J. "Caring for Collections Strategies for Conservation and Documentation." *Museum News* 63, no. 1 (1984): 68–71.

Biddle, Mark H. "The Legal Side of Buying a Computer." *Museum News* 66, no. 6 (1988): 76–77.

Blackaby, James R. "Managing Historical Data: The Report of the Common Agenda Task Force." *History News* 44, no. 5 (1989): 17–32.

Blackaby, James R., Patricia Greeno, and the Nomenclature Committee. *The Revised Nomenclature for Museum Cataloging*. Nashville, Tenn.: American Association for State and Local History, 1988.

Buck, Richard D. "Describing the Condition of Art Objects." *Museum News* 56, no. 6 (1978): 29–33.

Burcaw, G. Ellis. *Introduction to Museum Work*. 2d ed. Nashville, Tenn.: American Association for State and Local History, 1983.

Chenall, Robert G. *Museum Cataloging in the Computer Age*. Nashville, Tenn.: American Association for State and Local History, 1975.

———. *Nomenclature for Museum Cataloging: A System for Classifying Man-Made Objects*. Nashville, Tenn.: American Association for State and Local History, 1978.

Dudley, Dorothy H., and Irma Bezold Wilkinson. *Museum Registration Methods*. Washington, D.C.: American Association of Museums, 1979.

Fabing, Suzannah. "Facts On File." *Museum News* 70, no. 2 (1991): 56–60.

Fleming, David, and Robert Higginson. "Collections Management—An Independent Approach." *Museums Journal* 84, no. 2 (1984): 87–91.

Guthe, Carl E. *Documenting Collections: Museum Registration and Records*. Technical Leaflet, no. 11. Nashville, Tenn.: American Association for State and Local History, 1970.

Horne, Stephen A. *Way to Go! Crating Artwork for Travel*. New York: Gallery Association of New York State, 1985.

Jones, Barclay G. "Litany of Losses." *Museum News* 69, no. 3 (1990): 56–58.

Keck, Caroline, et al. *A Primer on Museum Security.* Cooperstown, N.Y.: New York State Historical Association, 1966.

LeBlanc, Steven A., and Peter H. Welsh. "Up and Running: Computerized Collections Management at the Southwest Museum." *Museum Studies Journal* 2, no. 3 (1986): 33–45.

Malaro, Marie C. "Collections Management Policies." *Museum News* 58, no. 2 (1979): 57–61.

———. "Deaccessioning: The Importance of Procedure." *Museum News* 66, no. 4 (1988): 74–75.

———. *A Legal Primer on Managing Museum Collections.* Washington, D.C.: American Association of Museums, 1985.

Manning, Anita. "Self-Study: How One Museum Got a Handle on Collections Management." *Museum News* 65, no. 6 (1987): 61–67.

Metzler, Richard. "The Long and Winding Tax Road." *Museum News* 66, no. 1 (1987): 32–35.

Miller, Ronald L. *Personnel Policies for Museums: A Handbook for Management.* Washington, D.C.: American Association of Museums, 1977.

Miller, Steven. "A State Museum Looks to the Twenty-first Century." *Curator* 32, no. 4 (1989): 249–55.

Neal, Arminta, Kristen Haglund, and Elizabeth Webb. "Evolving a Policy Manual." *Museum News* 56, no. 3 (1978): 26–30.

Phelan, Marilyn. *Museums and the Law.* Nashville, Tenn.: American Association for State and Local History, 1983.

Phillips, Charles. "The Ins and Outs of Deaccessioning." *History News* 38, no. 6 (1983): 7–13.

Porter, Daniel. *Current Thoughts on Collections Policies: Producing the Essential Document for Administering Your Collections.* Technical Report, no. 1. Nashville, Tenn.: American Association for State and Local History, 1985.

Reibel, Daniel B. *Registration Methods for the Small Museum.* 2d ed. Yardley, Pa.: DBR, 1991.

Sarasan, Lenore. "What to Look for in Automated Museum Collections Systems." *Museum Studies Journal* 3, no. 4 (1987): 1–17.

Texas Association of Museums and the Mountain Plains Museums Association. *The Museum Forms Book.* Austin: Texas Association of Museums and the Mountain Plains Museums Association, 1990.

Thomson, Garry. *The Museum Environment.* London: Butterworths, 1986.

Turner, Judith Axler. "Museum Computerization: The Evolution Has Begun." *Museum News* 66, no. 6 (1988): 22–28.

Ullberg, Allan D., and Robert C. Lind. "Personal Collecting: Proceed with Caution." *Museum News* 69, no. 5 (1990): 33–35.

Walker, Terry J. "Cutting Through the Legal Fog that Envelops Unclaimed Loans." *Museum News* 69, no. 3 (1990): 33–35.

Washburn, Wilcomb E. "Collecting Information, Not Objects." *Museum News,* 62, no. 3 (1984): 5.

Weil, Stephen E. "Deaccession Practices in American Museums." *Museum News,* 65, no. 3 (1987): 44–50.

Welsh, Peter H., and Steven A. LeBlanc. "Computer Literacy and Collections Management." *Museum News* 65, no. 5 (1987): 42–51.

Williams, David W. *A Guide to Museum Computing.* Nashville, Tenn.: American Association for State and Local History, 1987.

Williams, Stephen L., and Catharine A. Hawks. "Inks for Documentation in Vertebrate Research Collections." *Curator* 29, no. 2 (1986): 93–108.

Yang, Meipu. "Manuals for Museum Policy and Procedures." *Curator* 32, no. 4 (1989): 269–74.

Chapter 5

Storage

Bartlett, John, and Norman Reid. "The Planning of Museums and Art Galleries: Storage and Study Collections." *Museums Journal* 63, nos. 1, 2 (1963): 62–73.

Blackshaw, S. M., and Daniels, V. D. "The Testing of Materials for Use in Storage and Display in Museums." *The Conservator* 3 (1979): 16–19.

Craddock, Anne Brooke. *Construction Materials for Museum Storage.* Bulletin no. 18. New York: New York State Conservation Consultancy, 1988.

Dudley, Dorothy H., and Irma Bezold Wilkinson. *Museum Registration Methods.* Washington, D.C.: American Association of Museums, 1979.

Dunn, Walter S., Jr. *Storing Your Collections: Problems and Solutions.* Technical Leaflet, no. 5. Nashville, Tenn.: American Association for State and Local History, 1970.

Hatchfield, Pamela, and Jane Carpenter. *Formaldehyde: How Great Is the Danger to Museum Collections?* Boston: Center for Conservation and Technical Studies, Harvard University Art Museums, 1987.

Hughes, Olga. "Storage on a Shoestring." *Museum News* 51, no. 3 (1972): 37–38.

Jachimowicz, Elizabeth. "Storage and Access." *Museum News* 56, no. 2 (1977): 32–36.

Johnson, E. Verner, and Joanne C. Horgan. *Museum Collection Storage.* Washington, D.C.: American Association of Museums, 1989.

Miles, C. E. "Wood Coatings for Storage and Display Cases." *Studies in Conservation* 31 (1986): 114–24.

Packman, D. F. "The Acidity of Wood." *Holzforschung* 14, no. 6 (1960): 178–83.

Padfield, T., David Erhardt, and W. Hopwood. "Trouble in Store." Reprint from *Science and Technology in the Service of Conservation.* International Institute of Conservation, Washington, D.C., 1981.

Stolow, Nathan. *Conservation and Exhibitions: Packing, Transport, and Environmental Storage Considerations.* London: Butterworths, 1987.

Waddell, Gene. "Museum Storage." *Museum News* 49, no. 5 (1971): 14–20.

Glass and Ceramics

Andre, Jean-Michel. *The Restorer's Handbook of Ceramics and Glass.* Toronto: Van Nostrand, 1976.

Brill, R. H. "The Use of Equilibrated Silica Gel for the Protection of Glass with Incipient Crizzling." *Journal of Glass Studies* 20 (1978): 100–18.

Fall, Freida Kay. *Art Objects, Their Care and Preservation: A Handbook for Museums and Collections.* La Jolla, Calif.: Laurence McGilvery, 1973.

Lins, P. A. "Ceramics and Glass Conservation: Preventative Measures." *Museum News* 55, no. 3 (1977): 5–8.

Organ, R. M. "The Safe Storage of Unstable Glass." *Museums Journal* 56 (1957): 265–72.

Plenderleith, H. J., and A. E. Werner. *The Conservation of Antiquities and Works of Art.* London: Oxford University Press, 1977.

Rottenberg, Barbara Lang. *Care and Display of Glass Collections.* Technical Leaflet, no. 127. Nashville, Tenn.: American Association for State and Local History, 1980.

Werner, A. E. "The Care of Glass in Museums." *Museum News* 44, no. 10 (1966): 45–49.

Textiles and Costumes

Buck, Anne, and Jentina Leene. "Storage and Display." In *Textiles Conservation,* edited by J. E. Leene, pp. 113–27. Washington, D.C.: Smithsonian Institution Press, 1972.

Butterfield, Mary Ann, and Lotus Stack. "An Ounce of Prevention," *Weavers Journal* 10, no. 1 (1985): 7–10.

Canadian Conservation Institute. *Anionic Detergent.* CCI Notes, vol. 13, no. 9. Ottawa: Canadian Conservation Institute, n.d.

———. *Hanging Storage for Costumes.* CCI Notes, vol. 13, no. 5. Ottawa: Canadian Conservation Institute, 1983.

Canadian Conservation Institute. *Rolled Storage for Textiles.* CCI Notes, vol. 13, no. 3. Ottawa: Canadian Conservation Institute, 1983.

Dunn, Walter S., Jr. *Storing Your Collections: Problems and Solutions.* Technical Leaflet, no. 5. Nashville, Tenn.: American Association for State and Local History, 1970.

Fikioris, Margaret. "A Model for Textile Storage." *Museum News* 52, no. 3 (1973): 34–41.

Fikioris, Margaret. "Textile Conservation for Period Room Settings in Museums and Historic Houses." In *Preservation of Paper and Textiles of Historic and Artistic Value II*, edited by John C. Williams, pp. 253–74. Washington, D.C.: American Chemical Society, 1981.

Hearle, J. W. S. *Moisture in Textiles*. New York: Textile Book Publishers, 1960.

Kajitani, Nobuko. "Care of Fabrics in the Museum." In *Preservation of Paper and Textiles of Historic and Artistic Value II*, edited by John C. Williams, pp. 161–80. Washington, D.C.: American Chemical Society, 1977.

MacLeish, A Bruce. *The Care of Antiques and Historical Collections: A Conservation Handbook for the Non-Specialist*. Nashville, Tenn.: American Association for State and Local History, 1985.

Nylander, Jane. *Care of Textiles and Costumes: Cleaning and Storage Techniques*. Technical Leaflet, no. 2. Nashville, Tenn.: American Association for State and Local History, 1970.

Thomson, Garry. "Textiles in the Museum Environment." In *Preservation of Paper and Textiles of Historic and Artistic Value II*, edited by John C. Williams, pp. 98–112. Washington, D.C.: American Chemical Society, 1981.

Photographs and Documents

Anderson, Linda, and Marcia R. Collins. *Libraries for Small Museums*. 2d ed. Columbia: University of Missouri, Museum of Anthropology, 1975.

Clapp, Anne. *Curatorial Care of Works of Art on Paper*. 2d ed. Intermuseum Conservation Association. New York: Nick Lyons Books, 1987.

Duckett, Kenneth W. *Modern Manuscripts: A Practical Manual for Their Management, Care and Use*. Nashville, Tenn.: American Association for State and Local History, 1975.

Kane, Lucille M. *A Guide to the Care and Administration of Manuscripts*. Nashville, Tenn.: American Association for State and Local History, 1966.

O'Connor, Joan L. "Conservation of Documents in an Exhibit." *American Archivist* 47, no. 2 (1984): 156–63.

Reilly, James M. *Care and Identification of 19th Century Photographic Print*. Rochester, N.Y.: Eastman Kodak, 1986.

Ritzenthaler, Mary Lynn, Gerald J. Munoff, and Marjery S. Long. *Archives and Manuscripts: Administration of Photographic Collections*. Chicago: Society of American Archivists, 1984.

Thompson, Enid. *Local History Collections: A Manual for Librarians*. Nashville, Tenn.: American Association for State and Local History, 1978.

U.S. Library of Congress Preservation Office. "Polyester Film Encapsulation." U.S. Library Congress Preservation Office, Washington, D.C., 1980.

Waters, Peter. "Archival Methods of Treatment for Library Document." In *Preservation of Paper and Textiles of Historic and Artistic Value II,* edited by John C. Williams, pp. 13–23. Washington, D.C.: American Chemical Society, 1981.

Weinstein, Robert A., and Larry Booth. *Collections Use and Care of Historical Photographs.* Nashville, Tenn.: American Association for State and Local History, 1977.

Paintings and Prints

Canadian Conservation Institute. *Environmental and Display* Guideline for Paintings. CCI Notes, vol. 10, no. 4. Ottawa: Canadian Conservation Institute, 1986.

———. *Storage Systems for Paintings.* CCI Notes, vol. 10, no. 3. Ottawa: Canadian Conservation Institute, 1986.

Fall, Freida Kay. *Art Objects, Their Care and Preservation: A Handbook for Museums and Collections.* La Jolla, Calif.: Laurence McGilvery, 1973.

Keck, Caroline K. *A Handbook on the Care of Paintings.* Nashville, Tenn.: American Association for State and Local History, 1970.

———. *How to Take Care of Your Paintings.* New York: Scribner's, 1978.

Hughes, Olga. "Storage on a Shoestring." *Museum News* 51, no. 3 (1972): 37–38.

Sandwith, Hermione, and Sheila Stainton. *The National Trust Manual of Housekeeping.* London: National Trust, 1984.

Shelley, Marjorie. *The Care and Handling of Art Objects: Practices in the Metropolitan Museum of Art.* Washington, D.C.: American Association of Museums, 1987.

Stout, George L. *The Care of Pictures.* New York: Dover, 1975.

Wood

Barclay, R., R. Eames, and A. Todd. *The Care of Wooden Objects.* Technical Bulletin, no. 8. Ottawa: Canadian Conservation Institute, 1982.

MacLeish, A. Bruce. *The Care of Antiques and Historical Collections.* Nashville, Tenn.: American Association for State and Local History, 1972.

McGriffin, Robert. *Furniture Care and Conservation.* Nashville, Tenn.: American Association for State and Local History, 1983.

Williams, Marc A. *Keeping It All Together: The Preservation and Care of Historic Furniture.* Washington, D.C.: American Association of Museums, 1988.

Metalwork

Canadian Conservation Institute. *The Cleaning, Polishing and Protective Waxing of Brass and Copper Objects.* CCI Notes, vol. 9, no. 3. Ottawa: Canadian Conservation Institute, 1983.

Fales, Mrs. Dean A. *The Care of Antique Silver.* Technical Leaflet, no. 40. Nashville, Tenn.: American Association for State and Local History, 1967.

Fall, Freida Kay. *Art Objects, Their Care and Preservation: A Handbook for Museums and Collections.* La Jolla, Calif.: Laurence McGilvery, 1973.

Lewis, Ralph. *Manual for Museums.* Washington, D.C.: National Park Service, 1976.

MacLeish, A. Bruce. *The Care of Antiques and Historical Collections.* 2d ed. Nashville, Tenn.: American Association for State and Local History, 1985.

Sandwith, Hermione, and Sheila Stainton. *The National Trust Manual of Housekeeping.* London: National Trust, 1984.

Chapter 6

Alpert, Gary, and L. Michael Alpert. "Integrated Pest Management: A Program for Museum Environments." Unpublished paper, available through Archos, Inc., Cambridge, Massachusetts.

American Association for Museums. *Caring for Collections: Strategies for Conservation, Maintenance and Documentation.* Washington, D.C.: American Association of Museums, 1984.

Brandt, Charles Alfred Edwin. "Planning An Environmentally Benign Fumigator/Freezer Dryer for the Provincial Archives of Manitoba." Provincial Archives of Manitoba, Winnipeg, 1983.

Butcher-Younghans, Sherry, and Gretchen Anderson. *A Holistic Approach to Museum Pest Management.* Technical Leaflet, no. 171. Nashville, Tenn.: American Association for State and Local History, 1990.

Canadian Conservation Institute. *Silica Gel.* Technical Bulletin, no. 10. Ottawa: Canadian Conservation Institute, 1991.

————. *Using a Camera to Measure Light Levels.* CCI Notes, vol. 2, no. 5. Ottawa: Canadian Conservation Institute, 1983.

Deschiens, Robert, and Christine Coste. "The Protection of Works of Art in Carved Wood from the Attacks of Wood-eating Insects." *Museum* 10, no. 1 (1957): 55–59.

Dillon, Phyllis. "Conservation Planning—Where Can You Find the Help You Need?" *History News* 42, no. 4 (1987): 10–15.

Douglas, Alan R. "A Commonsense Approach to Environmental Control." *Curator* 15, no. 2 (1972): 139–44.

Edwards, Stephen, B. M. Bell, and M. E. King. *Pest Control in Museums: A Status Report.* Lawrence, Kans.: Association of Systematic Collections, 1988.

Ellis, Margaret Hoben. *The Care of Prints and Drawings.* Washington, D.C.: American Association of Museums, 1987.

Feller, Robert L. "Control of Deteriorating Effects of Light upon Museum Objects." *Museum* 17, no. 2 (1964): 72–98.

Fikioris, Margaret. "Textile Conservation for Period Room Settings in Museums and Historic Houses." In *Preservation of Paper and Textiles of Historic and Artistic Value II,* edited by John C. Williams, pp. 253–74. Washington, D.C.: American Chemical Society, 1981.

Florian, Mary-Lou. "Control of Biodeterioration: Methodology Used in Insect Pest Surveys in Museum Buildings—A Case History." International Council of Museums Committee for Conservation, 1987.

———. "The Effect on Artifact Materials of the Fumigant Ethylene Oxide and Freezing Used in Insect Control." International Council of Museums Committee for Conservation, 1987.

———. "The Freezing Process—Effects on Insects and Artifact Materials." *Leather Conservation News* 3, no. 1 (1986): 1–13, 17.

Lewis, Ralph. *Manual for Museums.* Washington, D.C.: National Park Service, 1976.

Lull, William P., and Linda E. Merk. "Lighting for Storage of Museum Collections: Developing a System for Safekeeping of Light-Sensitive Material." *Technology and Conservation* 7, no. 1 (1982): 20–25.

———. "Preservation Aspects of Display Lighting." *Electrical Consultant* 62, no. 6 (1982): 8–14, 20, 39.

MacLeish, A. Bruce. *The Care of Antiques and Historical Collections.* 2d ed. Nashville, Tenn.: American Association for State and Local History, 1985.

Macleod, K. J. *Museum Lighting.* Technical Bulletin, no. 2. Ottawa: Canadian Conservation Institute, 1975.

———. *Relative Humidity: Its Importance Measurement and Control in Museums.* Technical Bulletin, no. 1. Ottawa: Canadian Conservation Institute, 1975.

McGriffin, Robert F. *A Current Status Report on Fumigation in Museums.* Technical Report, no. 4. Nashville, Tenn.: American Association for State and Local History, 1985.

Peltz, P., and Monona Rossol. *Safe Pest Control Procedures for Museum Collections.* New York: Center for Occupational Hazards, 1983.

Plenderleith, H. J., and P. Philippot. "Climatology and Conservation in Museums." *Museum* 13, no. 4 (1960): 242–89.

Sandwith, Hermione, and Sheila Stainton. *The National Trust Manual of Housekeeping.* London: National Trust, 1984.

Stolow, Nathan. "The Action of Environment on Museum Objects, Part 1: Humidity, Temperature, Atmospheric Pollution." *Curator* 9, no. 3 (1966): 175–85.

———. "The Microclimate: A Localized Solution." *Museum News* 56, no. 2 (1977): 52–63.

Story, Keith O. *Approaches to Pest Management in Museums.* Washington, D.C.: Smithsonian Institution Press, 1985.

Thomson, Garry. *The Museum Environment.* London: Butterworths, 1986.

Watson, Edwin W. *Oriental Carpets: Selection, Use and Care.* Technical Leaflet, no. 122. Nashville, Tenn.: American Association for State and Local History, 1979.

Williams, Marc A. *Keeping It All Together: The Preservation and Care of Historic Furniture.* Washington, D.C.: American Association of Museums, 1988.

Chapter 7

American Association for State and Local History. *Housekeeping Techniques for the Historic House.* Nashville, Tenn.: American Association for State and Local History, 1978. Slide and tape production.

Canadian Conservation Institute. *The Cleaning, Polishing and Protective Waxing of Brass and Copper Objects.* Ottawa: Canadian Conservation Institute, 1983.

Chambers, J. Henry. *Cyclical Maintenance for Historic Buildings.* Washington, D.C.: National Park Service, 1976.

Clapp, Anne. *Curatorial Care of Works of Art on Paper.* Rev. ed. Oberlin, Ohio: Intermuseum Laboratory, 1973.

Fales, Mrs. Dean A. *The Care of Antique Silver.* Technical Leaflet, no. 40. Nashville, Tenn.: American Association for State and Local History, 1967.

Fall, Frieda Kay. *Art Objects, Their Care and Preservation: A Handbook for Museums and Collections.* La Jolla, Calif.: Laurence McGilvery, 1973.

Frangiamore, Catherine L. *Rescuing Historic Wallpaper: Identification, Preservation, Restoration.* Technical Leaflet, no. 76. Nashville, Tenn.: American Association for State and Local History, 1974.

Keck, Caroline. *A Handbook on the Care of Paintings.* Nashville, Tenn.: American Association for State and Local History, 1967.

Lewis, Ralph H. *Manual for Museums.* Washington, D.C.: National Park Service, 1976.

MacLeish, A. Bruce. *The Care of Antiques and Historical Collections.* Nashville, Tenn.: American Association for State and Local History, 1985.

Moss, Roger W. *Lighting for Historic Buildings.* Washington, D.C.: Preservation Press, 1988.

Nylander, Richard C. *Wallpapers for Historic Buildings.* Washington, D.C.: Preservation Press, 1983.

Paine, Shelly Reisman. *Basic Principles for Controlling Environmental Conditions in Museums and Historical Agencies.* Technical Report, no. 3. Nashville, Tenn.: American Association for State and Local History, 1985.

Sandwith, Hermione, and Sheila Stainton. *The National Trust Manual of Housekeeping.* London: National Trust, 1984.

Von Rosenstiel, Helene, and Gail Caskey Winkler. *Floor Coverings for Historic Buildings.* Washington, D.C.: Preservation Press, 1988.

Chapter 8

Bock, Gordon. "Inspecting Chimneys." *Old-House Journal* 17, no. 2 (1989): 34–37.

———. "Wood-Shingle Roof Care." *Old-House Journal* 18, no. 3 (1990): 36–37.

Bullock, Orrin M., Jr. *The Restoration Manual: An Illustrated Guide to the Preservation and Restoration of Old Buildings.* New York: Van Nostrand Reinhold, 1983.

Butcher-Younghans, Sherry, and Gretchen E. Anderson. *A Holistic Approach to Museum Pest Management.* Technical Leaflet, no. 171. Nashville, Tenn.: American Association for State and Local History, 1990.

Chambers, J. Henry. *Cyclical Maintenance of Historic Buildings.* Washington, D.C.: National Park Service, 1976.

Coney, William B. *Preservation of Historic Concrete: Problems and General Approaches.* Preservation Briefs, no. 15. Washington, D.C.: National Park Service, 1987.

Cotton, J. Randall. "Repairing Ornamental Concrete Block." *Old-House Journal* 12, no. 9 (1984): 201–4.

"Detecting and Defeating Rot in Old Houses." *Old-House Journal* 2, no. 10 (1974): 6–8.

Evers, Christopher. *The Old-House Doctor.* Woodstock, N.Y.: Overlook Press, 1986.

Glass, James A. *The Beginnings of a New National Historic Preservation Program, 1957 to 1969.* Nashville, Tenn.: American Association for State and Local History, 1990.

Grimmer, Anne E. *Dangers of Abrasive Cleaning to Historic Buildings.* Preservation Briefs, no. 6. Washington, D.C.: National Park Service, 1979.

Hanson, Shirley, and Nancy Hubby. *Preserving and Maintaining the Older Home.* New York: McGraw-Hill, 1983.

Holstrom, Ingmar, and Christina Sandstrom. *Maintenance of Old Buildings: Preservation from the Technical and Antiquarian Standpoint.* Stockholm: National Swedish Building Research, 1972.

Hosmer, Charles B., Jr. *Preservation Comes of Age: From Williamsburg to the National Trust, 1926–1949.* 2 vols. Charlottesville: University Press of Virginia, 1981.

Insall, Donald. *The Care of Old Buildings Today.* London: Architectural Press, 1973.

"Inspection Checklist for Older Buildings." *Old-House Journal* 15, no. 5 (1987): 40–47.

Judd, Henry A. *Before Restoration Begins: Keeping Your Historic House Intact.* Technical Leaflet, no. 67. Nashville, Tenn.: American Association for State and Local History, 1973.

Kahn, Eve M., ed. *The Old-House Journal Catalog.* Brooklyn, N.Y.: Old-House Journal Corporation, 1986.

Kitchen, Judith L. *Caring for Your Old House: A Guide for Owners and Residents.* Washington, D.C.: Preservation Press, 1990.

Labine, Clem. "Old-House Maintenance: Dull, But Essential." *Historic Preservation* 39, no. 1 (1987): 21–23.

———. "Repairing Slate Roofs." *Old-House Journal* 3, no. 12 (1975): 6–7.

Lewis, Ralph H. *Manual for Museums.* Washington, D.C.: National Park Service, 1976.

London, Mark. *Masonry: How to Care for Old and Historic Brick and Stone.* Washington, D.C.: Preservation Press, 1988.

Mack, Robert C. *The Cleaning and Waterproof Coatings of Masonry Buildings.* Preservation Briefs, no. 1. Washington, D.C.: National Park Service, 1975.

Mack, Robert C., de Teel Patterson Tiller, and James S. Askins. *Repointing Mortar Joints in Historic Brick Buildings.* Preservation Briefs, no. 2. Washington, D.C.: National Park Service, 1980.

"Maintenance of Gutters, Part 1." *Old-House Journal* 7, no. 10 (1979): 109, 116–18.

"Maintenance of Gutters, Part 2." *Old-House Journal* 7, no. 11 (1979): 129–30.

Mallis, A. *Handbook of Pest Control: The Behavior, Life History, and Control of Household Pests.* 6th ed. Cleveland: Franzak and Foster, 1982.

Moore, Harry. *Wood-Inhabiting Insects in Houses: Their Identification, Biology, Prevention and Control.* Washington, D.C.: Department of Agriculture, 1979.

Moss, Roger W. *Lighting for Historic Buildings.* Washington, D.C.: Preservation Press, 1988.

Murtagh, William J. *Keeping Time: The History and Theory of Preservation in America.* Pittstown, N.J.: Main Street Press, 1988.

Myers, John H. *The Repair of Historic Wooden Windows.* Preservation Briefs, no. 9. Washington, D.C.: National Park Service, 1981.

Nelson, Lee H. *Architectural Character—Identifying the Visual Aspects of Historic Buildings as an Aid in Preserving Their Character.* Preservation Briefs, no. 17. Washington, D.C.: National Park Service, 1988.

Nylander, Jane C. *Fabrics for Historic Buildings.* Washington, D.C.: Preservation Press, 1990.

Nylander, Richard C. *Wallpapers for Historic Buildings.* Washington, D.C.: Preservation Press, 1983.

O'Donnell, Bill. "Gutter Repairs." *Old-House Journal* 15, no. 2 (1987): 27–31.

Park, Sharon C. *The Repair and Replacement of Historic Wooden Shingle Roofs.* Preservation Briefs, no. 19. Washington, D.C.: National Park Service, 1989.

————. *The Repair and Thermal Upgrading of Historic Steel Windows.* Preservation Briefs, no. 13. Washington, D.C.: National Park Service, n.d.

————. *The Use of Substitute Materials on Historic Building Exteriors.* Preservation Briefs, no. 16. Washington, D.C.: National Park Service, 1988.

Phillips, Morgan W. *The Eight Most Common Mistakes in Restoring Houses (And How to Avoid Them).* Technical Leaflet, no. 118. Nashville, Tenn.: American Association for State and Local History, 1979.

Poore, Patricia, and Clem Labine, eds. *The Old-House Journal New Compendium.* Garden City, N.Y.: Doubleday, 1983.

Preservation of Historic Adobe Buildings. Preservation Briefs, no. 5. Washington, D.C.: National Park Service, 1978.

"Preventing Rot in Old Houses." *Old-House Journal* 2, no. 11 (1974): 1, 5–6.

"Protecting the Aging House from Winter Storms." *Old-House Journal* 1, no. 1 (1973): 2.

Seale, William. *Recreating the Historic House Interior.* Nashville, Tenn.: American Association for State and Local History, 1979.

"Sealing Leaky Windows." *Old-House Journal* 1, no. 1 (1973): 5–6.

Simonson, Kaye Ellen. *Maintaining Historic Buildings: An Annotated Bibliography.* Washington, D.C.: National Park Service, 1990.

Stephen, George. *New Life for Old Houses.* Washington, D.C.: Preservation Press, 1989.

Sweetser, Sarah M. *Roofing for Historic Buildings.* Preservation Briefs, no. 4. Washington, D.C.: National Park Service, 1978.

Tindall, Susan M. "Repointing Masonry—Why Repoint?" *Old-House Journal* 15, no. 1 (1987): 24–31.

Von Rosenstiel, Helene, and Gail Caskey Winkler. *Floor Coverings for Historic Buildings.* Washington, D.C.: Preservation Press, 1988.

Weeks, Kay, and David W. Look. *Exterior Paint Problems on Historic Woodwork.* Preservation Briefs, no. 10. Washington, D.C.: National Park Service, 1982.

Ziegler, Arthur P., Jr., and Walter C. Kidney. *Historic Preservation in Small Towns.* Nashville, Tenn.: American Association for State and Local History, 1980.

Chapter 9

Advisory Council on Historic Preservation and the General Services Administration. *Fire Safety Retrofitting in Historic Buildings.* Washington, D.C.: Advisory Council on Historic Preservation, 1989.

American Association of Art Museum Directors. *Planning for Emergencies: A Guide for Museums.* Washington, D.C.: American Association of Museums, 1987.

American Society for Industrial Security and the Standing Committee on

Museum, Library and Archival Security. *Suggested Guidelines in Museum Security*. Arlington, Va.: American Society for Industrial Security, 1990.

Babcock, Phillip. "Ready for the Worst." *Museum News* 69, no. 3 (1990): 50–54.

Barton, John P., and Johanna G. Wellheiser. *An Ounce of Prevention: A Handbook on Disaster Contingency Planning for Archives, Libraries, and Record Centers*. Ontario: Toronto Area Archivists Group Education Foundation, 1985.

Blair, C. Dean. *Protecting Your Exhibits: Security Methods and Devices*. Technical Leaflet, no. 99. Nashville, Tenn.: American Association for State and Local History, 1977.

Bostick, William A. "What Is the State of Museum Security." *Museum News* 46, no. 5 (1968): 13–18.

Burcaw, G. Ellis. *Introduction to Museum Work*. 2d ed. Nashville, Tenn.: American Association for State and Local History, 1983.

Burke, Robert, and Sam Adeloye. *A Manual of Basic Museum Security*. Washington, D.C.: American Association of Museums, 1986.

Canadian Conservation Institute. *Planning for Disaster Management: Introduction*. CCI Notes, vol. 14, no. 1. Ottawa: Canadian Conservation Institute, 1984.

———. *Planning for Disaster Management: Emergency or Disaster?* CCI Notes, vol. 14, no. 2. Ottawa: Canadian Conservation Institute, 1984.

———. *Planning for Disaster Management: Hazard Analysis*. CCI Notes, vol. 14, no. 3. Ottawa: Canadian Conservation Institute, 1988.

Chapman, Joseph. "Fire." *Museum News* 50, no. 5 (1972): 32–35.

Dunn, Joy B. "The Calm Before the Storm." *History News* 45, no. 1 (1990): 22–24.

Fay, John J. *Butterworths' Security Dictionary: Terms and Concepts*. Boston: Butterworths, 1987.

Fennelly, Lawrence J. *Museum, Archive and Library Security*. Boston: Butterworths, 1983.

Garfield, Donald. "Out of Harm's Way." *Museum News* 69, no. 3 (1990): 67–70.

Ginell, William S. "Making It Quake-Proof." *Museum News* 69, no. 3 (1990): 60–63.

Gossin, Francis. "A Security Chief Comments on Guards." *Museum News* 50, no. 5 (1972): 30–31.

Hunter, John E. *Preparing a Museum Disaster Plan*. Omaha: National Park Service, 1984.

Historic House Association of America, "Fire Protection for the Historic House." *Historic House* 4, no. 1 (1982): 10.

Hunter, John E. *Emergency Preparedness for Museums, Historic Sites, and Archives: An Annotated Bibliography*. Technical Leaflet, no. 114. Nashville, Tenn.: American Association for State and Local History, 1979.

Jones, Barclay G. "Litany of Losses." *Museum News* 69, no. 3 (1990): 56–58.

———, ed. *Protecting Historic Architecture and Museum Collections from Natural Disasters.* Boston: Butterworths, 1986.

Keck, Caroline K., Huntington T. Block, Joseph Chapman, John B. Lawton, and Nathan Stolow. *A Primer on Museum Security.* Cooperstown, N.Y.: New York State Historical Society, 1966.

Leo, Jack. "How to Secure Your Museum: A Basic Checklist." *History News* 35, no. 3 (1980): 10–12.

Lewis, Ralph H. *Manual for Museums.* Washington, D.C.: National Park Service, 1976.

McGriffin, Robert F. "Health and Safety in the Museum Workplace." *Museum News* 64, no. 2 (1985): 36–43.

McQuarie, Robert J. "Security." *Museum News* 49, no. 7 (1971): 25–27.

Menkes, Diana., ed. *Museum Security Survey.* Washington, D.C.: American Association of Museums, 1981.

Musgrove, Stephen W. "Keep Your Guard Up: Contracted Security Might Save You a Few Hassles, But Can It Replace Your Own Loyal Employees?" *Museum News* 68, no. 1 (1989): 68–69.

Peever, Mary. *Closing a Museum for the Winter.* CCI Notes, vol. 1, no. 3. Ottawa: Canadian Conservation Institute, 1988.

Probst, Tom. "Fire Detection/Fire Protection." *Museum News* 44, no. 9 (1966): 10–17.

Roth, Evan. "Romania's Revolution Rocks Museums, Too—For Good and Ill." *Museum News* 69, no. 3 (1990): 24–26.

"Smoke Detectors." *Consumer Reports* 41, no. 10 (1976): 555–59.

Society for the Protection of Ancient Buildings and The Fire Protection Association. *Fire Safety of Historic Buildings.* Technical Pamphlet, no. 6, London: Society for the Protection of Ancient Buildings and The Fire Protection Association, 1978.

U.S. Consumer Projects Safety Commission. *Smoke Detectors.* Washington, D.C.: Government Printing Office, 1979.

Weldon, Stephen. "Winterthur: Security at a Decorative Arts Museum." *Museum News* 50, no. 5 (1972): 36–37.

Williams, R. Scott. *Display and Storage of Museum Objects Containing Cellulose Nitrate.* CCI Notes, vol. 15, no. 3. Ottawa: Canadian Conservation Institute, 1988.

Wilson, Andrew. "Fire Fighters." *Museum News* 68, no. 6 (1989): 68–72.

"Your Security Questions Answered." *Museum News* 50, no. 5 (1972): 22–25.

Chapter 10

Alderson, William T., and Shirley Payne Low. 2d ed. *Interpretation of Historic Sites.* Nashville, Tenn.: American Association for State and Local History, 1985.

Alexander, Edward P. "Artistic and Historical Period Rooms." *Curator* 7, no. 4 (1964): 263–81.

———. *Museums in Motion: An Introduction to the History and Function of Museums.* Nashville, Tenn.: American Association for State and Local History, 1979.

Ames, Kenneth L. "Meaning in Artifacts: Hall Furnishings in Victorian America." *Journal of Interdisciplinary History* 9, no. 1 (1978): 19–46.

Ames, Michael M. "Biculturalism in Exhibitions." *Museum Anthropology* 15, no. 2 (1991): 7–15.

Anderson, Jay. *The Living History Sourcebook.* Nashville, Tenn.: American Association for State and Local History, 1985.

Anderson, Jay. *Time Machines: The World of Living History.* Nashville, Tenn.: American Association for State and Local History, 1984.

———. "Almost Gone: Historic Houses of Our Own Times." *Museum News* 61, no. 3 (1983): 45–53.

Benedict, Paul L. *Historic Site Interpretation: The Student Field Trip.* Technical Leaflet, no. 19. Nashville, Tenn.: American Association for State and Local History, 1971.

Blatti, Jo, ed. *Past Meets Present: Essays About Historic Interpretation and Public Audiences.* Washington, D.C.: Smithsonian Institution Press, 1987.

Bridal, Tessa. "Interpretation Through Theater." *Journal of the International Association of Zoo Educators* 22 (1989): 7–9.

Butcher-Younghans, Sherry. *The American Swedish Institute: A Living Heritage.* Dubuque, Ia.: Kendall/Hunt, 1989.

———. "Diversity in Dwellings." *Museum News* 70, no. 5 (1991): 57–59.

Chavis, John. "The Artifact and the Study of History." *Curator* 7, no. 2 (1964): 156–62.

Coats, Peggy. "Survey of Historic House Museums." *History News* 45, no. 1 (1990): 26–28.

Cohen, Lizabeth A. "How to Teach Family History by Using an Historic House." *Social Education* 39, no. 7 (1975): 466–69.

Cohen, Lizabeth A. "Embellishing a Life of Labor: An Interpretation of the Material Culture of American Working-Class Homes, 1885–1915." In *Material Culture Studies in America,* edited by Thomas J. Schlereth, pp. 289–305. Nashville, Tenn.: American Association for State and Local History, 1982.

Coleman, Laurence Vail. *Historic House Museums.* Washington, D.C.: American Association of Museums, 1933.

Colwell, Wayne. "Windows on the Past." *Museum News* 50, no. 10 (1972): 36–38.

Conaway, Mary Ellen. "A Made-for-Television Historic House Series: From Opera to Sitcom." *History News* 43, no. 3 (1988): 18–23.

Craig, Tracey Linton. "The Play's the Thing." *Museum News* 66, no. 5 (1988): 58–59.

———. " 'Reinterpreting' the Past." *Museum News* 68, no. 1 (1989): 61–69.

De Cunzo, Lu Ann. *Historical Archeology as a Tool for Researching and Inter-*

preting Historic Sites. Technical Leaflet, no. 173. Nashville, Tenn.: American Association for State and Local History, 1990.

Deetz, James. *In Small Things Forgotten: The Archeology of Early American Life.* New York: Anchor Press, 1977.

Drury, John. *Historic Midwest Houses.* 1947. Reprint. Chicago: University of Chicago Press, 1977.

Ellacott, S. E. *A History of Everyday Things in England.* London: Batsford, 1968.

Fischer, David Hackett. *Historians' Fallacies: Toward a Logic of Historical Thought.* New York: Harper & Row, 1970.

Fleming, E. McClung. "The Period Room as a Curatorial Publication." *Museum News* 50, no. 10 (1972): 38–42.

Floyd, Candace. "Too Close for Comfort." *History News* 40, no. 9 (1985): 9–14.

Folsom, Merrill. *Great American Mansions and Their Stories.* 1963. Reprint. New York: Hastings House, 1976.

Geertz, Clifford. "The Uses of Diversity." *Michigan Quarterly Review* 25, no. 1 (1986): 105–23.

George, Gerald. "Historic Property Museums: What Are They Preserving?" *Preservation Forum* 3, no. 2 (1989): 2–5.

Hall, Edward. *The Hidden Dimension.* New York: Doubleday, 1969.

Hamp, Steven K. "Subject over Object: Interpreting the Museum as Artifact." *Museum News* 63, no. 2 (1984): 33–37.

Harvey, Bruce. "Inside the Treasure Houses: The English National Trust Wrestles with Interpretation as It Attempts to Gain American Support." *History News* 42, no. 3 (1987): 16–18.

Hills, Patricia. "Turn-of-the-Century America." *Museum News* 56, no. 1 (1977): 30–34.

Historic House Association of America. "Digging into Your House's Past." *Historic Houses* 4, no. 5/6 (1982): 10–13.

———. "Fire Protection for the Historic House." *Historic Houses* 4, no. 1 (1982): 10.

Howe, Barbara J., Dolores A. Fleming, Emory L. Kemp, and Ruth Ann Overbeck. *Houses and Homes Exploring Their History.* 2d ed. Nashville, Tenn.: American Association for State and Local History, 1987.

Kenney, Alice P. *Access to the Past: Museum Programs and Handicapped Visitors.* Nashville, Tenn.: American Association for State and Local History, 1982.

King, Thomas, Patricia Parker Hickman, and Gary Berg. *Anthropology in Historic Preservation Caring for Culture's Clutter.* New York: Academic Press, 1977.

Klein, Janet S. "Houses as Artifacts." *Museum News* 68, no. 1 (1989): 56–57.

Leon, Warren, and Roy Rosenzweig. *History Museums in the United States.* Champaign: University of Illinois Press, 1989.

Little, Nina Fletcher. *Historic Houses: An Approach to Furnishings.* Technical

Leaflet, no. 17. Nashville, Tenn.: American Association for State and Local History, 1970.

Molloy, Larry. "Museum Accessibility: The Continuing Dialogue." *Museum News* 60, no. 2 (1981): 50–57.

Montgomery, Charles. "The Historic House—A Definition." *Museum News* 38, no. 1 (1959): 12–16.

Murtagh, William J. *Keeping Time: The History and Theory of Preservation in America*. Pittstown, N.J.: Main Street Press, 1988.

"National Symbols Presidential Homes." *History News* 45, no. 1 (1990): 8–17.

Noble, Joseph Veach. "More Than a Mirror to the Past." *Curator* 16, no. 3 (1973): 271–76.

Parr, A. E. "Habitat Group and Period Room." *Curator* 6, no. 4 (1963): 325–36.

Perrin, Richard W. E. *Outdoor Museums*. Milwaukee: Milwaukee Public Museum Publication, 1975.

Place, Linna Funk, Joanna Schneider Zangrando, James W. Lea, and John Lovell. "The Object as Subject: The Role of Museums and Material Culture Collections in American Studies." *American Quarterly* 26, no. 3 (1974): 281–94.

Reque, Barbara. "From Object to Idea." *Museum News* 56, no. 3 (1978): 45–47.

"Revising Colonial America." *Atlantic* 262, no. 6 (1988): 26–32.

Rosenburg, Sarah Z. "The Elusive Interpretive Experience Museums, Libraries and Humanities Scholars." *Museum News* 61, no. 6 (1983): 30–35.

Schlereth, Thomas. *Historic Houses as Learning Laboratories: Seven Teaching Strategies*. Technical Leaflet, no. 105. Nashville, Tenn.: American Association for State and Local History, 1978.

———. "It Wasn't that Simple." *Museum News* 56, no. 3 (1978): 36–44.

Schroeder, Fred E. H. *Interpreting and Reinterpreting Associative Historic Sites and Artifacts*. Technical Report, no. 6. Nashville, Tenn.: American Association for State and Local History, 1986.

Seale, William. *Recreating the Historic House Interior*. Nashville, Tenn.: American Association for State and Local History, 1979.

Seemann, Charlie. "Living History or Living Culture? One Alternative to Historical Re-creation." *History News* 44, no. 1 (1989): 32.

Smith, Jeffery E. "Living with a Legend." *History News* 40, no. 9 (1985): 14–19.

———. "Rites of Passage." *History News* 44, no. 1 (1989): 29–31.

Tackach, James. *Historic Homes of America*. New York: Moore and Moore, 1990.

Talbot, George. *At Home: Domestic Life in the Post Centennial Era, 1879–1920*. Madison: State Historical Society of Wisconsin, 1976.

Tilden, Freeman. *Interpreting Our Heritage*. 3d ed. Chapel Hill: University of North Carolina Press, 1957.

Tramposch, William J. "On Interpretation." *Minnesota History Interpreter* 11, no. 5 (1983): 3–5.

———. "Put There a Spark: How Colonial Williamsburg Trains Its Interpretative Crew." *History News* 37, no. 4 (1982): 21–23.

Wall, Charles. "The Mount Vernon Experience, 1859–1959." *Museum News* 38, no. 1 (1959): 18–23.

Wolins, Inez S. "Teaching the Teachers." *Museum News* 69, no. 3 (1990): 71–75.

Woods, Thomas A. "Perspectivistic Interpretation: A New Direction For Sites and Exhibits." *History News* 44, no. 1 (1989): 14, 27–28.

Chapter 11

Alexander, Edward P. *Museums in Motion.* Nashville, Tenn.: American Association for State and Local History, 1979.

American Association of Museums. *Museum Ethics.* Washington, D.C.: American Association of Museums, 1991.

Bandes, Susan J., and Selma Holo. "Interns Ins and Outs." *Museum News* 68, no. 4 (1989): 16–18.

Brown, Kathleen M. *Nine Keys to a Successful Volunteer Program.* Rockville, Md.: Taft Group, 1990.

———. "Thoughts on the Supervision of Volunteers." *Voluntary Action Leadership* (Spring 1984): 14–16.

Butcher-Younghans, Sherry. "Using Volunteers in History." *History News* 43, no. 4 (1988): 11–14.

Chadwick, Alan, and Eilean Hooper-Greenhill. "Volunteers in Museums and Galleries: A Discussion of Some of the Issues." *Museums Journal* 84, no. 4 (1984): 177.

Conrad, William R., Jr., and William E. Glenn. *The Effective Voluntary Board of Directors: What It Is and How It Works.* Athens, Ohio: Swallow Press, 1983.

Daly, Virginia. *Establishing a Volunteer Program.* Technical Leaflet, no. 170. Nashville, Tenn.: American Association for State and Local History, 1990.

Dean, Laurel Stulken. "Learning About Volunteer Burnout (It Can Improve Your Retention Rate)." *Voluntary Action Leadership* (Winter 1985): 17–19.

Fletcher, Kathleen Brown. *The Nine Keys to Successful Volunteer Programs.* Washington, D.C.: American Association of Museums, 1987.

Hill, Donna. "How to Prevent Volunteer Burnout: An Interview with Martha Bramhall." *Voluntary Action Leadership* (Winter 1985): 20–23.

Krockover, Gerald H., and Jeanette Hauck. *Training for Docents: How to Talk to Visitors.* Technical Leaflet, no. 125. Nashville, Tenn.: American Association for State and Local History, 1980.

Lowenthal, Helen. "The Volunteer in the Museum, as Well as Churches and Historic Houses: Experience of the National Association of Decorative and Fine Arts Societies." *International Journal of Museum Management and Curatorship* 2, no. 3 (1983): 275–78.

Lynch, Richard. "Preparing an Effective Recruitment Campaign." *Voluntary Action Leadership* (Winter 1984): 23–27.

Meltzer, Phyllis. "Help Volunteers Help You." *Museum News* 68, no. 2 (1989): 60–62.

Minnesota Office on Volunteer Services. *Handbook for Volunteer Recognition.* St. Paul: Minnesota Office on Volunteer Services, 1984.

Morrison, Emily Kittle. *Skills for Leadership: Working with Volunteers.* Tucson, Ariz.: Jordan Press, 1983.

Nickerson, Ann T. "How to Set Up a Corporate Volunteer Program." *History News* 38, no. 9 (1983): 34–37.

Sullivan, Patricia. "Volunteers: How to Build a Strong Support Staff for Your Institution." *History News* 37, no. 10 (1982): 19–21.

Vineyard, Sue. *Finding Your Way Through the Maze of Volunteer Management.* Downers Grove, Ill.: Heritage Arts, 1981.

Wilson, Marlene. *The Effective Management of Volunteer Programs.* Boulder, Colo.: Volunteer Management Associates, 1976.

———. *Survival Skills for Managers.* Boulder, Colo.: Volunteer Management Associates, 1981.

Wolins, Inez, Sherry Spires, and Helene Silverman. "The Docent as Teacher: Redefining a Commitment to Museum Education." *Museum News* 64 (1986): 41–50.

INDEX